The African Continental Free Trade Area

Benjamin Ofori-Amoah

The African Continental Free Trade Area

Prospects, Problems and Challenges

Springer

Benjamin Ofori-Amoah
Western Michigan University
Kalamazoo, MI, USA

ISBN 978-3-031-59180-8 ISBN 978-3-031-59181-5 (eBook)
https://doi.org/10.1007/978-3-031-59181-5

This Springer imprint is published by the registered company Springer Nature Switzerland AG
The registered company address is: Gewerbestrasse 11, 6330 Cham, Switzerland

Paper in this product is recyclable.

Acknowledgments

I am indebted to many people for this book. First and foremost is Mr. Zachary Romano, the Publishing Editor in Geography at Springer Nature, who contacted me in March 2019 to consider publishing an extended version of my paper titled "Sustainable Energy and Storage as Forms of Green Energy in Africa" which I had presented at the annual meeting of the American Association of Geographers (AAG) in Washington, DC, with Springer. That paper was part of an edited volume of another publisher, so I was not able to do as Mr. Romano requested. However, he contacted me and in the following year, 2020 about my AAG paper titled "African Free Trade Area: Problems and Prospects, which I was going to present at the Denver meeting but was cancelled because of the COVID-19 pandemic. Throughout 2020 and 2021, he kept in touch to nudge me on until we finally got a contract in September 2021. Over the next 3 years, he patiently worked with me to get the work completed. Clearly, this book would not have been possible without him, and for this, I am most grateful.

Second, I am thankful to Western Michigan University for granting me an administrative sabbatical leave after serving for 17 years as a department chair of Department of Geography, Environment, and Tourism. In particular, I am grateful to my colleagues in the department, who supported my sabbatical, Dr. Kathleen Baker who agreed to serve as acting chair, Dr. Carla Koretsky, the Dean of the College of Arts and Sciences, who enthusiastically approved my sabbatical leave application and recommended me to the then Provost Jennifer Bott, who approved it. Though this book was not my original sabbatical project, it became the default, when due to COVID-19 travel restrictions, I was not able to do my original project which was a comparative study of economic development of South Korea and Ghana. To this I would be remiss if I do not acknowledge the Milton and Ruth Scherer Endowment Fund of the former Geography, Environment, and Tourism Department of Western Michigan University. This fund dedicated to the research on Asia provided financial support for my partial stay in Ghana, when I completed the Ghana portion of my original sabbatical leave project. Given that I was not able to go to South Korea, I spent the rest of my sabbatical leave in Ghana where I completed the first draft of this book.

Third, special mention also goes to Mary Lou Brooks, my former Administrative Assistant, who spent her first year of retirement compiling and processing a large amount of trade data that is used in this book, and Esther Akoto Amoako, my former student and "adopted" daughter, who drew the maps used in the book. I also thank the reviewers of the manuscripts as well as my colleagues Dr. Senyo Adjibolosoo, Professor Emeritus of Economics at Point Loma the Nazarene University, and Dr. Michael Ryan, Professor and Chair of Economics at Western Michigan University, for their valuable inputs and advice on the theoretical sections of the book.

The last group of people I would like to acknowledge is my family. First is my wife Agnes, my rock and chief supporter, who had to endure over and over again the pain of complaining and grumpy behavior when things appeared to be going nowhere. To my children David, Jonathan, and Abigail, as well as my daughters-in-law, Monica and Jimini, I am very grateful for their incredible support during my sabbatical leave. Any errors in the book, however, are completely mine.

Contents

Chapter 1
Introduction

1.1 A Familiar Act

On March 21, 2018, an act that has become all too familiar to observers, policymakers, researchers, and students of Africa's development story played out with a big fanfare in Kigali, Rwanda's capital city. Forty-four African countries signed an agreement to launch a new institution, the African Continental Free Trade Area (AfCFTA), considered the largest free trade area in the world (African Union, 2018). The aims of the AfCFTA, among other things, were to

- Create a single market for goods and services. This task is to be facilitated by the movement of persons in order to deepen the economic integration of the African continent, in accordance with the Pan-African Vision of an integrated, prosperous, and peaceful Africa that is unconditionally enshrined in Agenda 2063.
- Establish a liberalized market for goods and services through successive rounds of negotiations.
- Contribute to the movement of capital and natural persons and facilitate movements building on the initiatives and developments in the member states and RECs, and.
- Lay the foundation for the establishment of a Continental Customs Union at a later stage (African Union, 2018, p. 14).

The growing literature on the problems and prospects of this act was predictable, and rightly so given the checkered history of similar efforts on the continent. Aniche (2020) classified this growing literature into three categories—the Afro-optimists, the Afro-pessimists, and the Afro-realists. The Afro-optimists focus on the prospects of the AfCFTA, the Afro-pessimists focus on the nagging challenges facing the AfCFTA, while the realists fall in between.

Rooted in neoliberalism, the optimists see the prospects of AfCFTA as opportunities to unlock the potential of Africans for continued development, unconditional

B. Ofori-Amoah, *The African Continental Free Trade Area*,
https://doi.org/10.1007/978-3-031-59181-5_1

boosting of their own state of intraregional trade, continuing stimulation of trade performance, integration of the global trading system, and perennial reduction of the continent's dependence on foreign aid and borrowing. In contrast, the pessimists draw inspiration from radical pan-Africanist approach of Presidents Kwame Nkrumah and Julius Nyerere in the early 1960s. These leaders were more aligned with the views of the neo-Marxists. The pessimists see a return to African socialism that is delinked from colonial ties, more aggressive protectionist trade policies, and import-substitution type of industrialization. For the pessimists, the key to success lies in proper implementation. For its part, the realists propose a middle approach. This approach is aimed at the attainment as well as the continued people-to-people integration pathway that will ultimately transcend the limitations neoliberals pursue through functionalism. Without ever denying the foregoing realities, the primary objectives of neoliberalists remain perennially committed to neoliberalists to the organization of the private sector, which is aimed at large cartels, conglomerates, and multinationals. Government role should be limited to coordination, harmonization, implementation, enforcement, and establishment national security apparatus that will allow trade to go on peacefully. It also emphasizes implementation as key (Aniche, 2020).

Within these broad categorizations, more attention has focused on the potential advantages or achievements of the agreement and what is required to attain those advantages or achievements. With respect to the first, the potential advantages of the agreement are many and are best summarized by a report issued by Saygili et al. (2017) on behalf of the United Nations Conference on Trade and Development. Such significant advantages include

> (1) creating bigger and integrated regional market for African products; (2) permitting producers to benefit from economies of scale and to access cheaper raw materials and intermediate inputs; (3) improving conditions for forming regional value chains and integrating to global value chains (GVCs); (4) allowing consumers to have access to cheaper imported products from other African countries; (5) leading to better allocation of resources and faster economic and trade growth; (6) catalyzing the structural transformation of the countries from resource and low technology based economies to more diversified knowledge based economies; (7) eliminating some challenges associated with multiple and overlapping trade agreements in Africa (spaghetti bowl); (8) encouraging both intra-African and external direct capital flows to African countries; and (9) stimulating cooperation in other areas such as technology transfer, innovation, investment and continent-wide infrastructure development. (Saygili et al., 2017, p. 5)

These advantages have been echoed by others including Mevel and Karingi (2012), Abrego et al. (2020), Luke and MacLeod (2019), Mene (2020), Chauvin et al. (2016), Charles (2021) and Oloruntoba and Tsowou (2019). It has also been suggested that the AfCFTA presents an opportunity to examine the relevance of the theory of comparative advantage which underlies international trade (Ezeani, 2018), and a framework for re-writing international economic laws (Kuhlmann & Agutu, 2020). Much of this potential view is based on the theoretical advantages of regional trade agreements (RTAs) and presumed success of existing RTAs on the continent. In this regard, there is a view that current RTAs in Africa have been successful (Chacha, 2008; Elbadawi, 1997; Foroutan & Pritchett, 1993; Gunning, 2001; Yang

& Gupta, 2007; Darku & Appau, 2015), and for that matter, the AfCFTA will work as well.

At the same time, there is an agreement that many obstacles need to be overcome in order to achieve these potential advantages. These include tariff and nontariff barriers (Mevel & Karingi, 2012) lack of coherent framework of cooperation among countries, lack of effective mechanisms to poll regional resources; and the high cost of trade among neighbor countries (Kamau, 2010); fear of losing significant tariff revenue sources; uneven distribution of cost and benefits among countries—some countries will benefit more while others will lose out (UNCTAD, 2013); overcoming systemic, continental, and subregional asymmetries (Hout & Mohamed Salih, 2019); and political will and commitment for implementation; and poor infrastructure. Undeniably, there is also a perennial lack of coherent framework for cooperation among African countries.

However, where there is no agreement is what is needed to achieve those advantages. Thus, the list is long and includes (a) making customs procedures more efficient and introducing nontariff measures to ease trade (Mevel & Karingi, 2012); (b) strict implementation and enforcement (Aniche, 2020); (c) providing information to national economies about how RTA will benefit them (Charles, 2021); (d) removal or reduction in tariffs, non-trade barriers and transportation cost (Gelan & Omore, 2014; Ngepah & Udeagha, 2018); (e) combination of trade liberalization, industrial development, and infrastructure development (Ismail, 2017); (f) reconfiguration of supply chain through establishment of regional value chains (Mene, 2020); (g) dealing with coordination problems that might impede industrialization policy (Odijie, 2018); (h) need to go beyond trade barriers (UNCTAD Paper 15); (i) incorporation of services (Simo, 2020); (j) innovative approaches to export competitiveness and regional focus diversification (Geda & Krebet, 2008); (k) a strong industrial development policies by governments, and a strong leadership commitment (Signe, 2018; van der Ven, 2017).

1.2 The Purpose of This Book

All the factors presented above and also discussed in this book are important. However, this book seeks to build on the call for strong industrial development policies and their implementation. It argues that the linchpin of the success of the AfCFTA is how much African economies tenaciously as well as meticulously restructure themselves to create natural complementarities among them. In particular, such restructuring requires emphasis on continuous manufacturing as well as the promotion of professional services. This argument rests on five indisputable facts about Africa's trade relations and experience with regional trade agreements. First, Africa is not a major player when it comes to world trade. Second, the AfCFTA is not the first free trade agreement in Africa. There have been many pre-AfCFTA regional trade agreements signed by African countries that have fallen short of their goals and objectives. So, what guarantees that the AfCFTA will be different? Third, these pre-AfCFTA agreements have failed to raise intra-African trade because the direction of Africa's trade is still toward external trade partners rather than internal trade partners. Fourth, the direction of trade continues to be externally oriented because of the composition of Africa's commodities trade. Fifth, the composition and the direction of trade indicate that removal of trade and non-trade barriers will not necessarily increase the volume of trade among African countries unless there are some complementarities. Since these facts constitute the basis of the book, it will be important to elaborate on them.

1.2.1 Africa's Role in World Trade

Africa is not a major player when it comes to world trade. In the 1960s Africa accounted for 5.6% of the world's merchandise export trade, in 2019 it was 2.5% (Table 1.1). Over the same period, Asia's share of world export trade went from 14.6% to 41.1%. Europe went from 50.4% to 38.2%, while Northern America (USA and Canada) went from 19.6% to 11%. Thus, the share of all major regions with exception of Asia declined over the same period, but the fact that Africa had the second lowest share throughout the period is concerning.

The story is not different with world import trade. In 1960, Africa accounted for 6% of the world's import trade. In 2019 its share of world import trade was 3% (Table 1.2). Compared to other major regions, Asia went from 15.4% to 37.8%,

Table 1.1 Percent share of world merchandise export trade by major regions 1960–2019

Major Region	1960	1970	1980	1990	2000	2005	2010	2015	2019
Africa	5.6	5.1	5.9	3.0	2.3	3.0	3.4	2.4	2.5
Asia	14.6	14.7	24.8	25.4	32.0	34.2	38.9	41.5	41.1
Europe	50.4	53.8	48.0	51.0	42.3	44.0	39.3	37.6	38.2
Lat. America & Carib.	7.5	5.4	5.4	4.2	5.7	5.6	5.8	5.5	5.5
Northern America	19.6	18.9	14.3	14.9	16.4	12.0	10.9	11.6	11.0
Oceania	2.4	2.1	1.4	1.5	1.3	1.3	1.7	1.4	1.7
World	100	100	100	100	100	100	100	100	100

Source: Author's calculation based on data from UNCTADStat

Table 1.2 Percent share of world merchandise import trade by major regions, 1960–2019

Major Region	1960	1970	1980	1990	2000	2005	2010	2015	2019
Africa	6.2	4.4	4.6	2.6	2.0	2.4	3.1	3.4	3.0
Asia	15.4	14.7	20.6	22.9	27.4	29.9	35.4	37.4	37.8
Europe	52.1	56.0	52.1	51.7	40.8	42.2	38.7	35.1	36.4
Lat America & Carib.	7.3	5.5	5.9	3.5	5.8	5.0	5.8	6.2	5.6
Northern America	16.3	17.2	15.3	17.8	22.6	19.1	15.4	16.4	15.7
Oceania	2.7	2.2	1.5	1.6	1.4	1.5	1.6	1.5	1.5
World	100	100	100	100	100	100	100	100	100

Source: Author's calculation based on data from UNCTADStat

Table 1.3 Percent share of world merchandise export trade by developing regions 1960–2019

Region	1960	1970	1980	1990	2000	2005	2010	2015	2019
Developing Africa	5.6	5.1	5.9	3.0	2.3	3.0	3.4	2.3	3.0
Developing America	7.5	5.4	5.4	4.2	5.7	5.6	5.8	5.6	6.0
Developing Asia	11.2	8.4	18.2	16.9	23.8	27.6	32.8	36.5	34.0
Developing Oceania	0.1	0.2	0.1	0.1	0.1	0.1	0.1	0.1	0.1

Source: Author's calculation based on data from UNCTADStat

Table 1.4 Percent share of world merchandise import trade by developing regions 1960–2019

Region	1960	1970	1980	1990	2000	2005	2010	2015	2019
Developing Africa	6.2	4.4	4.6	2.6	2.0	2.4	3.1	3.3	3.0
Developing America	7.3	5.5	5.9	3.5	5.8	5.0	5.8	6.1	6.0
Developing Asia	11.7	8.4	13.3	15.9	20.9	24.3	30.0	32.3	32.0
Developing Oceania	0.2	0.3	0.2	0.1	0.1	0.1	0.1	0.07	0.1

Source: Author's calculation based on UNCTADStat data

Europe from 52.1% to 36.4%, and Northern America from 16.3% to 15.7%. Once again Asia was the only region that saw a rise in its import trade over the period, while Africa's participation was the second lowest of all the major regions.

Comparing Africa's role in world trade with other developing regions of the world tells similar stories. Thus, in 1960, Africa ranked second from the bottom in terms of its contribution to world merchandise export trade (5.6%). By 2019, the situation had not changed and Africa's percentage share had declined (3%). In contrast Developing America's share of world export trade went from 7.5% to 6%, while Developing Asia went from 11.2% to 24% over the same period. Only Developing Oceania had a lower percentage share than Africa (Table 1.3). The share of import trade was the same (Table 1.4).

This low participation reflects the structure of Africa's economies, which is a harbinger of the structure of Africa's intraregional trade and the performance of its RTAs.

1.2.2 *Regional Trade Agreements in Africa: A Brief History*

Africa is not new to regional integration in general and regional trade agreements, in particular. With all the trade, conquests, and empire-building, it is more likely than not that some form of trade agreements and alliances were formed in pre-colonial Africa. Even so, the idea of integration was very prominent in the colonial period. As early as 1899, a customs union between the British colony of the Cape of Good Hope and the Boer Republic of the Orange Free State was established (Gerout et al., 2019). Throughout the rest of the colonial period, both the British and the French ruled their colonies as integrated territories. As a result, several regional institutions were established for British West Africa, British East Africa, and British

Central Africa, as well as for French West Africa and French Equatorial Africa. While many of these regional institutions were dismantled in the early post-independence period, in 1963, African countries were able to come together to form the Organization of African Unity (OAU), albeit not with a trade mandate but rather with a mandate to promote peace, unity, and cooperation and to end of colonialism in Africa. However, the idea of trade agreements did not entirely disappear from the ideals and aspirations of Africa's newly independent countries.

Dinka and Kennes (2007) identified two waves of regional organizations or trade agreement formation, to which we may add a third wave. The first wave occurred from late 1950s through mid-1970s; the second wave from mid-1970s through early 1980s and the third wave in the early 1990s. The result of these waves of regional trade agreements was that by the mid-1990s, African countries had created at least 13 regional trade agreements, which on paper ranged from free trade areas to common markets and beyond (Table 1.5). Many agreements have also resulted in overlapping membership, which has been referred to in the literature as the spaghetti bowl effect, a complex web of interactions and divided loyalties as illustrated in both Table 1.6 and Fig. 1.1.

Table 1.5 Regional trade agreements in Africa

Organization	Member states	Goals and objectives
1959: The Equatorial Customs Union (UDE) (1959–65)	Chad, Cent. African Republic (CAR), Congo, Gabon	To maintain some form of economic and political integration
1964: The Central African Customs and Economic Union (UDEAC)	Congo, Chad, CAR, Gabon, Cameroon (1966), Equatorial Guinea (1985)	Establish closer union and strengthen regional solidarity; promote gradual and progressive establishment of a Central Africa Common market; remove trade barriers to trade; pursue policies that are of common interest.
1966 West African Customs Union (UDEAO)	Burkina Faso, Cote d'Ivoire, Mali, Mauritania, Niger, and Senegal	To stimulate intraregional trade through a 50% tariff reduction on imports from members
1967: East African Community (EAC) (1967–1977)	Kenya, Tanzania, Uganda	To strengthen and regulate industrial, commercial, and other relations among members; removal of trade barriers; establishment of a common tariff and excise duties; free exchange of currency
1969: Southern African Customs Union (SACU)	South Africa, Botswana, Lesotho, Swaziland, Namibia (1990)	To maintain a common external tariff; share customs revenues, and coordinate policies and decision-making on a wide range of trade issues.
1973 West Africa Economic Community (CEAO) replaced UDEAO	Burkina Faso, Cote d'Ivoire, Mali, Mauritania, Niger, and Senegal	Implement an active cooperation and economic integration policy, to increase trade among members

(continued)

Table 1.5 (continued)

Organization	Member states	Goals and objectives
1975 Economic Community of West African States (ECOWAS)	Benin, Burkina Faso, Cape Verde Is, Cote d'Ivoire, Gambia, Ghana, Guinea, Guinea-Bissau, Liberia, Mali, Mauritania, Niger, Nigeria, Senegal, Sierra Leone, Togo	Elimination of customs duties, abolition of quantitative and administrative restrictions on trade; establishment of a common tariff and a common commercial policy; promote freedom of movement of people, services, and capital; harmonization of agricultural, industrial, and monetary policies; and joint development of infrastructure.
1980; Southern African Development Coordination Conference (SADCC)	Angola, Botswana, Lesotho, Malawi, Mozambique, Swaziland, Tanzania, Zambia, Zimbabwe. Namibia (1990)	To promote cooperation among members to lessen dependence on South Africa
1982 Preferential Trade Area (PTA)	Angola, Burundi, Djibouti, Kenya, Lesotho, Malawi, Mozambique, Rwanda, Somalia, Sudan, Uganda, Tanzania, Zambia, Zimbabwe	To promote cooperation and integration in all areas of economic activity; To raise the standards of living of the people of the region; To create a common market by the year 2000; to contribute to the progress and development of Africa
1983. Central African Economic Community (CEAC).	Congo, Chad, CAR, Gabon, Cameroon, Equatorial Guinea, DRC, Burundi, Rwanda, Sao Tome	To attain economic community status.
1992. Southern African Development Community (SADC) Replaced SADCC	Angola, Botswana, Lesotho, DRC, Malawi, Mauritius, Mozambique, South Africa, Seychelles, Swaziland, Tanzania, Zambia, Zimbabwe	Reduce economic dependence; create a genuine and equitable regional integration; promote national, interstate, and regional policies; secure international cooperation within the framework of the SADC's strategy for economic liberalization
1993. The Common Market for Eastern and Southern Africa (COMESA) replaced PTA	Burundi, Comoros, Djibouti, Egypt, Eritrea, Ethiopia, Kenya, Libya, Madagascar, Malawi, Mauritius, Rwanda, Seychelles, Somalia, Sudan, Swaziland, Uganda, Zambia, Zimbabwe	Establishment of customs union through removal of trade barriers; establishment of a common tariff and rules of origin; coordination of macroeconomic policy; free movement of services and capital; work toward currency convertibility; cooperation in economic and social development; redistribution of benefits from integration
1994 Economic and Monetary Union of West African States (UEMOA) Replaced CEAO	Burkina Faso, Cote d'Ivoire, Mali, Niger, and Senegal	To develop a national economic policy; harmonize the legal and regulatory framework for economic activity; harmonize fiscal policy, and unify national economic space

Table 1.6 Overlapping membership in regional trade agreements in Africa

Country	AMU	CEN-SAD	COMESA	EAC	ECCAS	ECOWAS	IGAD	SADC	Total
Algeria	X								1
Angola					X			X	2
Benin		X				X			2
Botswana								X	1
Burkina Faso		X				X			2
Burundi			X	X	X				3
Cameroon					X				1
Cape Verde						X			1
Cent. African Rp.		X			X				2
Chad		X			X				2
Comoros		X	X					X	3
Congo, DR			X	X	X			X	4
Congo Rep.			X		X				2
Cote d'Ivoire		X				X			2
Djibouti		X	X				X		3
Egypt	X	X	X						3
Equat. Guinea					X				1
Eritrea		X	X				X		3
Eswatini			X					X	2
Ethiopia			X				X		2
Gabon					X				1
Gambia		X				X			2
Ghana		X				X			2
Guinea						X			1
Guinea-Bissau		X				X			2
Kenya			X	X			X		3
Lesotho								X	1
Liberia						X			1
Libya	X	X	X						3
Madagascar			X					X	2
Malawi			X					X	2
Mali		X				X			2
Mauritania	X	X							2
Mauritius			X					X	2
Morocco	X	X							2
Mozambique								X	1
Namibia								X	1
Niger		X				X			2
Nigeria		X				X			2
Rwanda			X	X					2

(continued)

Table 1.6 (continued)

Country	AMU	CEN-SAD	COMESA	EAC	ECCAS	ECOWAS	IGAD	SADC	Total
Sao Tome & Principe					X				1
Senegal		X				X			2
Seychelles			X					X	2
Sierra Leone		X				X			2
Somalia		X					X		2
South Africa								X	1
South Sudan				X			X		2
Sudan		X	X				X		3
Tanzania				X				X	2
Togo		X				X			2
Tunisia	X	X							2
Uganda			X	X			X		3
West. Sahara									
Zambia			X					X	2
Zimbabwe			X					X	2

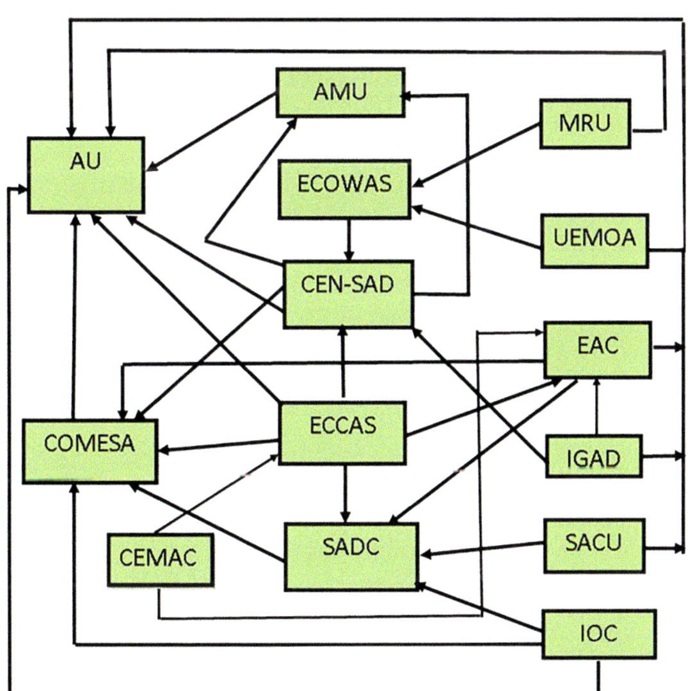

Fig. 1.1 Overlapping membership of Africa's regional trade agreements. Arrows indicate RTAs with overlapping memberships

1.2.3 *The Unimpressive Track Record of Pre-AfCFTA Regional Trade Agreements*

The number of pre-AfCFTA should not be a problem if they had lived up to their objectives, but the fact is they have not especially in changing the direction of Africa's trade. The track record of these groups has been relatively mediocre compared to RTAs elsewhere (UNECA, 2006, 2012; Ross-Larsen et al., 2006; African Union Commission & ECA, 2008; UNECA et al., 2010; Ofori-Amoah, 2019; International Trade Centre, 2019). Thus, after more than six decades when the first regional trade agreement was signed followed by a dozen more such agreements, African countries trade less among themselves than they do with countries or groups outside the continent. This in itself is not uncommon since Europe is the only continent that has the highest percentage of international trade within its borders. What is remarkable is that Africa's percentage of intracontinental trade ranks among the lowest in the world (Ofori-Amoah, 2019). For example, from 1960 to 1962, only 5.6% of Africa's total exports were intracontinental, compared to Latin America's 16%, Asia's 21%, Northern America's 26%, and Europe's 61.4% (UNCTAD, 2009). Recent data show that Africa's intracontinental trade has increased a bit, but it still fell short compared to other major regions of the world. For example, in 2019, Africa's intracontinental export trade was only 16.3% of its total export trade (Table 1.7). In comparison, intraregional trade accounted for 59.4% of Asia's export trade, 68% of Europe's, and 30.1% of Northern America's exports. Only Latin America and Oceania fell below Africa.

Intra-regional merchandise import trade follows a similar trend. In 2019, intraregional merchandise trade accounted for 14.3% of Africa's total import trade. Comparable numbers were 62.2% for Asia, 64.9% for Europe, 18.5% for Northern America, and 15% for Latin America and the Caribbean. Only Oceania had a lower percentage of intraregional trade than Africa in both export and import trade (Table 1.8). Many researchers have identified overlapping membership as one of the reasons why Africa's intraregional trade is low, but at the continental level, this is a moot point since overlapping membership should not matter at that level.

The main objectives of the AfCFTA are to (1) create a single continental market for goods and services, with free movement of business persons and investments, and thus pave the way for accelerating the establishment of the Continental Customs

Table 1.7 Intra-regional merchandise export trade of world major regions

Region	1995	2000	2005	2010	2015	2019
Africa	11.8	10.0	9.6	13.7	18.7	16.3
Asia	53.0	51.7	56.0	59.7	59.9	59.4
Europe	67.9	72.8	74.1	70.8	66.8	68.0
Lat. America & Caribb.	20.4	17.9	18.7	20.0	17.3	14.8
Northern America	35.9	39.7	40.8	32.4	31.1	30.1
Oceania	12.9	11.6	12.1	8.6	8.0	6.5

Source: Author's calculation based on data from UNCTADStat

Table 1.8 Intra-regional merchandise import trade of world major regions, 1995–2019

Region	1995	2000	2005	2010	2015	2019
Africa	9.2	14.2	13.8	14.7	13.4	14.3
Asia	54.5	60.0	63.7	63.5	62.3	62.2
Europe	66.8	68.4	70.0	66.8	66.3	64.9
Lat. America & Caribb.	19.0	17.8	21.3	20.0	16.2	15.0
Northern America	27.6	26.7	23.2	20.4	19.3	18.5
Oceania	11.4	10.3	9.4	8.5	6.8	6.5

Source: Author's calculation based on data from UNCTADStat

Union and the African customs union; (2) expand intra-African trade through better harmonization and coordination of trade liberalization and facilitation regimes and instruments across RECs and across Africa in general; (3) resolve the challenges of multiple and overlapping memberships and expedite the regional and continental integration processes; and (4) enhance competitiveness at the industry and enterprise level through exploiting opportunities for scale production, continental market access and better reallocation of resources. In order to achieve these, the agreement decided to use existing regional trade agreements to form the basis of the AfCFTA. Those existing RTAs that had achieved free trade status were automatically absorbed into AfCFTA, those that had not were given the chance of adopting a free trade agreement before joining the AfCFTA. Of the eight regional trade agreements recognized by the African Union at the formation of the AfCFTA, only four had achieved free trade area status—COMESA, ECOWAS, EAC, and SADC. The remaining four—AMU, CEN-SAD, ECCAS, and the IGAD—were not. However, as we have seen, none of these has lived up to expectations, and for that reason, they provide a very poor model to follow (Shacinda, 2001; Geda & Krebet, 2008; Kamau, 2010; Ofori-Amoah, 2019).

1.2.4 The Composition of Africa's Trade

The composition of Africa's merchandise trade has changed but only slightly. Since the 1960s, most of Africa's exports have been primary commodities broadly categorized as foods, agricultural raw materials, ores and metals, and fuels (Ofori-Amoah, 2019). In 1960, primary commodities accounted for 82.8% of total export trade with manufacturing accounting for only 17.2%. In 2019, primary commodities accounted for 77% of total exports, while manufacturing constituted the remaining 23%, an improvement of 6% over 59 years (Fig. 1.2).

Fuel was by far the largest group of primary commodity exports accounting for 41% of the total exports in 2019, followed by foods and ores and metals with 12% each, and then machinery and equipment and other manufactures with each accounting for 9%. In comparison, the composition of Asia's export trade though consisted of the same general products as Africa's, but the proportions were different (Fig. 1.3).

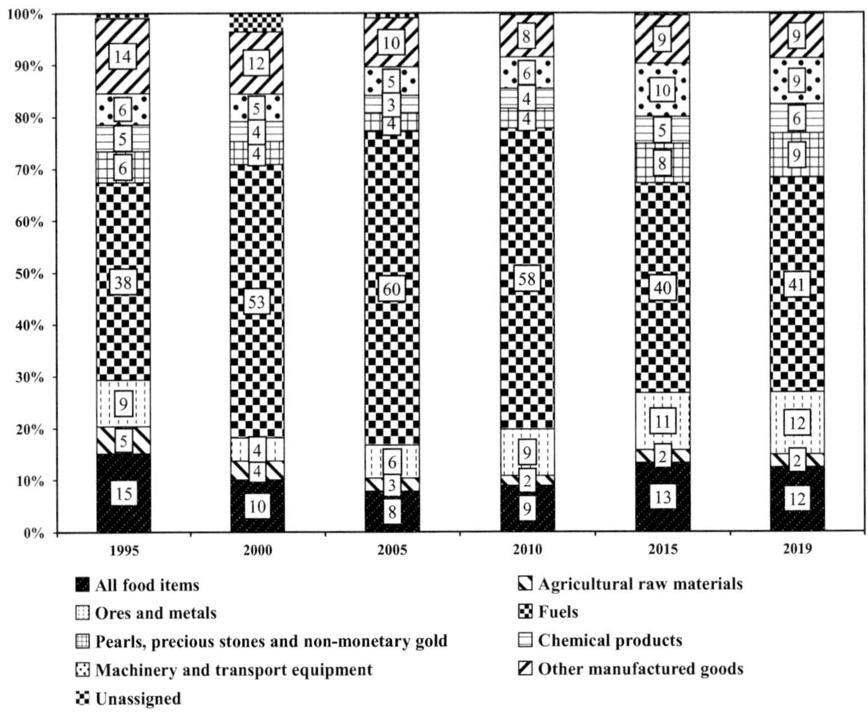

Fig. 1.2 Composition of Africa's export trade, 1995–2019. (Source: Data from UNCTADStat)

Manufactured goods accounted for between 68% and 80% of total merchandise exports since 1995. In 2019, it constituted 76% of its export trade, primary commodities accounted for 21%, while the remaining 3% were unassigned products (Fig. 1.3). Manufactured goods in the merchandise export trade of Latin America and Caribbean accounted for 49–58% over the period from 1995 to 2019. In 2019, manufactured goods accounted for 48% of its total export trade. In contrast, manufactured products have dominated Africa's merchandise imports since the 1960s. However, from the 1990s through 2019, the percentage of primary commodities in Africa's total imports grew slowly to over 30%. Most of the increase in primary commodities imports came from fuels and food. In 2019, manufactured products accounted for 63% of Africa's total merchandise imports, while primary commodities accounted for 35%, with remaining 2% being unassigned. The main import commodities in 2019 were machinery and transportation equipment (30%), other manufactures (22%), food (15%), fuels (15%), and chemical products (12%) (Fig. 1.4).

Comparable numbers of Asia's merchandise import trade were 64% manufactured goods, 35% primary commodities, and 1% unassigned. Asia too has seen an increase in primary commodities, but most of the increase was due to fuels (Fig. 1.5). The main import merchandise in 2019 were machinery and transportation equipment (37%), other manufactured goods (17%), fuels (16%), and chemical products

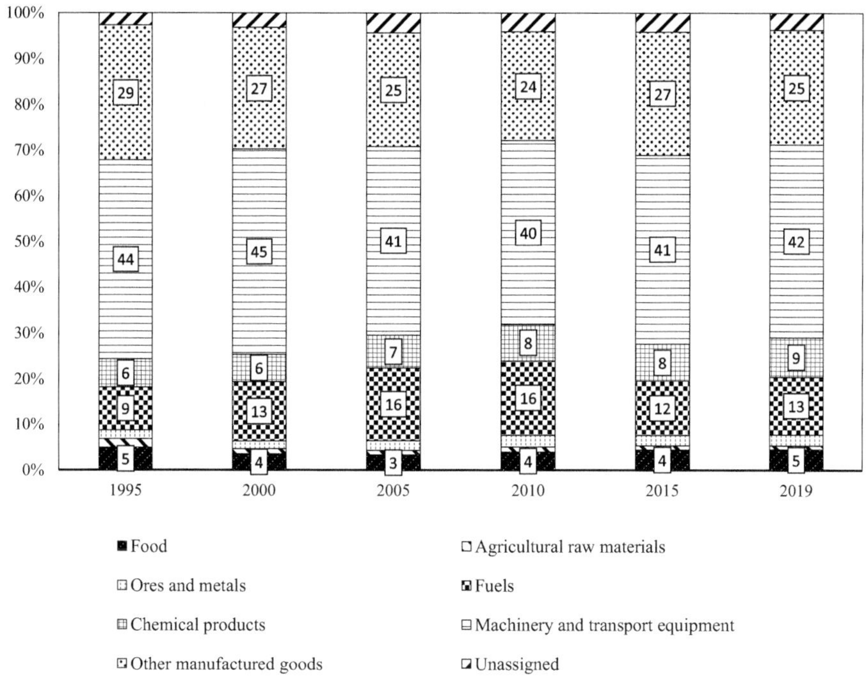

Fig. 1.3 Composition of Asia's merchandise export trade, 1995–2019. (Source: Data from UNCTADStat)

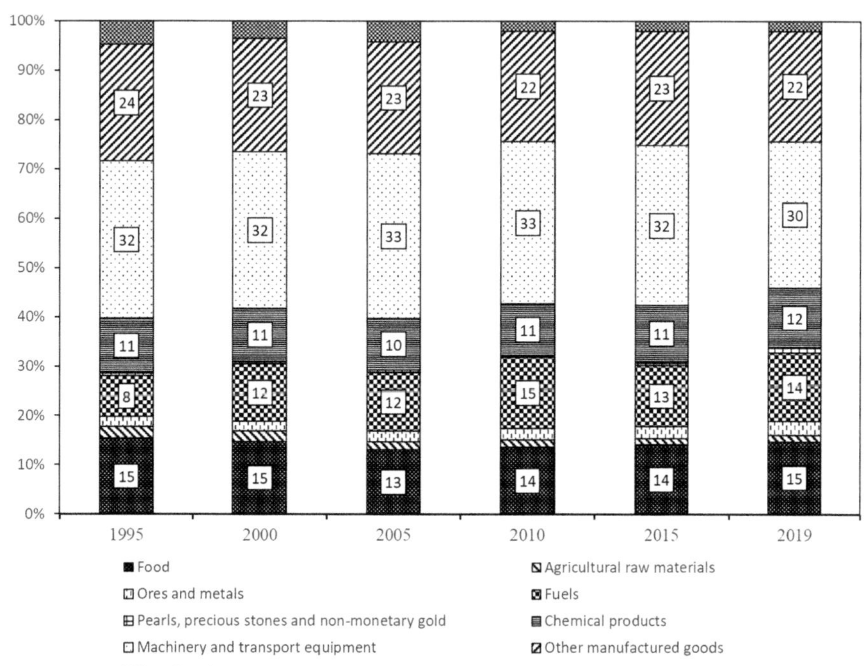

Fig. 1.4 Composition of Africa's merchandise import trade, 1995–2019. (Source: UNCTADStat)

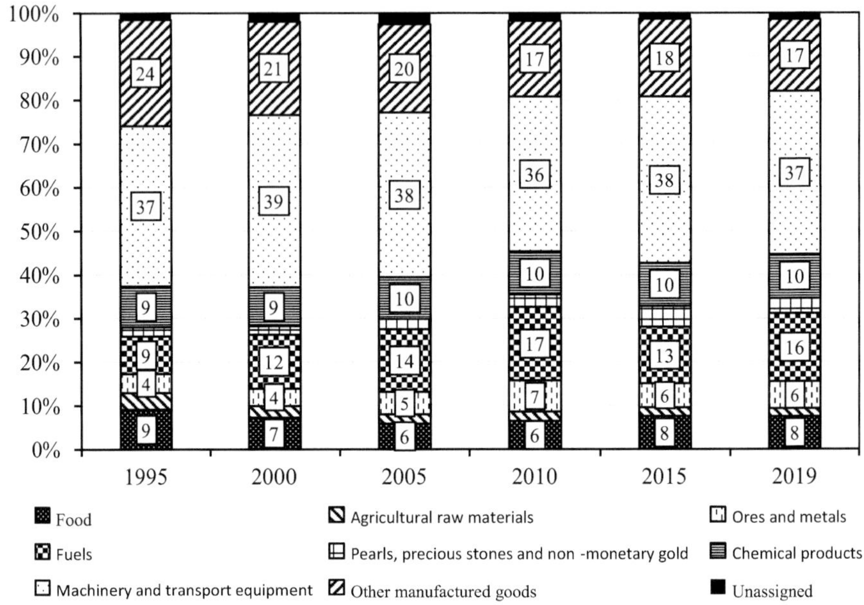

Fig. 1.5 Composition of Asia's merchandise import trade, 1995–2019. (Source: UNCTADStat)

(10%). Latin America and the Caribbean had the highest proportion of manufactured products in its import merchandise import, accounting for 74% in 2019. Transport and machinery equipment accounted for 39%, other manufactured goods 20%, chemical products 15%, and fuels 12%.

The story told by the current composition of Africa's trade is that Africa is a supplier of primary commodities, most of which it does not have the capacity to process, and a consumer of manufactured products, most of which it does not produce. This could therefore be an important determinant of Africa's low-level intraregional trade, but let us look at the direction of trade, which we discuss below.

1.2.5 The Direction of Africa's Merchandise Trade

Like everywhere else, the direction of Africa's merchandise trade can be divided into two categories: inside Africa, or intracontinental trade, and trade outside of Africa, or intercontinental trade. As already mentioned, intracontinental trade takes only a small percentage of African countries' international trade. In contrast, intercontinental trade accounted for 83.7% of total export trade and 85.7% of import trade in 2019. The question is who did Africa trade with and why? Africa's colonial roots committed much of its international trade to Europe, a commitment that has been maintained by such agreements as the Yaoundé Agreements and the Lomé Conventions (Ofori-Amoah, 2019). It is only in recent years starting from about

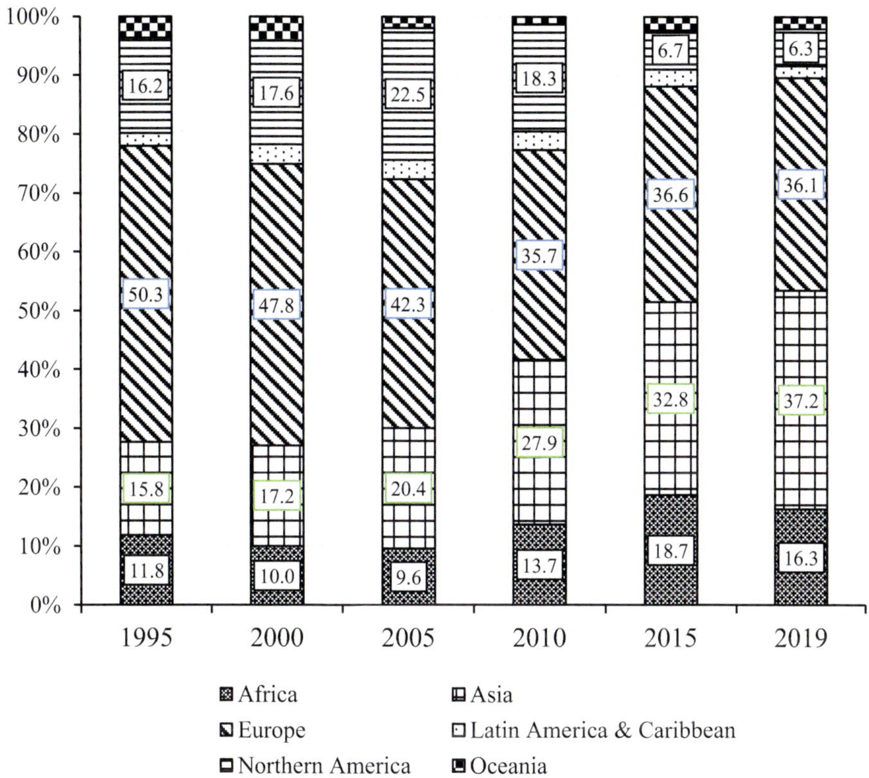

Fig. 1.6 Direction of Africa's merchandise export trade, 1995–2019. (Source: UNCTADStat)

2010, that Europe's position in Africa's trade has been declining. Figure 1.6 shows two main changes since 1995. The first is the gradual decline of Europe as the top destination of Africa's merchandise export trade, from 50% in 1995 to 36% in 2019. The second is the increasing importance of Asia as the destination of Africa's export. Accounting for only 16% of Africa's export trade in 1995, Asia's role as the destination of Africa's export grew slowly but steadily till about 2009, when it overtook Northern America as the second most important export trade partner of Africa. By 2019, Asia had become Africa's top export market (Fig. 1.6). In the meantime, Africa's trade with itself languished barely above 10% until 2010, when it rose above 10%.

Similar trends can be seen with respect to Africa's import trade. In 1995, Europe accounted for 46.5% of Africa's import trade. Europe was followed by Asia (24%), Africa (14%), and Northern America (9%). By 2019, Asia was the leading import market with 43% of Africa's import trade, followed by Europe (33%) and Africa (14.3%) (Fig. 1.7).

Trade within existing trade blocs before the formation of AfCFTA has not been encouraging either. For example, in 2019, the most intra-regional export trade

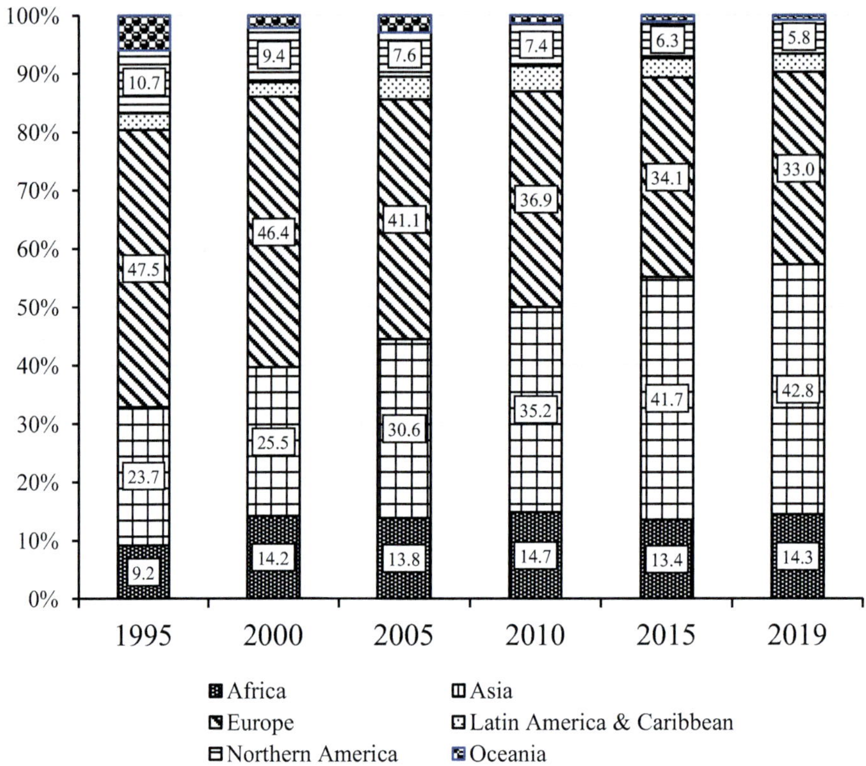

Fig. 1.7 Direction of Africa's merchandise import trade, 1995–2019. (Source: UNCTADStat)

occurred in the SADC (24.4%) followed by SACU (18.1%), CEN-SAD (17%), ECOWAS (10.3%), and COMESA (10%). Import trade was not different from the export trend. SADC accounted for 26%, SACU, 18.1%, COMESA, 15.6%, CEN-SAD, 15.7%, and ECOWAS, 7.7%.

So, why is it that Africa has about 13 active regional trade agreements, some of which have been around for decades, yet most of Africa's trade is with external entities? Ropivia (1999, p. 125) asked "How can African leaders succeed in establishing at the continental level what they have failed to promote within smaller regions and sub-regions?" In this book, we ask: If pre-AfCFTA trade blocs in Africa did not encourage more intracontinental trade, what guarantees that the newly formed AfCFTA will do that? The formation of the AfCFTA will definitely remove overlapping membership that existed with previous trading blocs on the continent, but what is different about the AfCFTA that will get rid of cumbersome regulations, boost manufacturing, and create jobs? This book builds on the several excellent studies initiated by the United Nations Conference on Trade and Development (UNCTAD) (E.g. UNCTAD, 2009, 2013), as well as those of the United Nations Economic Commission for Africa (UNECA), African Union, and the African Development Bank (UNECA, 2006, 2012; UNECA et al., 2010). However, it takes the view that the dreams of AfCFTA will not be realized unless African countries make efforts to address the industry mix of their economies and enforce the rules and regulations they set down on paper.

1.3 The Plan of This Book

This book has at least five unique features. First, discussions about regional trade agreements in Africa have gone beyond trading activities and have included security and other areas of cooperation. This book is deliberately limited to trading activities, nothing more nothing less. For that reason, it leans more toward trade theory from economic perspective than international relations perspective. Second, much commentary about the prospects of AfCFTA has been based on theoretical expectations of what Free Trade Area is supposed to achieve, instead of the performance of pre-AfCFTA trading blocs. This book is based on the premise that we can learn a lot from the past. So, in addition to discussing the theoretical benefits of regional integration, the book will do a critical analysis of the past trading performance of existing regional trade agreements (RTAs) in Africa to examine whether the theoretical projections could be realized.

Third, there appears to be an assumption that removal of trade and non-trade barriers will increase intra-African trade by boosting industrialization, productivity, and competition. This book argues that that may not necessarily be the case, because the basic reason why African countries trade less among themselves is due more to a lack of complementarity or supply and demand relationship between and among them than existence of trade and non-trade barriers. It has been argued elsewhere that complementarity does not fully explain why countries trade with each other and that there are other factors that come into play such as trade infrastructure (UNCTAD, 2009). However, the composition and direction of Africa's trade tell a different story.

Fourth, Africa has the lowest intraregional trade in the world. It is therefore important to study the trade relations of other regions as part of understanding what is going on in Africa. Much has been learned about removal of trade and non-trade barriers, but not much has focused on the actual composition and direction of trade in other regions to see how they compare with the current and future prospects of intra-African trade. This book is of the view that such knowledge will be relevant to the prospects of AfCFTA. Fifth, the book uses the results of the analysis of existing regional integrations in Africa and the trade patterns and trend of other major regions to illustrate the problems and prospects of the AfCFTA.

The book consists of 11 chapters, including this chapter. Chapter 2 discusses the various perspectives on the theory of trade and development. Chapter 3 focuses specifically on the general role of regional trade agreements in intraregional trade. It discusses the theory, purpose, different types, and expectations and constraints of regional trade agreements. The chapter raises a series of questions that are verified by case studies in the remaining chapters. Chapters 4, 5, 6, 7, 8, and 9 focus on the trade performances of the eight RTAs that were recognized by the African Union at the formation of the AfCFTA. Each case study begins with a brief background of the formation, objectives of the RTA and moves to an analysis of how well it has lived up to its objectives with particular reference to intra-regional and extra-regional trade. The analysis focuses on two aspects of trade of these RTAs the composition and direction of trade. It is acknowledged that RTAs have other objectives, including security but the main focus here is trade. Chapter 4 discusses the Economic Community of West African States (ECOWAS). Chapter 5 is about Southern African Development Community (SADC). Chapter 6 focuses on the East African Community (EAC). The Economic Community of Central African States (ECCAS) is the topic of Chap. 7. Chapter 8 discusses the Southern Africa Development Community (SADC). The Community of Sahel-Saharan States (CEN-SAD) follows in Chap. 9. Chapter 10 summarizes a select number of RTAs outside of Africa. Chapter 11 wraps up with a synthesis and a conclusion.

The analysis makes heavy use of trade data from the United Nations Conference on Trade and Development (UNCTAD), the International Trade Center (ITC), and the World Trade Organization (WTO). These data are estimated from data reported by member states. So, they are subject to underestimation or overestimation errors. However, they are the best global data on trade available for the kind of analysis done in this book. Due to the COVID-19 pandemic, the analysis uses 1995–2019 data. The author is very much aware of international trade works that have used sophisticated methods such as gravity models to analyze factors affecting trade. This book does not do that. Instead, it uses the data to illustrate the nature and trends of international trade in Africa and their implications for policy. Researchers interested in applying more rigorous economic methods to examine Africa's trade on a larger are welcome to do so.

References

Abrego, L., de Zamaróczy, M., Gursoy, T., Issoufou, S., Nicholls, G. P., Perez-Saiz, H., & Rosas, J.-N. (2020). *The African continental free trade area: Potential economic impact and challenges*. IMF Staff Discussion Note.

African Union. (2018). *Agreement establishing the African continental free trade area*. Kigali.

African Union Commission and United Nations Economic Commission for Africa. (2008). *Assessing regional integration in Africa III: Towards monetary and financial integration in Africa*. UNECA. https://hdl.handle.net/10855/15035

Aniche, E. T. (2020). African continental free trade area and African Union agenda 2063: The roads to Addis Ababa and Kigali. *Journal of Contemporary African Studies*. https://doi.org/10.1080/02589001.2020.1775184

Chacha, M. (2008). Regional integration and trade: Overlapping memberships and the challenges of regionalism in Africa. In *International studies association conference*, March 26–29.

Charles, F. D. (2021). African continental free trade area: Is there a trade potential for Côte d'Ivoire? *Cogent Economics & Finance, 9*, 1.

Chauvin, N. D., Ramos, M. P., & Porto, G. (2016). Trade, growth, and welfare impacts of the CFTA in Africa. *Proceedings of CSAE conference: Economic development in Africa*. Oxford.

Darku, A. B., & Appau, A. B. (2015). Analysing sub-Saharan Africa trade patterns in the presence of regional trade agreements – The case of COMESA, SADC, ECCAS, and ECOWAS. *African Finance Journal, 17*(1), 41–66.
Dinka, T., & Kennes, W. (2007). *Africa's regional integration arrangements: History and challenges.* Maastricht.
Elbadawi, I. (1997). The impact of regional trade and monetary schemes on intra-sub-Saharan Africa trade. *Regional Integration and Trade Liberalization in Sub-Saharan Africa, 1*, 210–255.
Ezeani, E. (2018). Comparative advantage in de-globalisation Brexit, America first, and Africa's continental free trade area. *Journal of International Trade Law and Policy, 17*(1/2), 46–61.
Foroutan, F., & Pritchett, L. (1993). Intra-Sub-Saharan African trade: Is it too little? *Journal of African Economies, 2*(1), 74–105.
Geda, A., & Kebret, H. (2008). Regional economic integration in Africa: A review of problems and prospects with a case study of COMESA. *Journal of African Economies, 17*(3), 357–394.
Gelan, A., & Omore, A. (2014). Beyond tariffs: The role of non-tariff barriers in dairy trade in the East African community free trade area. *Development Policy Review, 2*, 523–543.
Gerout, G., Macleod, J., & Desta, M. (2019). The AfCFTA as yet another experiment towards continental integration: Retrospect and prospect. In D. Luke & J. MacLeod (Eds.), *Inclusive trade in Africa: The African continental free trade area in comparative perspective* (pp. 15–34). Routledge.
Gunning, J. W. (2001). Trade blocs: Relevant for Africa? *Journal of African Economies, 10*(3), 311–335.
Hout, W., & Mohamed Salih, M. A. (2019). *A political economy of African regionalisms: An overview of asymmetrical development.* Edward Elgar.
International Trade Centre. (2019). *Diversifying trade in Africa: New strategy approaches for the African continental free trade area.* ITC.
Ismail, F. A. (2017). Advancing regional integration in Africa through the continental free trade area (CFTA). *Law Developmental Review, 10*(1), 119–146.
Kamau, N. L. (2010). The impact of regional integration on economic growth: Empirical evidence from COMESA, EAC and SADC trade blocs. *American Journal of Social and Management Sciences, 1*(2), 150–163.
Kuhlmann, K., & Agutu, A. (2020). The African continental free trade area: Toward new legal model for trade and development. *Georgetown Journal of International Law, 51*(4), 753–808.
Luke, D., & MacLeod, J. (Eds.). (2019). *Inclusive trade in Africa: The African continental free trade area in comparative perspective.* Routledge.
Mene, W. (2020). The African Continental Free Trade Area (AfCFTA): Boosting intra-Africa trade. *Georgetown Journal of International Law, 51*(4), 751–752.
Mevel, S., & Karingi, S. (2012). Deepening regional integration in Africa: A computable general equilibrium assessment of the establishment of a continental free trade area followed by a Continental Customs Union. In *7th African economic conference*, 30.
Ngepah, N., & Udeagha, M. C. (2018). African regional trade agreements and intra-African trade. *Journal of Economic Integration, 33*(1), 1176–1199.
Odijie, M. E. (2018). The need for industrial policy coordination in the African continental free trade area. *African Affairs, 118*(470), 182–193.
Ofori-Amoah, B. (2019). *Africa's geography: Dynamics of place, cultures, and economies.* Wiley.
Oloruntoba, S. O., & Tsowou, K. (2019). Afro-continental free trade areas and industrialization in Africa: Exploring Afro-Canadian partnership for economic development. *Canadian Foreign Policy Journal, 25*(3), 237–240.
Ropivia, M.-L. (1999). Failing institutions & shattered space: What regional integration in Central Africa? In D. C. Bach (Ed.), *Regionalisation in Africa: Integration & disintegration* (pp. 125–127). Indiana University Press.
Ross-Larson, B. C., United Nations Economic Commission for Africa, & African Union Commission. (2006). *Assessing regional integration in Africa II: Rationalizing regional economic communities.* UNECA.

Saygili, M., Peters, R., & Knebel, C. (2017) *African continental free trade area: Challenges and opportunities of tariff reductions*, UNCTAD research paper No. 15.
Shacinda, S. (2001). COMESA – Africa's first free trade area. *Review of African Political Economy, 28*(87), 121–122.
Signe, L. (2018). Why Africa's free trade area offers so much promise. *Forum, 2*, 12–13.
Simo, R. Y. (2020). Trade in services in the African continental free trade area: Prospects, challenges and WTO compatibility. *Journal of International Economic Law, 23*, 65–95.
UNECA. (2006). *Assessing regional integration in Africa*. Economic Commission of Africa.
UNECA. (2012). *Assessing regional integration in Africa V: Towards a continental free trade area, Customs Union and common market*. UNECA.
UNECA, Regional Cooperation and Integration Division, African Union Commission, & African Development Bank. (2010). *Assessing regional integration in Africa IV: Enhancing Intra-African trade*. UNECA.
UNCTAD. (2009). *Economic development in Africa: Strengthening regional economic integration for Africa's development*. United Nations Conference on Trade and Development.
UNCTAD. (2013). *Economic development in Africa report intra-African trade: Unlocking private sector dynamism*. United Nations Conference on Trade and Development.
van der Ven, C. M. A. (2017). Trade, development and industrial policy in Africa: The case for a pragmatic approach to optimizing policy coherence between industrial policy and the WTO policy space. *Law Developmental Review, 10*(1), 29–80.
Yang, Y., & Gupta, S. (2007). Regional trade arrangements in Africa: Past performance and the way forward. *African Development Review, 19*(3), 399–431.

Chapter 2
Perspectives on International Trade and Development

2.1 Introduction

Trade, the exchange of goods and services, is an essential component of life. We only need to take stock of what we eat, and wear, how we get from one place to another, and what we do to get comfortable in just a single day to realize that without trade life will be different indeed. Thus, we consume a lot of things we do not produce and can aspire to live the lifestyle that we would like to enjoy because of trade. If we define development as a collective effort to improve our living conditions, then trade is an integral part of that effort. Many thinkers before us have shed their views about the role of trade in development as well as the mechanics of trade. The purpose of this chapter is to review some of these views in order to provide the appropriate foundation and context for the overall objective of this book. The review covers trade theories, barriers to trade, and how the world in general, and Africa in particular, has dealt with trade barriers. The chapter consists of three sections and a conclusion. The first section reviews trade theories. The second reviews the barriers to trade, and the third section reviews how African countries in particular have dealt with barriers to trade.

2.2 Trade Theories

Economic theory provides different classifications of trade theories. One example is classical trade theories and modern trade theories. Another one is positive trade theories and normative trade theories. In this section, we review three classes of trade theories: classical, neoclassical, and Marxist and Marxian theories of trade.

B. Ofori-Amoah, *The African Continental Free Trade Area*,
https://doi.org/10.1007/978-3-031-59181-5_2

2.2.1 Classical Trade Theories

2.2.1.1 From Antiquity to Mercantilism

Evidence of trade as a human activity dates back to the first human civilization (Mariadoss, 2019). However, ideas about international trade per available written records can only be traced back to Ancient Greece, particularly in the writings of Plato, Xenophon, and Aristotle (Dorobăț, 2015). Plato believed that no city state could be self-sufficient, and that division of labor and specialization was better than autarky because it led to increased productivity through the use of human aptitudes and available natural resources. Xenophon talked about the advantages of larger international markets for Greek city-states. However, there were also concerns that international trade could lead to foreign influences on Greek city-states. Thus, Aristotle advocated for self-sufficiency to reduce foreign dependence (Dorobăț, 2015). Early Christian theologians through the fifteenth century held similar views about international trade. For example, both St. Augustine and St. Thomas Aquinas believed that international trade was beneficial to society but worried about the deleterious effects it could have on society (Dorobăț, 2015). By the sixteenth century, however, the thinking about international trade had become largely favorable, due in part to the rise of nation-states and mercantilism in Europe.

Mercantilism was based on the idea that a nation's wealth was measured in terms of its stock of gold and silver. Exports increased a nation's gold stock while imports reduced it. However, mercantilism believed that nation-states were in perpetual conflict with each other, and national wealth building through trade was a zero-sum game in which nation-states—accumulated wealth at the expense of each other. As a result, governments were encouraged to support their producers to export more manufactured goods and import only raw materials through price controls, tariffs, and other trade barriers. For the next two centuries, mercantilism served as the main philosophy behind international trade.

However, due to its inability to fulfill the promise of wealth creation and due to the rise of the Industrial Revolution, mercantilism came under severe criticism during the rise of economic liberalism in the late eighteenth and nineteenth centuries. Among these critics were philosophers and liberal economists such as Josiah Tucker, David Hume, Roger Postlethwayt, and Adam Smith. Tucker and Hume opposed the mercantilist idea of wealth accumulation. Hume argued that an increase in gold accumulation would result in an increase in the money supply of the nation. This would cause commodity prices to rise, which in turn would make the nation's exports more expensive (Rotwein, 1955). The nation would then increase imports and wipe out its trade surpluses. Postlethwayt discussed the ideas of comparative advantage as far back as 1751 (Whitened, 1996). Perhaps, the most potent criticism of mercantilism came from the Physiocrats who believed that a nation's wealth depended solely on the development of its agriculture and saw trade liberalization as a better approach to wealth accumulation than the protectionist's philosophy of mercantilism. Notable among them were François Quesnay and A-R. J. Turgot.

2.2.1.2 Absolute and Comparative Advantage

Economic historians tell us that the formal articulation of international trade theory came from two schools—the British Classical School of Adam Smith, John Stuart Mill, and David Ricardo, and the French Liberal School of Jean Baptiste Say, Frederic Bastiat, and Paul Leroy-Beaulieu. Under assumption of perfect competition, homogenous products, and constant returns to scale, Adam Smith (1776) challenged the mercantilist philosophy of wealth accumulation. He argued that a nation's wealth should not be measured in terms of its gold stock but by the standard of living of its people—the amount of goods and services consumed. Given that no country could produce all its needs, countries should specialize in the production of goods in which they had an absolute advantage. This would lead to specialization, increased productivity, and surplus production, which would then be exchanged for goods produced elsewhere through trade. The benefits of trade for Smith are contained in one of his most cited pieces below:

> Between whatever places foreign trade is carried on, they all of them derive two distinct benefits from it. It carries out that surplus part of the produce of their land and labor for which there is no demand among them, and brings back in return for it something else for which there is a demand. It gives a value to their superfluities, by exchanging them for something else, which may satisfy a part of their wants, and increase their enjoyments. By means of it, the narrowness of the home market does not hinder the division of labor in any particular branch of art or manufacture from being carried to the highest perfection. By opening a more extensive market for whatever part of the produce of their labor may exceed the home consumption, it encourages them to improve its productive powers, and to augment its annual produce to the utmost, and thereby to increase the real revenue and wealth of society (Cannan, 1977, Vol 1., p. 413).

For Smith, international trade occurred because of absolute advantage and specialization.

Expounding on this quotation, Myint (1958) identified two benefits. The first is that international trade overcomes the narrowness of the home market and provides an outlet for the surplus product above domestic requirements, which has been referred to as the "vent for surplus" theory of international trade. The second benefit is that by widening the extent of the market, international trade also improves the division of labor and raises the general level of productivity within the country, which is the "productivity" theory. Economists have debated the interpretation of these two benefits (see Schumacher, 2015), to which we will return later.

For now, suffice it to say that Smith's theory of absolute advantage was a triumph over mercantilist view of trade, but it raised some troubling questions. For example, consider a two-country world model—Country A and Country B. Both countries need cocoa and coffee. Country A has an absolute advantage in producing both, while Country B does not but can produce cocoa better than coffee with its resources. Smith's law of absolute advantage says that in this world, Country A should produce both commodities. The question is what should Country B do? How will trade occur between the two countries if Country B does nothing? David Ricardo (1821) addressed this loophole in the absolute advantage theory by arguing that countries did not need absolute advantage but instead comparative advantage to engage in the production and trading of goods and services. Ricardo argued that if a country did not have an absolute advantage in producing two or more goods, it could still specialize in the good it could produce relatively better cost-wise, and exchange its surpluses for the good it would cost it more to produce through trade. Thus, in the above example, it would be best for Country A to produce cocoa and Country B to produce coffee. Both countries would produce surpluses and exchange for what they lacked through trade. For Ricardo, international trade occurred because of comparative advantage—a comparison of opportunity cost of producing an item and specializing in what it can produce relatively better (Mohtadi, 2017; Dorobăț, 2015).

Both absolute and comparative advantage advanced the notion that international trade was beneficial to all parties involved. However, Mill, the third member of the British Classical School, showed that the benefits of international trade to trading partners depended on other factors. In his theory of international values, Mill argued that—international trade was different from domestic trade and needed a new set of laws. Mill (1909) showed that the terms of trade between two countries depended on intensity of reciprocal demand for goods as a function of their exchange ratios. The gains from trade of a country could change with intensity of demand or the level of protective trade barriers. Mill's theory of international values shifted the unlimited gains from trade by all countries advocated for by Smith and Ricardo to a fixed gain from trade that could be shifted in favor of one country.

The French School, although did not receive the same popularity as its British counterpart, extolled the importance of free market, free trade, and production, like the British. However, they differed from the British in one respect. Ricardo and Mill proposed objective theory of value based on supply-side conditions meaning the cost of labor was the main determinant of formation of exchange prices in the market. The French School proposed a theory based on the demand-side conditions, which meant exchange prices were determined by demand for the product. [The difference between domestic price and world price is the basis for imports and exports. If the domestic price of the product is lower than the world price, the product will be exported. If the domestic price of the product is higher than the world price, the product will be imported (Mohtadi, 2017)].

2.2.2 Neoclassical and Modern Trade Theories

Throughout the late nineteenth and early twentieth centuries, various efforts were made to replace the labor theory of value in the international trade theory with other factors, in the neoclassical economic tradition. These included the subjective theory of value (Menger, 1871; Jevons, 1871; Walras, 2014), marginal utility (Pareto, 1895), opportunity cost (Haberler, 1935), and factor endowments (Heckscher, 1919; Ohlin, 1933). The Heckscher-Ohlin theory came to represent neoclassical theory of trade and dominated international trade for about half a century.

2.2.2.1 The Heckscher-Ohlin (H-O) Theory

The Heckscher-Ohlin international trade theory sought to replace the labor cost component in both absolute and comparative advantage with factor endowments. The theory assumed the following:

1. Two factors of production, labor measured in number of workers, and capital measured in the number of machines.
2. Two countries could be classified as labor-abundant or capital-abundant depending on their ratio of labor to capital. In addition, they have identical tastes and access to the same technology.
3. Two products, classified by factor intensities—capital intensive and labor intensive.
4. Perfect competition—a market of numerous small firms which are price takers.
5. Both capital and labor are internally mobile but externally immobile in the two countries.
6. No barriers to free trade and no transportation costs.

On the basis of these assumptions, the labor-abundant country will have lower wages relative to capital rent, while the capital-abundant country will have higher wages relative to capital rent. As a result, it would be cheaper for the labor-abundant country to produce the labor-intensive product, and for the capital-abundant country to produce the capital-intensive product. In Ricardo's terms, the labor-abundant country has comparative advantage in producing the labor-intensive product, while the capital-abundant country has comparative advantage in producing the capital-intensive product. The result is the same as Ricardo's model, by concentrating on their factor endowments both countries would consume more through specialization and trade than if each country produced both products itself. The overall implication of the H-O model is that capital-abundant countries such as the United States will export capital-intensive products—automobiles, paper products, and machinery, while labor-abundant country such as Egypt will export labor-intensive products—agricultural products, textiles, and garments.

The H-O theory though became dominant for over 50 years, was also plagued by the fact that its theoretical prescription was not borne by reality. For example, Stolper and Samuelson (1941) showed that while international trade brought gains to a country as a whole, within the country, some factors would gain while other factors would lose. For example, what may be a gain for capital owners, could be a loss for labor. Leontief (1956), found that the US exported more labor-intensive products than capital-intensive products contrary to the H-O theory, a finding that became known as the Leontief Paradox. Minhas (1962) and Linder (1961) argued that a representative demand—a range of goods in demand at a given per capita income level—should be present in order to have trade between countries. For trade to occur there must be some overlap within the representative goods. Linder thus put demand at the center of trade. The H-O theory is based on comparative advantage measured in terms of factor endowments. A consistent feature of trade models based on comparative advantage is the assumption that countries are the main agents of trade, and much of that trade is inter-industry—cars for textiles, and cows for airplanes. In reality, much of the world's merchandise trade occurs in industrialized countries and it is intra-industry (Mohtadi, 2017). This and other restrictive assumptions of trade theories based on comparative advantage have led to new thoughts about international trade, some of which are based on firms as trading agents and others on the removal of restrictive assumptions of both classical and neoclassical theory. The former group is usually referred to as firm-based trade theories and the latter as the new trade theory. We review these below.

2.2.2.2 Firm-Based Trade Theories

Firm-based trade theories stem from the recognition that it is firms and not countries that trade so they focus on how firms trade. They were motivated by the rise of multinational corporations and how their pursuit of profits influenced their location decisions. Following Mariadoss (2019) these theories may be classified as country similarity theory, the product life cycle theory, and the competitive advantage theory.

The *country similarity theory* originated from the work of Linder (1961). In search for an explanation of inter-industry trade, Linder observed that firms begin by producing for their domestic markets. As a result, when they start thinking about exporting, they look for places or markets with consumers that look like their own domestic markets in terms of consumer preferences because they offer the most potential for success. Linder's theory thus states that "most trade in manufactured goods will be between countries with similar per capita income and interindustry trade." (Mariadoss, 2019).

The *product life cycle theory* advanced by Vernon (1966) was an attempt to address some missing elements in the mainstream trade theory. It shifted the emphasis of international trade theory from "comparative cost doctrine to timing of innovation, effects of economies of scale, and the roles of ignorance and uncertainty in influencing trade patterns" (Vernon, 1966, p. 190). The theory states that a product's life has three distinct stages—new product, maturing product, and standardized product. While the requirements for each stage may be the same, their relative importance varies at each stage. Thus, in the new product stage—the degree of freedom and flexibility to change inputs, high degree of production differentiation, and swift and effective communication between producers and consumers as well as suppliers tend to be crucial. All these make location in the home country necessary. In the maturing product stage, the product moves toward more standardization than differentiation. Possibilities for achieving economies of scale through mass production, and concerns about production cost become more important. These changes have implications for the firm's location. In particular, firms begin to look for locations outside their home countries to serve the markets there, and take advantage of lower labor cost. If the labor cost is large enough to overcome transportation cost, then it is even possible for the firm to export back to the home country. At standardized product stage, the production process has become highly standardized and does not require a sophisticated industrial environment. At this stage, less-developed areas may become more attractive locations. However, this assumes that information and knowledge about less-developed areas are free and available to all. In reality, this information and knowledge about foreign areas are not free. They have a cost and not all firms can afford that. Location in less-developed areas would also depend upon other factors including demand characteristics, the role of scale economies in the production process, and transportation cost. Thus, products that have high elasticity of demand, products that do not rely on scale economies to produce, and products that are cheaper to transport over longer distances are potential candidates to be located in less-developed or remote areas. The product life cycle model was a useful theory in the 1960s and added a new perspective on international trade. However, it could not anticipate the behavior of multinational corporations in the late twentieth and early twenty-first centuries whereby new products are produced outside of the home country and R&D can occur now at home as well as in other countries.

Another firm-based theory of trade is *the global strategic rivalry theory* originated from the work of Krugman (1979, 1980) and Lancaster (1980, 1996). The theory focuses on multinational corporations and their need to gain competitive advantage over each other, and how their strategic decisions affect international trade. This struggle revolves around barriers of entry to new markets; so, what firms do is to find ways to overcome these entry barriers. They do this by leveraging assets they have developed over the years such as R&D capabilities; intellectual property rights, achieving economies of scale, unique business processes, rich history, and control of resources.

Last but not the least of the firm-based trade theories is *the theory of competitive advantage* (Porter, 1985, 1990). The theory of comparative advantage assumes that trade will naturally flow once countries have determined their comparative advantage in production. In reality, however, not all nations are able to trade. The theory of competitive advantage seeks to explain why some countries are competitive in certain businesses and others are not. The theory argues that a nation's competitiveness in an industry depends on the capacity of the industry to innovate and upgrade. Porter (1985) identifies five factors in order for this to occur. The first is local market resources and capabilities, which include natural resources, labor skills, investment in education, technology, and infrastructure. The second is local market demand conditions that are sophisticated enough to stimulate continuous innovation, trendsetting, and development of new products. The third is local suppliers and complementary industries needed to remain competitive, and efficient and related industries to supply large companies. The fourth is local firm characteristics, including firm strategy, firm structure, and industry rivalry. The fifth is government policies and actions.

2.2.2.3 The New Trade Theory (NTT)

As we have already noted, both classical and neoclassical theories of trade assume among other things perfect competition, homogenous products, and absence of economies of scale. Taking their cue from industrial organization theories, and the work of Krugman (1979, 1980) and Lancaster (1980), Brander and Spencer (1981, 1985) questioned the conventional trade theories on the basis of these elements that led to the new trade theory (NTT). Thus, instead of discarding imperfect competition, homogenous products, and economies of scale, NTT embraced them in addition to the other assumptions of conventional trade theories. With respect to imperfect competition, NTT argues that many markets in international trade are oligopolies (Krugman, 1987). These firms make super abnormal profits by charging a lot more than their marginal costs of production. This gives the right to governments to intervene by shifting competition in favor of domestic firms as a form of national welfare.

This profit-shifting policy can be implemented in three ways. The first and simplest is to use tariffs to extract rent from a foreign oligopolistic firm. The second is to provide a subsidy to domestic firms competing against a foreign firm in a third market. These will enhance national welfare by reducing the marginal cost of the domestic firm. This allows the domestic firms to capture a larger foreign market share, which increases domestic profit and reduces foreign profit. The third is to apply or extend the infant-industry argument, which is a protected home market that allows domestic firms to leverage their internal economies of scale over foreign producers thereby enabling domestic forms to raise market share in the domestic and unprotected foreign markets. Such government policies are referred to as "strategic trade policies" because they "serve much the same role that "strategic" moves such as investment in excess capacity or research and development (R & D) serve in many models of oligopolistic competition" (Krugman, 1987, p. 135). With respect to scale economies, the NTT argues that certain firms and industries generate positive externalities that are characterized by such low levels of appropriability that those firms and industries will not be able to grow to their optimum without government promotion. Typical examples are knowledge-intensive high-tech and R&D firms and industries in which competitors can easily reverse-engineer a new product.

At a glance it appears that the NTT is arguing against free trade and for that reason, the criticisms have been very swift. These criticisms have come from two sources—economics and political economy (Krugman, 1987; Alam, 2001). The economic critique first charges that the NTT assumes Cournot competition (competition by product variety) which does not work in the Bertrand competition (competition by prices). Thus, in duopoly if the firms behave consistently the same, profit shifting does not work, but defaults to free trade. Second, if the domestic firms are both duopoly but large, an export subsidy creates a negative externality since domestic firms compete against each other without taking into consideration the effects of their actions on their domestic competitors (Dixit, 1984). Also, export subsidies can lead to inefficient entry into the global market and push the domestic firm up its average cost curve (Horstmann & Markusen, 1986). Third, oftentimes, the size of excess profit may be overestimated. The cost of R&D is quite high and we may not see the full cost and losses until the firms begin to turn profits (Grossman, 1986). If profits are not large then the whole basis of profit-sharing postulate falls apart. Fourth, there are differences in results between partial and general equilibrium analysis. Much of the NTT intervention arguments have been based on partial equilibrium analysis, which limits itself to a few factors that operate in the sub-economy.

In general equilibrium analysis, where all factors in the macroeconomy are taken into consideration, things are different. For example, in partial equilibrium, a targeted industry will grow because it can draw resources from other industries. But in general equilibrium conditions, there are chances that some industries will crowd out due to competition, and their inability to draw resources from anywhere. Thus, when all export industries are symmetric, that is, face similar demand conditions in export market, have similar production technologies, and face similar degrees of foreign competition, free trade is the optimum policy since the losses outweigh the gains if one or more firms are targeted for subsidization.

Political economy critique says the prescription of the NTT will first attract foreign retaliation, which can be bad for small countries. Second, inefficient government intervention may worsen the welfare objectives of the NTT. It is argued that many developing countries tried that in the past but failed (Bhagwati, 1987). Besides, the information needed by the government to target or select an industry is difficult to gather and analyze. Third, due to special interest groups that can lobby government actions, government interventions may be ill-advised but its consequences can affect the whole economy. Fourth, government interventions may transfer benefits to owners and employees of protected industries instead of the society at large. Fifth, with respect to developing countries, the NTT prescription is not helpful because of the nature of market structure, especially the lack of anti-trust laws; small size of domestic markets that make it difficult to explore economies of scale; and small size of economy that makes it difficult for governments to play strategic games. Finally, small countries are not repositories of global industries or if they are their small size will prevent them from being first movers. As a result, they stand to lose more in global retaliation.

Classical and neoclassical trade theories based on the law of comparative advantage in terms of comparative costs and factor endowments respectively, advocate for free trade. Firm-based theories while shifting from country as traders to firm as traders highlighted how firms trade and raised the idea of competitive advantage. In addition, they also argued strongly for free trade. Taking its point departure from restrictive assumptions of classical and neoclassical trade theories, such as perfect competition, homogenous products, and absence of scale economies in existing trade theories, the NTT embraced a world of imperfect competition, product differentiation, and economies of scale. The result though still closely tied to comparative and competitive advantage, revealed that both comparative and competitive advantage could be manipulated for "strategic" reasons, questioning the doctrine of free trade that has dominated the theory of international trade for centuries. The result is that as Sen (2005) points out there appear to be two theories of international trade—one for developing countries that promote free trade through trade liberalization, and the other for developed countries that promote "strategic trade policy." Granted the criticism of "strategic trade policy" has been swift, and we will have more to say in subsequent chapters. In the meantime, there is one other disturbing aspect of international trade theory and that is its relationship or impact on development. So much has been written about gains from trade but how these translate into development is at best not explicit in the international trade theory. So, we ask how does international trade relate to or promote development?

2.3 Marxist Trade Theories

A fundamental tenet of classical and neoclassical international trade theories is that trade is beneficial to all parties. However, throughout its history international trade theories have also had some implicit and explicit dissenting views. One of the explicit dissenting views can be traced to Karl Marx. In this section, we examine Marx's original views on international trade and how those views have inspired further theories on trade.

2.3.1 Marx and the International Trade Theory

It is well-known among international trade scholars that Karl Marx did not develop an explicit international trade theory in his lifetime, but his theories of surplus value and money had some relevance to international trade (Marx, 1867, 1885; Shaikh, 1980; Brewer, 1990; Macheda, 2014). Marx agreed with Ricardo and the classical economists about the benefits of free trade but he saw free trade as a vehicle for the impending crisis of capitalism that would transition society into socialism. He attributed this to the unequal development that resulted from capitalist free trade. This unequal development stemmed from two flaws with the labor theory of commodity value, and the quantity theory of money that formed the basis of classical theory of trade (Shaik, 1980; Brewer, 1990).

First, Marx agreed with the labor theory of commodity value of classical economists such as Smith and Ricardo, but for Marx, the price of a commodity was not equivalent to the value of the commodity. Instead, Marx distinguished between the use value and exchange value of commodities. The former is the satisfaction gained from using the commodity, while the latter is the price of the commodity (Marx, 1867; Shaikh, 1980; Brewer, 1990; Macheda, 2014). Marx argued that for the exchange value to be profitable, the capitalist must pay labor what is socially necessary for survival as wages. Marx referred to the difference between this and the actual value as surplus value. The surplus value appropriated by all firms producing the same commodity is not the same because of the differences in technology employed by the capitalist. More capital-intensive firms must sell their products above their direct prices while more labor-intensive firms must sell below their direct prices. The result was an unequal exchange of commodity trade, in which there was a net transfer of value from the labor-intensive firms or technological laggards to the capital-intensive or technological leaders.

Second, Marx disagreed with the theory of comparative advantage that trade would make countries equal. He argued that as a result of competition, firms in low-productivity nations would see declining market shares, contrary to the promise of comparative advantage. Marx elaborated on how this occurred with a critique of the quantity theory of money, which was assumed in Ricardo's theory of comparative advantage. The quantity theory of money states that an increase in the money supply will result in a similar increase in inflation. Marx argued that there was no correlation between changes in money supply and changes in commodity prices and that prices of commodities were not determined by the quantity of money. Marx explained this with a two-country model that was used by Ricardo—namely A and B, engaged in the production of two commodities cocoa and textiles. Country A was more competitive in the production of both items and as a result, was able to undersell firms in Country B. This would cause an outflow of capital from B to A, causing a decrease in money-capital for investment in B and an increase in money-capital in A. Interest rates would rise in B curtailing investment capital, while the exact opposite would occur in A. At some point, the need to invest capital would cause an outflow of capital from A to B, reversing the trend, but only for a short time, because eventually, investment capital that went to B must be paid back with interest, thereby reinstating the status quo of A running a trade surplus and B running a trade deficit (Shaikh, 1980; Brewer, 1990; Macheda, 2014). As a result of all these Marx concluded that free trade would not make all countries competitive but would make weaker trading partners more vulnerable. Second, trade liberalization would be more beneficial to firms in technologically advanced nations than those in technologically impeded nations. Finally, technologically impeded countries would find themselves in a cycle of trade deficit and international borrowing. Marx did not develop an explicit theory of international trade but his ideas would directly or indirectly spurn further thoughts about the role of international trade in economic development. These ideas include imperialism, terms of trade, unequal exchange, and dependency theories.

2.3.2 *Imperialism and International Trade*

Stathakis (2008) asserts that theories of imperialism initially emerged from attempts to explain the rivalry among industrialized nations, especially from 1890 to 1910, that culminated in the catastrophic world event that was antithetical to the ideals of international trade—World War I. International trade was supposed to promote peace and not conflict. These attempts included the works of Hobson (1938), Hilferding (1910), Luxemburg (1913), Bukharin (1917), and Lenin (1917).

Hobson (1938) attributed imperialism to underconsumption, which in turn was caused by monopoly of the capitalist mode of production. Profits obtained through monopolistic control concentrated wealth in the hands of a few, which led to decline in demand. For capital to survive, external markets and new outlets for capital exports were needed, which in turn put pressure on the annexation of new territories. Hobson argued that for the nation, imperialism was bad, but it was good for the monopolists or the few who controlled capital.

Luxemburg (1913, 1921) saw the world economy as consisting of two sectors—a capitalist sector consisting of capitalist firms and states, and a non-capitalist or pre-capitalist sector consisting of non-capitalist firms and states. These two conflicted with each other. Thus, while the non-capitalist sector was stagnant, the capitalist sector was constantly expanding due to competition within it and among its firms. As competition in the capitalist sector intensified, capitalist firms and states were forced to trade with the pre-capitalist sector, which eventually dismantled that mode of production. Capital did this through one of two means—introducing the capitalist mode of production and installing a commodity production that was then undermined by competition for cheaper alternatives of the commodity (Brewer, 1990). In this case, international trade was just another tool of imperialism.

Hilferding (1910) wrote about a new entity in the evolution of capitalism, namely the joint-stock company. Unlike the previous capitalist organizations of individual ownership that were limited in capital and other resources, these joint-stock companies combined a large number of capital from smaller shareholders into one large one, which he referred to as finance capital, and defined as the fusion of industrial and financial capital. Finance capital according to Hilferding, originated from bank deposits which grew as a result of monopoly business. This led to a decline in investment in commerce, which turn forced banks to invest directly in production (Brewer, 1990). The more banks invested in industrial production the more they became part of the industrial capitalists. Hilferding (1910) argued that finance capital had three objectives—the first was to establish the largest possible economic territory. The second was to close the territory with protective tariffs, and the third was to reserve it as an area of exploitation by national monopolies. Finance capital achieved these objectives in several ways. The first was through capital export, which found a way around tariffs by locating production facilities within the tariff wall. The second was by annexing the capital-importing country into the capital-exporting country, and the third was by undermining the protective tariff of the capital-importing country. Hilferding's work was more of the rivalry among industrial nations, but he noted that finance capital used violent methods when it came to dealings with underdeveloped areas. In particular, he noted that capital exports to underdeveloped areas were done through the force of colonialism, and targeted the production of raw materials for export, which in the end led to political and economic dependence.

Bukharin (1917) followed Hilferding's work except that he linked finance capital more explicitly to imperialism, which he saw both as policy and ideology. Thus, imperialism was a policy of conquest and at the same time a phase in the evolution of capitalism. Apart from this, Bukharin saw two processes at work—the internationalization and nationalization of capital, and the division of world economy into national economic blocs. International trade established social relations of production on a world scale. This international division of labor was in turn based on different natural conditions in different areas and the uneven development of countries.

Lenin (1917) explained why Marx's prediction of the collapse of capitalism did not occur, in his theory of imperialism. He argued that as capitalism matured and monopolies caused the concentration of wealth and falling profits, capitalist economies were forced to find new territories or colonies to serve as market and investment outlets as well as sources of raw materials. It was this that postponed the collapse of capitalism as Marx had predicted. Thus, for Lenin, imperialism was the last phase of capitalism.

Classical theories of imperialism, neither focused explicitly on international trade nor developing countries but they all implied that international trade and foreign direct investments were not meant to benefit all partners equally, but rather to benefit the countries that have control of investment capital. Besides, they laid the foundation for subsequent works that explicitly challenged the ideals of international trade with particular reference to developing countries.

2.3.3 Structuralists and the Terms of Trade Arguments

According to Negeshi (2013), the role of terms of trade in determining the benefit of international trade to a country was first identified by Edgeworth (1894) in his theory of international values, in which he showed that trade expansion can have a detrimental effect on a country due to changing terms of trade. However, it would not be until the mid-twentieth century that the terms of trade argument received more attention from structuralist economists, who sought to understand elements of human economic conditions by relating those conditions to broader systems. Thus, structuralists believe that problems facing developing countries stem from rigidities in the economies of those countries.

Manoilesco (1929, 1934) attacked the existing international division of labor and denounced the prescription of classical trade theories that agricultural countries should continue to specialize in agriculture. For Manoilesco, the productivity of industrial workers was much higher than that of agricultural workers, and that would continue as long as agricultural countries did not industrialize. As a result, Manoilesco saw the international division of labor as prescribed by international trade theory as a swindle—a way to exploit one group of people by another (Love, 1980).

In 1937, Raul Prebisch, an Argentine economist, became critical of the idea that international trade was beneficial to all trading countries. He began to investigate why agricultural markets collapsed and found that it was due to long-term deterioration of terms of trade of agricultural products and raw materials. Prebisch (1950) argued that in a world where developed countries exported all manufactured goods and developing countries exported only agricultural products and raw materials, all the benefits of trade would go to developed countries. This idea received support from Hans Singer, the British economist. Singer (1950, p. 477) wrote:

> The specialization of underdeveloped countries on export of food and raw materials to industrialized countries, largely as a result of investment by the latter, has been unfortunate for the underdeveloped countries for two reasons: (a) because it removed most of the secondary and cumulative effects of investment from the country in which the investment took place to the investing country; and (b) because it diverted the underdeveloped countries into types of activity offering less scope for technical progress, internal and external economies taken by themselves, and withheld from the course of their economic history a central factor of dynamic radiation which has revolutionized society in the industrialized countries. But there is a third factor of perhaps even greater importance which has reduced the benefits to

underdeveloped countries of foreign trade-cum-investment based on export specialization on food and raw materials. This third factor relates to terms of trade.

Singer argued that developed countries benefit more from trade than developing countries because of their export industry mix—exporting mostly manufactured products—the impact of technological progress, and elasticity of demand. This led to the Prebisch-Singer Hypothesis that as a result of continuous technological progress, the prices at which less-developed countries will sell at the world market will decline while the prices of what they import will stay just about the same.

This sentiment was expressed by several leading economists toward the end of the 1950s. For example, Myrdal (1957) argued that backwash effects of investments in an open economy often overruled its spread effects. In his theory of immiserizing growth, Bhagwati (1958) showed how an expansion of a country's international trade and economic growth could lead to a loss of welfare as a result of deteriorating terms of trade. Haberler et al. (1958) spelled out factors that led to lack of demand for exports from semi-industrialized countries in advanced countries as technological change, low prices in advanced countries, and income elasticity of demand for export from developing countries. Nurkse (1959) identified the role of agricultural protectionism in advanced countries and lagging demand for imported inputs from developing countries as the causes of underdevelopment.

Basing himself on what he identified as the "vent-for-surplus" theory of international trade by Adam Smith, Myint (1958) pointed out that the international trade expansion that occurred in less-developed countries in the nineteenth century could be better explained by the "vent-for-surplus" theory than the comparative cost theory of international trade. Myint (1958) argued that the expansion was due to production increase without any additional input except the development of a transportation system by colonial powers. Many of the colonies started off with sparse populations which allowed for rapid expansion of export trade. This participation in international trade did not benefit only the colonial powers but the colonies as well. As already pointed out the vent-for-surplus interpretation has attracted a lot of debate among economists, some in support of Myint's interpretation and others completely against it. For Schumacher (2015) the two benefits of trade Adam Smith were talking about were exports and imports.

2.3.4 Dependency Theories and International Trade

Dependency theories may be seen as modern theories of imperialism or theories of imperialism that emerged after World War II. (Baran (1957), a pioneer of these theories, divided the world economy into two—the advanced capitalist countries and underdeveloped countries. These two parts of the world economy interacted in three ways—trade flows, surplus flows, and political-military relations. Trade flows served as a conduit for cheaper manufactured goods and a deterrent to development of manufacturing capacity in developing countries. Surplus flow occurred in the form of profits and dividends that were appropriated by industrialized countries, while political-military helped support governments in underdeveloped countries in return for their loyalty to advanced countries (Brewer, 1990). Baran (1957) identified three pre-conditions for capitalism—the first was an increase in agricultural output and displacement of a large number of agricultural population; the second was a growth of commodity production and division of labor, and the third was the accumulation of capital by merchants and rich peasants (Brewer, 1990). Baran saw the accumulation of capital as the most crucial and pointed out that it was the accumulation of merchant capital in Europe that supported the European expansion across the world, to the detriment of underdeveloped countries. The persistence of underdeveloped regions, according to Baran was due to a uniform and characteristic social and economic structure that has come to exist in underdeveloped regions that blocked development. For Baran, these included a large and very backward agriculture sector characterized by small-scale peasant production and parasitic landlords; a relatively advanced but small industrial sector dominated mostly by foreign ownership and producing for the limited local market; a large group of small-scale enterprises producing raw materials for export; a large trading sector consisting of large-scale merchants who controlled foreign trade; and a small-scale trading sector which operated in rural areas. The weakest point in such an economic structure was the lack of industrial development, which in turn was due to competition from abroad that stifled infant industry, narrow markets that discouraged development, and monopolies that became barriers instead of progress (Brewer, 1990).

Seeking to extend the work of structuralists such as Prebisch and Singer and the Marxist theory of Baran, Frank (1966) argued that the uneven development across the world could be traced directly to global capitalism. Following Baran (1957), Frank (1966) divided the world economy as consisting of metropolitan (developed) and satellite (underdeveloped) countries and argued that underdevelopment was not an initial stage, but rather a conditioning process to make satellite countries become dependent on metropolitan countries (Dos Santos, 1970). This process was started with the European voyages of exploration which then morphed into international trade and colonialism. Furtado (1973) added that the consumption pattern of the elite in underdeveloped countries was another part of the process since such a pattern was adopted from the metropolitan countries, forcing the production of goods to meet such a limited market. So, while the present-day advanced countries were undeveloped in the past, they were not underdeveloped, because they did not go through the conditioning process. For Frank, it was the link with the capitalist system of metropolitan countries that was the problem. He argued that from 1929 to the 1950s Latin America showed the greatest level of industrialization because its links with metropolitan countries were disrupted by Great Depression and World War II. Unfortunately, because Latin America still relied on raw material exports and because raw material prices fell, the opportunity for Latin America's growth was short-lived (Kay, 2005).

Frank's theory of underdevelopment was extended to the modern World Systems theory by Wallerstein (1979). This theory conceived of a global economy that consisted of three parts—the core, the semi-periphery, and the periphery. The core was dominated by the advanced capitalist countries and the periphery was characterized by poor countries, while the semi-periphery countries were between the core and the periphery. This system began in the sixteenth century after the European voyages of discovery and culminated in the nineteenth century with European colonialism. In this world system, there is a transfer of net wealth from the periphery to the core. The semi-periphery states consisted of states of labor aristocracy that sought to prevent the systems from the two polar extremes of the core and the periphery. This system is maintained by the core states' ability to manipulate it through such measures as protecting their own manufacturing industries without reciprocal protection of industries in the periphery, the international division of labor of the capitalist mode of production, and its associated international institutions such as the World Bank and the International Monetary Fund (Milward, 2020).

Amin (1974, 1976) followed a similar trend of thought to explain how capital accumulation on a world scale resulted in unequal development and its associated problems for developing countries. Contrary to the belief that capital accumulation led to uniformity, Amin argued that accumulation led to division of the world economy into the center, consisting of developed countries, and the periphery, consisting of developing countries. While accumulation at the center grew on its own dynamics, accumulation at the periphery was controlled by the center-periphery relationship. At the core of this relation is the unequal specialization between the center and the periphery that came to exist as a result of the initial advantage that the center had in productivity in many areas of industry. This made it possible for wages to be held low at both the center and the periphery. Later, wages rose at the center while the high productivity allowed the center to keep production costs down. This enabled capitalism at the center to invade pre-capitalist modes of production, subjecting them to production of only resource-based activities without the full development of capitalist industrialization—what Amin called "peripheral capitalism." High wages at the center and low wages at the periphery led to unequal exchange. For Amin, specialization was determined by absolute advantage not comparative costs. Trade could cause unemployment because when capital is mobile and productivity differences are higher than wage differences, capital will flow from the periphery to the center.

2.3.5 *Theories Unequal Exchange*

The concept of unequal exchange was not new in international trade discussions (Brewer, 1990; Milward, 2020). Milward (2020) states that Bauer and Grossman used the concept of organic composition of capital to illustrate the idea of unequal exchange during the 1920s and 1930s. Prebisch's (1937) work on terms of trade was also in the same tradition. However, it was Emmanuel's (1972) theory that revived the idea and brought it to the center of Marxian trade theories. Emmanuel's theory began with an attack on one of the most fundamental assumptions of Ricardo's law of comparative cost—immobility of labor and capital. Thus, Emmanuel began with the same factors in Ricardo's law of comparative cost—labor and capital. The value of a commodity consisted of three parts—the value of the material and machinery used in the production, the value of the labor that went into the production, and the surplus value. Prices of products also consisted of three parts—the cost of material and machinery, the cost of labor, and profits (Sau, 1976). Mobility of labor equalized wages while mobility of capital equalized profits. However, while Ricardo assumed the immobility of both labor and capital, Emmanuel assumed that capital was internationally mobile while labor was not (Shaikh, 1980). Thus, while there could be a single rate of profit globally, there were wage differences at the national level. In addition, he assumed free trade with no transportation cost. Under these conditions, two countries with different wage levels have two ways to reap equal rates of profits. First, they must produce the same items but the country with higher wages must have a higher productivity to make cost equal. Second, the countries may produce different commodities to avoid competition (Brewer, 1990). However, if one commodity was produced only in the high-wage country and the other only in the low-wage, the commodity produced in the high-wage country would be more expensive than the one produced in a low-wage country because the price of the commodities must reflect the wage differences. Emmanuel referred to this as unequal exchange, because the low-wage producer must pay more for its imports than it would if wages were the same. Similarly, the high-wage country would get more imports for its exports. Thus, the source of unequal exchange according to Emmanuel was the wage differentials between advanced and underdeveloped countries. As a result, there was a transfer of value from underdeveloped countries to developed countries through international trade, contrary to what neoclassical economic theory of international trade.

Emmanuel (1972, p. 265) wrote:

> Even if we agree that unequal exchange is only one of the mechanisms whereby value is transferred from one group of countries to another and that its direct effects account for only part of the difference in standards of living, I think it is possible to state that unequal exchange is the elementary transfer mechanism and that, as such it enables the advanced countries to begin and regularly to give new impetus to that unevenness of development that sets in motion all the other mechanisms of exploitation and fully explains the way that wealth is distributed.

Lewis (1969) also advanced an alternative view of unequal exchange, in which labor was the only cost in an economy in which all countries produced food that was traded on the world market at a single price. However, the productivity levels were lower in less developed countries than in more developed countries. As a result, less-developed countries had lower wages compared to more developed countries. At the same time, non-food commodities (manufactures) were produced only in advanced countries, so their prices were higher since they reflected the differences in wages in those countries. Under these conditions, the exchange for non-food commodities was unequal for the same reasons as wage differentials, but unlike Emmanuel, Lewis attributed the wage differentials to differences in productivity in the industries in the advanced and less-developed countries.

International trade theories in the Marxist tradition emerged as a critique of neoclassical trade theories, but they have been also criticized by both Marxist and non-Marxists (e.g. Lall, 1975; Sweezy, 1976; Brenner, 1977; Moles, 1999; Namkoong,

1999; Agbebi & Vertinan, 2017; Futerman & Block, 2020). Marx himself has been criticized for leaving an incomplete work that was largely based on European history (Shaikh, 1980). Futerman and Block (2020) argued that the terms of trade argument outlined by Prebisch-Singer thesis actually backfired because the cause of Argentina's plight was the protectionism and import-substitution industrialization that was promoted by the Prebisch-Singer thesis. Lall (1975) criticized dependency theories for their circular arguments—that is less-developed countries were poor because they were dependent. Dunn (2009) also noted that dependency theories fell out of favor in part because the experiences of export-oriented economies of Asia undermined the contention of the North's grip of an unchanging North-South hierarchy that perpetuated underdevelopment. Brenner (1977) criticized dependency, world systems, and unequal exchange theories. He disagreed with Wallerstein about the appropriate level and unit of analysis. For Brenner, the nation-state and class should be the appropriate level and unit of analysis, respectively, instead of using systems as level of analysis and several other factors including state and class as units of analysis. In addition, trade was not prominent in the development of capitalism as Wallerstein, projected. He also criticized Frank's theory of underdevelopment for attributing all the causes of underdevelopment to external exploitation, an argument that was echoed by Smith (1979) and Namkoong (1999). For Brenner, it was the type of class structure that developed that caused underdevelopment, not external exploitation. Finally, Brenner also questioned the relevance of the theory of unequal exchange in a world of equalization of profit rates due to international capital mobility.

However, Bergesen (1984) questioned Brenner's argument noting that indigenous class struggle in Latin America could not have produced the class relations of the underdeveloped colonial society. With respect to unequal exchange, Bergesen (1984) argued that core-periphery relations should not be seen only as unequal exchange, but as global class relations. Thus, it was not unequal exchange between Europe and the Aztecs and Incas that caused the underdevelopment, but the forceful conquest and continued ownership and control of these areas and their people, and their labor power by the core (Bergesen, 1984, p. 368). For Bergesen (1984) both traditional Marxists and World-System theorists were trapped in theoretical structure of the nineteenth century. Thus, while class was central to the transformation of Europe, it was not the case in the periphery. The central question is who controls the means of production. Given that more than 80% of the world's population was living in colonial possessions, Bergesen (1984) argued that colonialism represented the defining social relations of production for one global economy. Bergesen (1984, pp. 370–371) wrote

> There is, then, no "internal" and "external." There is only one world economy, one social formation, and, most important, one world or global mode of production. Contrary to Wallerstein, it is not defined by the unequal exchange of a core/periphery division of labor; nor, contrary to Brenner, do its class relations exist only within states. The global mode of production is defined by the global class relation of core ownership and control over peripheral production, which occurred in the past through formal colonial rule and persists today through a variety of less formal mechanisms (foreign investment, penetration by multinationals, arms dependence, periodic military interventions, and so on).

> The core/periphery relation is a power-dependence relation and only secondarily an exchange relation. … There is unequal exchange, yes, but it exists only because of a priori global power-dependence relations (global class relations) that frame these exchanges.

In a review of a debate between Brenner and Wallerstein, Denemark and Thomas (1988) concluded that while the world-systems framework offered a more powerful level of analysis, it alone was not sufficient to account for internal political and economic interactions of countries.

2.4 Trade Barriers

Trade theory in general espouses benefits for all, but international trade is also intertwined with politics and national interest. As a result, there are barriers. These barriers are of many different kinds but they generally fall into two categories—tariffs and non-tariff barriers.

2.4.1 Tariffs

Tariffs are the conventional tool for impeding trade between and among nations. They are taxes levied on imports with the rationale that those imports will be more expensive than domestically produced goods and services. Generally speaking, tariffs may benefit the domestic sector but economic theorists and especially the supporters of free trade frown on tariffs as a form of protectionist tool and a trade impedance. Tariffs are paid by the importers of the commodity into a country to the customs agency but in the end, it is the domestic consumers who pay the tax because importers pass on the cost to consumers. Tariffs are used for several reasons (Radcliffe, 2022). First, they are used to protect domestic employment. International competition can lead to declining revenues for domestic firms, which in turn can lead to the layoff of workers and a rise in unemployment. Second, tariffs may also be used to protect domestic consumers. This is when governments deem a particular product dangerous for human consumption, Third, tariffs may be used to protect infant industries. Infant industries are new or young industries that are particularly vital to the economies of countries that are just embarking on industrialization. The rationale is that without such protection, it will be difficult for the young industry to take off because of the relatively cheaper alternatives from countries that have established industries. In this case, a tariff raises the price of the competing product making it more expensive than the domestic product. This it is argued allows developing countries to jumpstart their manufacturing sector thereby enabling them to make the transition from primary producers to secondary producers. Fourth, tariffs may also be used for purposes of national security. This is common in developed countries where certain sectors of their economies are deemed strategic to their national security. As a result, governments impose tariffs to exclude foreign competitors from participating in such areas. The most common examples are defense-related industries. Fifth, tariffs also serve as retaliation tools. This often arises when trading partners become suspicious of each other for not playing by the rules (Radcliffe, 2022). We recently witnessed this about US trade with China, the EU, Canada, and Mexico during the Trump Administration. The Trump administration announced a 25% tariff on $16 billion worth of Chinese goods in 2018. It also announced tariffs on steel imports from the EU, Canada, and Mexico all as a retaliation for unfair trade. China retaliated with its own 25% tariff on $16 billion worth of US goods.

Theoretically, there are two main types of tariffs—specific tariffs and ad valorem tariffs. Specific tariffs are levied on a single product and tend to vary by product. Ad valorem tariff is based on the value of the product and it is usually based on the percentage of the product's value. That percentage is usually added to the price of the product, thereby making it more expensive in the domestic market.

Practically, the WTO, UNCTAD, and the World Bank database on tariffs use a different classification system for their purposes. They are the most favored nation (MFN), with preferential tariffs, and bound tariffs. MFN tariff is what a country proposes to charge for exports or imports from another country that is a member of WTO unless that country belongs to the same free trade area (FTA) or customs union (CU). It is the highest tariff a country can impose. Preferential tariffs are the rates offered to countries that are members of FTAs or CUs. So, virtually all countries of the world have at least one preferential tariff by being a member of a free trade area or customs union. These rates are usually zero among members of an FTA or CU. Bound tariffs are the maximum MFN tariffs a country agrees to commit on a given commodity during trade negotiations with its trading partners. It is not the actual tariff applied but serves as the upper limit to the tariff rate. Once agreed, countries are free to raise or decrease their tariff rates as long as the rates do not arise above the bound. If the rate rises above, other WTO members can take that country to dispute settlement. The binding coverage is the percentage of a country's commodities that have the bound tariff rate. This has varied from excluding certain commodities (e.g. agricultural products) to including all. At the moment they range from 15% to 100% depending on the country. The difference between the applied MFN tariff rate and the bound tariff is called the binding overhang (The World Bank, 2010).

2.4.2 *Non-tariff Barriers*

Besides tariffs, there are other barriers to trade. A survey of business conducted by the OECD (2005) listed 22 non-tariff barriers (NTB). Of these, the most frequently mentioned were technical barriers, internal taxes or charges, customs rules and procedures, and competition-related restrictions on market access. Others include licenses, import prohibitions and quotas, voluntary export restraints, and local content requirements.

2.4.2.1 Technical Barriers

These include regulations, product standards, testing, and certification procedures countries use for product entry into a country. Imported commodities must meet these requirements before they are allowed entry into a country (WTO et al., 2021). They serve two purposes. The first is to ensure product quality and the second is to protect the health of domestic consumers (Grundke & Moser, 2019). Products that do not comply with such standards are refused entry into the domestic markets. Most countries have government agencies that are charged with such responsibilities. In the US for example it is the Food and Drug Administration (FDA). Research shows that there appear to be two standards—a less stringent one for domestic products, and a more stringent one for imported products. In the United States, for example, the agency must have evidence of a violation to refuse a domestic product from entering the market. However, for imported products, an "appearance of a violation" would be enough to refuse the product's entry into the domestic market. Several studies show that the application or implementation of such standards tends to be more severe for developing countries than for countries that belong to the Organization for Economic Cooperation and Development (OECD). In addition, refusal of entry increases during a period of economic crisis (Grundke & Moser, 2019; Trefler, 1993; Essaji, 2008; Bagwell & Staiger, 2003; Kee et al., 2013). For the USFDA, Grundke and Moser (2019) state that there are two main reasons for refusing a product into a domestic market. They are adulteration and misbranding. The first refers to product quality including the health hazard concerns of the product's content. The second refers to not meeting US labeling standards or not providing full documentation or certificates for product assessment (Grundke & Moser, 2019). All these and the fact that refusal of entry without any sample product analysis dominates the total volume of refusals have led many researchers to see this as a form of hidden protectionism (Grundke & Moser, 2019; Rose, 2013; Bown & Crowley, 2013; Kee et al., 2013; Lamb, 2006).

The WTO collects data on notifications of technical barriers from member nations. From this database, WTO (2021) reported that technical barriers to trade have increased at an average rate of 11% since 1995. Over the past 5 years, notifications have topped more than 3000 a year. Of these, protection of human health accounts for about 45%. While notifications provide the opportunity for member countries to comment on intended new rules, concerns allow members to discuss new rules before they go into effect or before matters become fully disputed. Since 1995, the number of concerns raised has grown at an average rate of 11% per year (WTO, 2021). In 2020, a record number of 57 new concerns were discussed.

2.4.2.2 Administrative Barriers

These include complex customs regulations, large amounts of paperwork, cumbersome customs clearances, and frequent inspections (OECD, 2005; Hornok & Koren, 2015). These barriers have such a dampening effect on trade that in 2013 all members of the World Trade Organization agreed for the first on a trade facilitation package called the Bali Package. Administrative barriers are not a one-time cost but they are associated with every shipment. Research shows that these barriers are larger in developing countries and smaller in developed countries. Hornok and Koren (2015) assert that doubling the income of an importing country would be associated with a 6% decline in per shipment cost. Hornok and Koren (2015) also argue that because administrative barriers are associated with every shipment, exporters have to decide how to break up total trade into smaller shipment. At the same time, because consumers prefer their products within a certain time frame, delays due to shipment breaks lead to welfare loss to consumers. Administrative barriers reduce trade volumes, and it has been identified as one of the reasons why trade volumes are higher in a customs union than in a free trade area (Hornok & Koren, 2015; Krueger, 1997; Frankel, 1998).

2.4.2.3 Information Asymmetry

According to WTO (2005), information asymmetry refers to product information differences between producers and consumers of the product. Thus, producers may have information about the product's quality that is not available to consumers. These differences can create a lemons market mentality on the part of consumers which ends up impeding international trade (Potoski & Prakash, 2009; Akerlof, 1970; Chisik, 2003; Chiang & Masson, 1988). In general, consumers or buyers try to avoid lemons market in several ways. First, they associate product quality with the reputation of the producer and its brand (Potoski & Prakash, 2009; Greif, 1989; Kreps & Wilson, 1982; Milgrom & Roberts, 1986). Second, they associate the product quality with the country of the producer or seller. Third, they rely on the government to help solve the lemons market problem through regulations, mandatory disclosures, and product standards. This is an international trade problem that emerging industrialized countries face compared to established industrialized countries. Generally speaking, information asymmetry worsens when the product is from a developing country. A current example is products from China compared to products from other industrialized countries. Underlying this information asymmetry are spatial and cultural barriers. Potoski and Prakash (2009) show that the International Organization for Standardization (ISO) 9000 program has helped reduce the information asymmetry among countries and has thus increased international trade. This increase is particularly remarkable for developing countries, which as a group used to be more subjected to the lemons market problem.

2.4.2.4 Licenses, Import Prohibitions, Quotas, and Safeguards

Licenses authorize importers to import specific types of products into a country. These are granted by governments to specific businesses. By allowing a small segment of businesses to import certain products, licenses restrict the volume of trade. Import prohibitions are restrictions to imports that are usually applied at the border. Import quotas are quantitative limits on the number or volume of a given product that can be imported into a country. They sometimes operate within license agreements or on their own. For example, the government can set a limit on the number of cars that can be imported into a country in a year at 500,000, beyond which no imported cars will be allowed. Together, import prohibitions and quotas serve two purposes, to reduce the volume of imports or to completely stop the importation of the commodity (Czaga, 2005). Safeguards are actions taken by a country if its domestic economy is injured by a sudden surge of imports. Industries or companies may request the government to take a safeguard action. If investigations confirm the need for a safeguard action, the government can restrict imports.

Article XI of GATT provides that no restrictions be placed on imports and exports of goods. However, there are exceptions for economic and non-economic reasons whereby restrictions can be imposed by governments. The non-economic reasons include application of product standards or regulations for classification and marketing of the product, achievement of certain public goals such as morals, and human and animal health; and national security interests. Exceptions for economic reasons include safeguarding the external financial position of the country, protecting infant industry in developing countries; and protecting domestic producers from serious injury (Czaga, 2005).

2.4.2.5 Voluntary Export Restraints (VER)

VERs place limits on the volume of exports by exporting countries at the request of importing countries for reciprocity. For example, at the request of Ghana, Burkina Faso could place a VER on the amount of tomatoes it exports to Ghana. In return, Ghana could place a VER on the amount of textile prints it exports to Burkina Faso. Theoretically, both countries will enjoy price increases while protecting their domestic economies.

2.4.2.6 Local Content Requirements

Governments may also require some components or percentage of an imported product to be made domestically. For example, the requirement could be a percentage of the value of the commodity or a percentage of the components of the product. Such requirements protect the domestic markets from full competition from foreign firms and also create technological capability in the local economy.

When a company exports a commodity at a price lower than what it charges in its own home market, it is dumping. Anti-dumping regulations are set to counter-dumping. Countries may impose anti-dumping duty. Countervailing measures are the reactions to dumping and subsidies. They usually involve a tax or duty—countervailing duty. The duty is imposed only after the importing nation has conducted a thorough investigation into the matter (WTO et al., 2021).

2.4.2.7 Dealing with Trade Barriers and African Countries

In theory, trade barriers are counter to free trade and its welfare effect on economies; so as much as trade barriers have evolved with international trade so are the efforts to reduce them. Trade agreements, bilateral or multilateral, have been part of human history even though there is not much about them in received literature. Thus, most discussion takes its starting point from mercantilism, which was an anti-trade agreement because of its view of international trade as a zero-sum game. The end of mercantilism and the rise of nationalism in Europe in the eighteenth and nineteenth centuries thwarted any serious efforts at trade agreements until well after World War II. In 1948, as part of the post-World War II Bretton Woods, New Hampshire, Conference the General Agreements on Tariff and Trade (GATT) Treaty was signed. The original intent of GATT was to establish an International Treaty Organization (ITO), with the ultimate goal of removing trade barriers through a series of multilateral trade negotiations that were referred to as Rounds. The ITO was not established but GATT's mission of trade negotiations to reduce tariffs was pursed. In 1986, the Uruguay Round, which was the eighth and the last series of talks, made a significant breakthrough that eventually led to the formation of the WTO (Ofori-Amoah, 2019).

With respect to African countries, between the signing of the agreement and the establishment of the WTO, a number of developments occurred that were all related to removing trade barriers (Ofori-Amoah, 2019). First, only four African countries (Ethiopia, Liberia, South Africa, and Egypt) were politically independent when GATT was signed, yet by their status as colonies of Europe, they were all given associated states (AS) status of GATT except Morocco, which France did not sponsor to become a member of GATT. The return to independence of many African countries in the 1960s meant that a new form of agreement was needed. Thus, in July 1963, the European Economic Community (EEC) and former French colonies in Africa signed the Yaoundé Convention, which removed all customs duties on agricultural products not covered by EEC common agricultural policy and EEC tariffs, except for those that generated revenues for development (Sissoko et al., 1998). The treaty expired in May 1969 and was extended by Yaoundé II from January 1970 to January 1975.

Second, African countries and their developing world counterparts grew concerned about their terms of trade. At the same time foreign aid, which had been purported to be a fix for the problems, was not working, as it should. As a result, developing countries pushed for a forum for discussing trade and development issues. In 1961, African countries joined a group of developing countries that claimed to be non-aligned to either the West or the East to form the Non-Aligned Movement (NAM). In July 1962, the group issued the Cairo Declaration that (1) Developing countries should focus on the processing of raw materials and labor-intensive manufacturing; (2) Developed countries focus on higher capital goods production that did not require resources from developing countries; (3) There was no need to form another economic bloc; (4). Commodity price stabilization should be fixed; and (5). There was a need to convene an international conference on trade and development (Nesadurai, 2008).

The first United Nations Conference on Trade and Development (UNCTAD) convened in March 1964 in Geneva, Switzerland, but that conference as well as subsequent ones were wrecked by differences between developed and developing countries. In 1971, UNCTAD developed a list of least developed countries including 16 African countries to receive special treatment from developed countries. GATT adopted this system as the Generalized System of Preferences (GSP) in 1971, which consisted of preferential treatments that each developed country chose to give a particular developing country on a limited number of commodities. There was no general list and the preferences were limited because none of the commodities involved was duty-free (Minta, 1984). Apart from this, reciprocity was often enforced in multilateral trade negotiations.

Third, on May 1, 1974, a push from developing countries caused the UN General Assembly to adopt the Declaration on the Establishment of a New International Economic Order (NIEO) and a Program of Action for the Establishment of a New International Economic Order. The program contained seven proposals for change. (1) More stable prices for agricultural commodities and raw materials through the establishment of a Common Fund that would be used to stabilize prices similar to the buffer stock mechanism. (2). Transfer of resources from rich countries to poor countries through such mechanisms as generalized debt relief and increased aid that was less dependent on developed countries' politics and government. (3). Access to technology that would enable developing countries to industrialize and contribute about 25% of global manufacturing by 2000. (4) Stricter control of the activities of multinational corporations in developing countries so that the corporations would not only concern themselves with their bottom line but would take into consideration the wellbeing and development of their host countries. (5). More access to the market of developed countries by developing country manufactures through lowering of tariff and non-tariff barriers. (6). Reform of the international monetary system. In particular, developing countries complained about the conditionality attached to loans received from the International Monetary Fund (IMF), as well as the dominance of the IMF by developed countries. (7). Developed countries should give more voice to the developing countries in international trade and investment matters (Streeten, 1982). Developed countries initially opposed the NIEO, especially the idea of a Common Fund, which was to serve as a buffer stock for commodities. However, by the next UN meeting in 1975, the positions of both developing countries and the US, in particular, changed from confrontation to cooperation, because of mutual interests. Some sort of compromise between the general position of developing countries and the US position was attempted at the meeting, but overall, the meeting was a disappointment for developing countries. Subsequent conferences continued to discuss some elements of the NIEO, but by the 1980s, the NIEO idea was dead (Ofori-Amoah, 2019).

Fourth, African countries had entered into other trade deals on their own, while the NIEO dragged on. One of these trade deals was the International Cocoa Agreement of 1972 and the more comprehensive Lomé Convention. The convention was signed for the first time in 1975 between the European Economic Community (EEC), and African, (excluding North Africa) Caribbean, and Pacific (ACP) states. It was negotiated after Britain was admitted into the EEC to allow its former colonies to have a relationship with the EEC. Essentially the agreement gave preferential treatment to ACP countries, to trade with the EEC. In particular, sugar, beef, banana, and rum received special treatment. Commodities that fell under the Common Agricultural Policy (CAP) of the EEC, however, did not get free access due to quality and health restrictions imposed by the EEC. An important piece of the Lomé agreement was the establishment of the Export Earning Stabilization System (STABEX). This system provided funds from the EEC to ACP countries that fell short in export revenues (at least 7.5%) due to natural disasters. Initially, STABEX covered 34 commodities. The Lomé Convention was extended several times by Lomé II (1981–1985), Lomé III (1986–1990), and Lomé IV (1990–2000). Under Lomé II, STABEX was extended to cover 44 commodities, including mining, and the shortfall in export revenue that would make a country eligible for STABEX funds was reduced to 6.5% (Sissoko et al., 1998). Lomé III emphasized self-sufficiency in food production, while Lomé IV had a political dimension.

Analyzing the impact of these trade agreements on African countries, Sissoko et al. (1998) noted that the results were generally insignificant. Indeed, EEC imports from Associated States declined under both Yaoundé I and II, while exports from Associated States to others increased. Under Lome I and II, however, African countries did better. Their exports to the EEC grew to 62.1% even though African countries in the British Commonwealth did better than their counterparts in Yaoundé I and II. Much of the growth was however limited to a few commodities and countries. For example, since oil and coffee accounted for 33.7% and 4.6% of imports, respectively, the countries that benefited the most were Nigeria, Angola, Gabon, and Cote d'Ivoire. Imports by the EEC grew more slowly in sub-Saharan African countries compared to North African countries (Sissoko et al., 1998). With respect to STABEX, Sissoko et al. (1998) reported that the impact was positive for West and East Africa especially as it pertained to cotton production but was negative for Central and North African countries, especially Sudan because of political and social crises. Finally, effort to use GATT's GSP by the EEC within the framework of the Lomé Conventions was not successful because of too many restrictions. In the end, the Lomé Conventions failed to diversify exports of African countries.

Fifth, following the economic crises of the 1970s, African countries were from 1980 through late 1990s subjected to trade liberalization policies as part of the World Bank and the International Monetary Fund's structural adjustment programs (SAPs). These policies involved the reduction of tariffs, conversion of non-tariff barriers to tariffs, and devaluation of national currencies (UNCTAD, 2008). The argument was that such policies would encourage export trade through efficiency and production of tradable goods. The UNCTAD (2008) report revealed that between 1995 and 2006 tariffs in Africa went from 22% to 13%. Most of the non-tariff barriers were removed, while national currencies fell from 200% overrated levels in 1981–1985 to 50% in the 1990s. These policies also did away with the agricultural commodity marketing boards in many African countries, except in Ghana, that were using the buffer stock mechanism to support price fluctuations.

Sixth, the formation of the World Trade Organization (WTO) in January 1995 with the mandate to implement, administer, and manage all trade agreements reached under GATT, impacted African trade in many significant ways. First, the preferential treatment regarding the EU banana trade within the Lomé Convention was challenged by the banana producers of Central and South America backed by the US. WTO ruled that the EU banana regime, as the agreement was called, was inconsistent with WTO rules. After both an appeal and a revised proposal by the EU had failed, the EU agreed to phase out the ACP agreement by 2006. In its place, a new agreement, the Cotonou Agreement, was signed for a period of 20 years (2000–2020). The Agreement allowed African countries to export goods to the EU duty-free and retain their tariffs on goods imported from the EU. However, this applied to only the countries that were classified as least developed countries, most of which were in Africa. The countries that were relatively well off had to negotiate their own trade agreements with the EU.

Second, the WTO also has the mandate to administer the agreement on trade-related aspects of intellectual property rights (TRIPS). This agreement gives protection to inventors of new products and processes, especially in the pharmaceutical industry in developed countries for a period of 20 years before the product could be made by others or the process might be available to others. A test of this agreement arose when in 1998 the Pharmaceutical Association of South Africa filed a lawsuit against a South African law that allowed parallel importing and compulsory licensing of HIV/AIDS drugs to make them more accessible to HIV/AIDS patients. Parallel importing is when a product is resold by a third party without the consent of the patent holder and compulsory licensing is where a government allows a third party to produce a product without authorization of the patent holder, a practice permitted under public health emergency (Mshomba, 2009). Although HIV/AIDS infection in South Africa had become a national public health emergency, both the US and EU sided with the Pharmaceutical Association. The lawsuit was however dropped in 2001 due to international public outcry and the intervention of the World Health Organization (WHO).

The third and definitely the area of most concern to African countries is the trade in agricultural products. The agreement that established the WTO was an Agricultural Trade Agreement, which called for increased access to market, and a reduction in domestic support and export subsidies to agricultural products. However, the agreement had no clear commitment so not much happened. The sticking point in the agreement was the farm and export subsidies that the EU, the United States, and China gave to their respective farmers. At its meeting in Doha, Qatar, in November 2001, WTO members agreed to initiate a new round that would focus on development, and increase market access in agriculture, manufacturing, and service activities. However, what began with high hopes amidst fanfare has been a major disappointment after more than 20 years of negotiation due to the differences among developed countries on non-tariff barriers and differences between developing and developed countries on agricultural subsidies.

Fourth, the WTO launched a new initiative, called Aid for Trade in 2005, which had implications for African countries. The purpose of the initiative was to (1) develop trade strategies, negotiation, and implementation of outcomes; (2) build trade-supporting infrastructure such as roads, ports, and telecommunication networks, (3) improve productive capacities for export diversification; and (4) deal with the cost of trade due to loss of tariff revenue, preferential treatment, or declining terms of trade. A review of the Aid for Trade program in 2011 by the United Nations Economic Commission for Africa (UNECA) showed that from 2006–2009 African countries received more Aid for Trade commitments than years before, from \$7.6 billion from 2002 to 2005 to \$16.5 billion from 2006 to 2009. However, disbursements fell from 75% in 2006 to 62% in 2009 (UNECA, 2011). Apart from this, a disproportionate share went to a few countries including Egypt, Ethiopia, Ghana, Kenya, Morocco, Mozambique, Tanzania, and Uganda. The largest proportion, more than 50%, of this aid went to economic infrastructure, followed by improvement in productive capacity particularly in agriculture and banking sectors. About 60% of the economic infrastructure projects were in road transportation and storage facilities. The remaining 40% went into the energy sector (30%) and telecommunication (10%). Subsequent biennial reviews of Aid for Trade by the WTO indicate that the program is working. However, the amount of commitment and disbursement to Africa has declined from a peak of \$18.5 billion in 2010 to \$13.1 billion in 2011, a drop of 29%. Under WTO, African countries have continued to receive preferential treatment but that too has limited their ability to participate fully in the dispute settlement understanding (DSU) process, which in itself is a very complicated and expensive process (Mshomba, 2009). Last but not least, from 1959 through 1994, African countries formed 13 regional trade agreements that resulted in overlapping membership, which is the subject of this book.

2.5 Conclusion

International trade was not a favorite subject of antiquity thinkers. From ancient Greece through early Christian period, the leading thinkers of the day leaned more toward autarky than obtaining societal needs through trade. However, this view evolved over time to where international trade came to be seen as beneficial to society. Mercantilism provided the first formal rationale for international trade. It believed that a nation's wealth was determined by the amount of gold and silver it possessed. So, governments were encouraged to support more exports, which brought gold and silver in, and limit imports, which caused outflow of gold and silver. More importantly, mercantilism saw international trade as a zero-sum game, where one nation's gain was another nation's loss. This view was criticized by the Physiocrats and classical economists such as Adam Smith, David Ricardo, and John Stuart Mill criticized mercantilism. The Physiocrats charged that a nation's wealth depended on its agricultural development and that free trade was the best approach to amass wealth. Adam Smith also criticized mercantilism and argued that nations would benefit more if they specialized in producing goods in which they had absolute advantage and exchanged their surpluses through trade. Ricardo argued that nations did not need absolute advantage to engage in trade; rather they needed comparative advantage. For the next 100 years or so the law of comparative advantage became the main explanation for why international trade took place. During the 1930s the Heckscher-Ohlin theory sought to replace the labor cost component in the law of comparative advantage with factor endowments of countries. The theory argued that labor-abundant countries should specialize in producing labor-intensive goods, while capital-abundant countries should specialize in producing capital-intensive products. By so doing both countries would consume more through specialization and division of labor. For the next 50 years factor endowments dominated international trade theory although empirical evidence was woefully weak. This and other criticisms of the theory led to firm-based and new trade theories. Firm-based theories take their motivation from two ideas. The first is it is firms, not countries that trade. The second is the trading behavior of multinational corporation corporations. These theories highlight how corporate strategies influence when, where, and how firms conduct international trade. Still focusing on corporate behavior in a world of imperfect competition and economies of scale, the new trade theories argue that much of the world trade is conducted by oligopolies, which have the tendency to make abnormal profits. This gives national governments the legitimacy to shift some of the profits for "strategic "and other public welfare reasons using tariff and non-tariff measures. This new perspective has been criticized by proponents of free trade, yet the reality of international trade is that international trade has never been without obstacles. Apart from this, the fairness of trade has long been questioned by developing countries and researchers of Marxist and Marxian persuasions. They see international trade as an extension of the evolution of capitalism, that is meant to continue the core-periphery relationship of the world economy. In particular, this relationship is maintained they see the law of comparative advantage whether by factor cost or factor endowments is based on unequal exchange and other past and current exploitative rules that give primary producers the short end of the deal.

Despite the advantages of free trade, trade has never been free because of tariff and non-tariff barriers that national governments impose on trade for economic, social, and political reasons. At the same time, there appears to be a general agreement that the long-run benefit of these barriers is not commensurate with the cost. As a result, there has been a worldwide effort to reduce these trade barriers. African countries have been part of this worldwide movement, but the results have not been very encouraging. In the next chapter, we focus particularly on the most common efforts among countries to deal with trade barriers, namely regional trade agreements.

References

Agbebi, M., & Vertinan, P. (2017). Dependency theory: A conceptual lens to understand China's presence in Africa? *Forum for Development Studies, 44*(3), 429–451.

Akerlof, G. A. (1970). The market for "lemons": Quality uncertainty and the market mechanism. *Quarterly Journal of Economics, 84*, 488–500.

Alam, A. (2001). *The new trade theory and its relevance to trade policies in developing countries* (Policy, research working paper; no. WPS 1274). World Bank Group.

Amin, S. (1974). *Accumulation on a world scale*. Monthly Press Review.

Amin, S. (1976). *Unequal development*. Harvester Press.

Bagwell, K., & Staiger, R. (2003). Protection and the business cycle. *Advances in Economic Analysis and Policy, 3*, 1–43.

Baran, P. (1957). *The political economy of growth*. Penguin.

Bergesen, A. (1984). The critique of world-system theory: Class relations or division of labor? *Sociological Theory, 2*, 365–372.

Bhagwati, J. (1958). Immiserizing growth: A geometrical note. *The Review of Economic Studies, 25*(3), 201–205.

Bhagwati, J. (1987). Trade and development theory and policy: A synthesis exists. *Economic and Political Weekly, 22*(22), 859.

Bown, C. P., & Crowley, M. A. (2013). Import protection, business cycles, and exchange rates: Evidence from the great recession. *Journal of International Economics, 90*(1), 50–64.

Brander, J. A., & Spencer, B. J. (1981). International R & D Rivalry and industrial strategy. *Review of Economic Studies, 50*, 707–722.

Brander, J. A., & Spencer, V. J. (1985). Export subsidies and international market share rivalry. *Journal of International Economics, 18*, 83–100.

Brenner, R. (1977). The origins of capitalist development: A critique of Neo-Smithian Marxism. *New Left Review, 104*, 25–92.

Brewer, A. (1990). *Marxist theories of imperilaism: A critical survey* (2nd ed.). Routledge.

Bukharin, N. (1917). *Imperialism and world economy*. Merlin.

Cannan, E. (Ed.). (1977). *An inquiry into the nature and causes of the wealth of nations*. The University of Chicago Press. First Published 1776.

Chiang, S., & Masson, R. T. (1988). Domestic industrial structure and export quality. *International Economic Review, 29*, 261–270.

Chisik, R. (2003). Export industry policy and reputational comparative advantage. *Journal of International Economics, 59*, 423–451.

Czaga, P. (2005). Import prohibitions and quotas. In OECD (Ed.), *Looking beyond tariffs: The role of non-tariff barriers in world trade* (pp. 59–103). OECD.

Denemark, R. A., & Thomas, K. P. (1988). The Brenner–Wallerstein debate. *International Studies Quarterly, 32*(1), 47–65.

Dixit, A. K. (1984). Trade policies and oligopolistic industries. *Economic Journal Supplement, 94*, 1–16.

Dorobăț, C. E. (2015). A brief history of international trade thought: From pre-doctrinal contributions to the 21st century heterodox international economics. *The Journal of Philosophical Economics: Reflections on Economic and Social Issues, 2*, 106–137.

Dos Santos, T. (1970). The structure of dependence. *The American Economic Review*, 60(2), 231–236.

Dunn, B. (2009). *Global political economy: A Marxist critique*. Pluto Publishers.

Edgeworth, F. Y. (1894). The theory of international values, III. *Economic Journal, 4*, 424–443.

Emmanuel, A. (1972). *Unequal exchange: A study of the imperialism of trade*. Monthly Review Press.

Essaji, A. (2008). Technical regulations and specialization in international trade. *Journal of International Economics, 76*(2), 166–176.

Frank, A. G. (1966). The development of underdevelopment. *Monthly Review, 41*(2), 37–51.

Frankel, J. A. (Ed.). (1998). *The regionalization of the world economy*. University of Chicago Press.

Furtado, C. (1973). The concept of external dependence. In C. K. Wilber (Ed.). *The political economy of development and underdevelopment*. Random House.

Futerman, A. G., & Block, W. E. (2020). An Austrian critique of the Prebisch-Singer theory of the deterioration in the terms of trade. *Journal of Financial Economic Policy, 12*(4), 721–735.

Greif, A. (1989). Reputation and coalitions in medieval trade: Evidence on the Maghribi traders. *Journal of Economic History, 49*, 857–882.

Grossman, G. M. (1986). Targeted export promotion: A critique. In P. Krugman (Ed.), *Strategic trade policy and the new international economics* (pp. 47–68). MIT Press.

Grundke, R., & Moser, C. (2019). Hidden protectionism? Evidence from non-tariff barriers to trade in the United States. *Journal of International Economics, 117*, 143–157.

Haberler, G. (1935). *Theory of international trade: With its applications to commercial policy*. William Hodge.

Haberler, G., De Oiveira Campos, R., Meade, J. E., & Tinbergen, J. (1958). *Trends in international trade* (A report by a panel of experts). G.A.T.T.

Heckscher, E. (1919). The effects of foreign trade on the distribution of income. *Ekonomisk Tidskrift, 21*, 497–412.

Hilferding, R. (1910). *Finance capital: A study of the latest phase in capitalist development*. Routledge & Kegan Paul.

Hobson, J. A. (1938). *Imperialism: A study* (3rd ed.). Allen & Unwin.

Hornok, C., & Koren, M. (2015). Administrative barriers to trade. *Journal of International Economics, 96*, S110–S122.

Horstmann, I. J., & Markusen, J. R. (1986). Up the average cost curve: Inefficient entry and the new protectionism. *Journal of International Economics, 20*, 225–247.

Jevons, W. S. (1871). *Theory of political economy*. Macmillan and Co.

Kay, C. (2005). Andre' Gunder Frank: From the 'development of underdevelopment' to the 'world system'. *Development and Change, 36*(6), 1177–1183.

Kee, H. L., Neagu, C., & Nicita, A. (2013). Is protectionism on the rise? Assessing national trade policies during the crisis of 2008. *Review of Economics and Statistics, 95*(1), 342–346.

Kreps, D., & Wilson, R. (1982). Reputation and imperfect information. *Journal of Economic Theory, 27*, 253–279.

Krueger, A. O. (1997). Free trade agreements versus customs unions. *Journal of Development Economics, 54*(1), 169–187.

Krugman, P. (1979). Increasing returns, monopolistic competition and international trade. *Journal of International Economics, 9*, 858–864.

Krugman, P. (1980). Scale economies, product differentiation and the pattern of trade. *American Economic Review, 70*, 151–175.

Krugman, P. (1987). New theories of trade among industrial countries. *American Economic Review, 73*(2), 343–347.

Lall, S. (1975). Is 'dependence' a useful concept in Analyzing underdevelopment? *World Development, 3*(11–12), 799–810.

Lamb, R. L. (2006). Rent seeking in U.S. – Mexican avocado trade. *The Cato Journal, 26*(1), 159–177.

Lancaster, K. (1980). Intra-industry trade under perfect monopolistic competition. *Journal of International Economics, 10*, 151–175.

Lancaster, K. (1996). *Trade, markets and welfare*. Edward Elgar.

Lenin, V. I. (1917). *Imperialism, the highest stage of capitalism*. Foreign Language Publishing House.

Leontief, L. W. (1956). Factor proportions and the structure of American trade: Further theoretical and empirical analysis. *Review of Economics and Statistics, 38*(4), 386–407.

Lewis, W. A. (1969). *Aspects of Tropical Trade*. Almqvist & Wiksell.

Linder, S. (1961). *An essay on trade and transformation*. Wiley.

Love, J. A. (1980). Raul Prebisch and the origins of the doctrine of unequal exchange. *Latin American Research Review, 15*(3), 45–72.

Luxemburg, R. (1913). *The accumulation of capital*. Monthly Review Press.

Luxemburg, R (1921). *The accumulation of capital: an anti-critique*. Frankes Verlag. G.m.b.H

Macheda, F. (2014). *Marx on international trade*. https://www.academia.edu/7440362/Marx_on_International_Trade_Lesson_3_Macheda

Manoilesco, M. (1929). *Theorie du protectionnisme et de l'echange international*. Marcel Giard.

Manoilesco, M. (1934). *Le siecle du corporatisme: Doctrine du corporatisme integral et pur*. Felix Alcan.

Mariadoss, B. J. (2019). *Core principles of international marketing*. https://opentext.wsu.edu/cpim/front-matter/introduction/

Marx, K. (1885). *Capital, Vol. II* (Edited. F. Engels). Foreign Languages Publishing House; First published in German 1885.

Marx, K. (1867). *Capital, Vol. I*, (Edited F. Engels). Foreign Languages Publishing House.

Menger, C. (1871). *Principles of economics* (J. Dingwall and B. F. Hoselitz, Trans) The Free Press.

Milgrom, P., & Roberts, J. (1986). Price and advertising signals of product quality. *Journal of Political Economy, 94*, 796–821.

Mill, J. S. (1909). *Principles of political economy*. Longmans Green.

Milward, B. (2020). *International trade and sustainable development: Economic, history, and moral arguments for asymmetrical global trade*. Routledge.

Minhas, B. S. (1962). The homo-Hypallagic production function, factor-intensity reversals, and the Heckscher-Ohlin theorem. *Journal of Political Economy, 70*(2), 138–156.

Minta, I. K. (1984). *The Lomé convention and the new international economic order* (Vol. 27, pp. 953–973).

Mohtadi, S. (2017). *A guide to international economics*. Business Expert Press. ProQuest Ebook Central, http://ebookcentral.proquest.com/lib/wmichlib-ebooks/detail.action?docID=5781051

Moles, D. (1999). Dependencia and modernization. http://dmoles.files.wordpress.com/2014/06/dependencia.pdf

Mshomba, R. E. (2009). *Africa and the world trade organization*. Cambridge University Press.

Myint, M. (1958). The 'classical theory' of international trade and the underdeveloped countries. *Economic Journal, 68*, 313–337.

Myrdal, G. (1957). *Economic theory and underdeveloped regions*. Duckworth.

Namkoong, Y. (1999). Dependency theory: Concepts, classifications, and criticisms. *International Area Review, 2*(1), 121–150.

Negeshi, T. (2013). *Development of international trade theory*. Springer. Second Enhanced Edition.

Nesadurai, H. E. (2008). Bandung and the political economy of north-south relations: Sowing the seeds for re-visioning international society. In S. S. Tan & A. Acharya (Eds.), *Bandung revisited: The legacy of the 1955 Asian-African conference for international order* (pp. 68–104). National University of Singapore Press.

Nurkse, R. (1959). *Patterns of trade and development*. Blackwell.

Ofori-Amoah, B. (2019). *Africa's geography: Dynamics of place, cultures, and economies*. Wiley & Sons.

Ohlin, B. (1933). *Theory of interregional and international trade*. Harvard University Press.

Organization for Economic Co-operation and Development (OECD). (2005). *Looking beyond tariffs: The role of non-tariff barriers in world trade*. OECD.

Pareto, V. (1895). Teoria matematica del commercio internazionale. *Giornale degli Economisti, 2*(10), 476–498.

Porter, M. E. (1985). *Competitive advantage: Creating and sustaining superior performance*. Free Press.

Porter, M. E. (1990). *The competitive advantage of nations*. Free Press.

Potoski, M., & Prakash, A. (2009). Information asymmetries as trade barriers: ISO 9000 increases international commerce. *Journal of Policy Analysis and Management, 28*(2), 221–238.

Prebisch, R. (1950). *The economic development of Latin America and its principal problems* (UN document no. E/CN.12/89/Rev.1). United Nations.

Radcliffe, B. (2022). *The basics of tariffs and trade barriers.* https://www.investopedia.com/articles/economics/08/tariff-trade-barrier-basics.asp
Ricardo, D. (1821). *On the principles of political economy and taxation.* John Murray.
Rose, A. K. (2013). The march of an economic idea? Protectionism isn't counter-cyclic (anymore). *Economic Policy, 28*(76), 569–612.
Rotwein, E. (Ed.). (1955). *Writings on economics.* Edinburgh.
Sau, R. (1976) The theory of unequal exchange, trade and imperialism. *Economic and Political Weekly*, 11(10): 399, 401–404.
Sen, S. (2005). International trade theory and policy: What is left of the free trade paradigm? *Development and Change, 36*(6), 1011–1029.
Schumacher, R. (2015). Adam Smith's "two distinct benefits" from trade: The dead end of "vent-for-surplus" interpretations. *History of Political Economy, 47*(4), 577–603.
Shaikh, A. (1980). Laws of algebra and laws of production: Humbug II. In E. J. Nell (Ed.) . *Growth, profits and property: essays in the revival of political economy.* Cambridge University Press.
Singer, H. W. (1950). The distribution of gains between investing and borrowing countries. *The American Economic Review, 40*(2), 473–485.
Sissoko, M. M., Osuji, L. O., & Cheng, W. L. (1998). Impact of the Yaoundé and Lomé conventions on EC-ACP trade. *The African Economic & Business Review, 1*(1), 7–24.
Smith, A. (1776). *An inquiry into the nature and causes of the wealth of nations.* The Modern Library/Random House.
Smith, T. (1979). The ubderdevelopment of development literature: the case of dependency theory. *World Politics, 13*, 247–288.
Stathakis, G. (2008). Imperialism: old and new theories. *International Journal of Economic Sciences and Applied Research, 1*(1), 100–124.
Stolper, W. F., & Samuelson, P. A. (1941). Protection and real wages. *The Review of Economic Studies, 9*(1), 58–73.
Streeten, P. P. (1982). The new international economic order. *International Review of Education, 28*(4), 407–430.
Sweezy, P. (1976). A critique. In M. Dobb et al. (Eds.), *The transition from feudalism to capitalism.* New Left Books.
The World Bank. (2010). *Types of tariffs.* https://wits.worldbank.org/wits/wits/witshelp/content/data_retrieval/p/intro/c2.types_of_tariffs.htm
Trefler, D. (1993). Trade liberalization and the theory of endogenous protection: An econometric study of U.S. import policy. *Journal of Political Economy, 101*(1), 138–160.
UNCTAD. (2008). *Economic development in Africa: Export performance following trade liberalization: Some patterns and policy Perspectives.* United Nations.
UNECA. (2011). *Global review of aid for trade 2011: Africa case stories.* UNECA.
Vernon, R. (1966). International investment and international trade in the product cycle. *The Quarterly Journal of Economics, 80*(2), 190–120.
Wallerstein, I. (1979). *The capitalist world economy.* Cambridge University Press.
Walras, L. (2014) *Éléments d'économie politique pure (Elements of theoretical economics.* D. A. Walker and J. van Daal, trans) Cambridge: Cambridge University Press (Original work published 1871).
Whitened, D. J. (1996). The industrial revolution and birth of the anti-mercantilist idea: Epistemic communities and global leadership. *Journal of World-Systems Research, 2*(1), 2–35.
World Trade Organization (WTO). (2005). *World trade report.* WTO.
World Trade Organization (WTO). (2021). *Technical barriers to trade agreements: 10 key results from 2020.* World Trade Organization.
WTO, ITC, & UNCTAD. (2021). *World tariff profiles.* OECD.

Chapter 3
Regional Trade Agreements: Theory, Aspirations, and Realities

3.1 Introduction

This chapter focuses specifically on the general role of regional trade agreements (RTAs) in intraregional trade. It discusses the theory, purpose, different types, and expectations of regional trade agreements. The chapter raises a series of questions that will be verified by the case studies in subsequent chapters. It is divided into five sections. The first section places regional trade agreements within the broader context of integration theory. The second section defines regional trade agreements and outlines their origins. The third section outlines the conventional theory of regional trade agreements, the fourth section presents the political economy perspectives, and the final section concludes with a number of questions that are examined in the case study chapters.

3.2 Integration Theory and Regional Trade Agreements

Regional trade agreements fall within the general area of regional integration. It will therefore be appropriate to start with integration theory before honing in on regional trade agreements. According to Biswaro (2011), the theory of integration comes from two disciplinary sources—economics and political science.

3.2.1 Economic Theories of Regional Integration

Economic theories of regional integration began with Ricardo's law of comparative advantage and international trade, which articulated the view that cooperation between two countries in trade was necessary for countries to gain the full benefits

B. Ofori-Amoah, *The African Continental Free Trade Area*,
https://doi.org/10.1007/978-3-031-59181-5_3

of trade. The transformation of the European Coal and Steel Community (ECSC) into the European Economic Community in the early post-WWII period provided economists with a renewed interest to theorize about integration. Viner (1950) examined the effects of creating a customs union on member states. According to Viner, creation of a customs union would lead to elimination of trade barriers among member countries and a common tariff barrier for nonmembers. However, this would result in two effects—trade creation effects and trade diversion effects. Trade creation effects would occur if the output of inefficient industries was replaced by output of more efficient industries from within the union, making the country with inefficient industries better off. However, if nonmember states happened to be the lowest-cost suppliers compared to member states, the imposition of the tariff wall would now make the imports from nonmembers more expensive forcing members of the union to deal with high-cost suppliers in the union. This is trade-diversion effect. Viner (1950) surmised that the net benefits of a customs union will thus depend on the difference between the trade creation effects and the trade-diversion effects.

Other economists proposed an alternative approach that took into consideration the historical dimension of socio-economic developments (Tinbergen, 1959; Marchal, 1965; Perroux, 1966). Tinbergen (1954) noted that there were two aspects to all processes of economic integration—negative integration which involved elimination of obstacles to trade liberalization; and positive integration, which involved harmonization and coordination of existing instruments or setting up new institutions. Marchal (1965) focused on the question of whether integration resulted from development or led to development. In the first case, integration was seen as the result of historical evolution of technological and industrial development. In the second, integration was seen as a conscious effort by a group of people to improve their lives. In this latter case, Marchal argued that integration must be based on industrialization and social transformation, and since this could not take place anywhere, Perroux (1966) in particular argued that such integration could be organized around growth poles. Economists agreed that integration was not the same as regional cooperation, which implies a less defined structure, a sort of ad-hoc temporary arrangement to achieve a common purpose. Integration involves the establishment of some institutional mechanism and some degree of shared sovereignty. Other economists, in particular Balassa (1961) focused on types or stages of economic integration and distinguished among five such stages—free-trade area; customs union; common market, an economic union, and economic integration.

3.2.2 Political Science Theories of Integration

The theories of integration from political science are much more extensive and have been classified into federalism, functionalism, neo-functionalism, neo-institutionalism, intergovernmentalism, realism, and post-neofunctionalism. For **federalism**, integration is the creation of a new state through the merger of previously existing sovereign states. Here political rather than economic goals are the prime movers. In contrast, **functionalism** posits that international agreements around specific functions such as health, communications, and postal services, would save the world from another war. Mitrany (1966) the leading exponent of this view argued that the successful development of such institutions will eventually garner enough legitimacy and support to overcome the nationalistic tendencies of nation-states.

Haas (1958, 1964) focused more on how integration actually occurred rather than why it occurred and proposed a **neo-functionalist** approach to integration. For Haas integration was the work of domestic interest groups and political parties seeking to preserve their own interests. It was strongly driven by what he called "spill-over" effects, which was the result of previous integration efforts. Thus, as interest groups (political elites, business class, entrepreneurs, etc.) saw the benefits of a previous integration, they would push for more integration in other areas. Eventually, this would lead to political integration. However, Haas (1976) repudiated his own theory.

On its part the **neo-institutionalism** believes in the role of institutions in solving world problems. It argues that the success of international institutions in supporting states provides incentives to states wanting to solve their problems with one another. Closely related to this view and neo-functionalism is intergovernmentalism. **Intergovernmentalism** agrees with the neo-functionalism idea of integration due to functional roles and with the neo-institutionalism on the importance of international institutions in integration. However, its point of departure is the role of national governments in forging integration. Moravscik (1998) who is the leading advocate of this view argues that three factors have played a role in European integration since 1955—commercial interests, relative bargaining power of national governments, and incentive to enhance the credibility of interstate commitment. To Moravcsik the commercial interests and the rational choices made by various national governments to pursue such interests were the most important. It is thus due to national responses to a world that is becoming increasingly interdependent economically that is the prime motivation for integration.

The **realist approach** to integration places emphasis on power, national political interests, and interstate rivalry in forging integration. It argues that successful economic and political integration needs one or two states to champion it (De Melo & Panagariya, 1993). In the case of the EU—it has been France and Germany. At the same time, there are several factors that may hinder integration—the importance of relative gains and distribution of resources; expectations of economic advantage, existence of sociocultural bonds (Birch, 1966; Deutsch et al., 1957). This is why there is a need for a powerful leader who has the resources and capacity to forge integration. Ultimately realism sees the role of political will and anticipated gains as a prerequisite for successful integration (Biswaro, 2011). Recently, others have proposed a **post-neo-functionalism** approach to regional integration, especially with respect to integration in Africa. Post-neo-functionalism, according to Aniche (2021) combines neo-nationalism, post-nationalism, and humanism to drive regional integration. From this perspective, integration among countries will not work unless the myriad of problems face the countries, including security matters are resolved.

In summary, economists' emphasis on trade and political scientists' emphasis on political units have produced various concepts and forms of regional integration. From economists, Balassa's (1961) classification has become the Gold Standard. Thus, there are five forms of integration. The first is a free-trade area in which there are no trade barriers among members. However, each member maintains its own trading regulations with nonmembers. The second is a customs union, in which there are no trade barriers among members, but there is a common tariff wall against nonmembers, which means all the members maintain common trading laws with respect to nonmembers. The third is a common market, in which there are no trade barriers among members, all nonmembers face a common tariff wall, and there is free movement of factors—labor, capital, and technology—among members. The fourth is an economic union, in which there are no barriers to trade and factor movement, there is a common tariff against nonmembers and there is a common economic policy, which is binding on all members. The fifth is regional integration in which there is free movement of goods, services, and factors among members, a common tariff wall against nonmembers, and a common economic policy and a political union.

From political science, there are three forms of integration in a continuum—political cooperation, political federation, and a political union. Political cooperation involves arrangement among countries to achieve a common objective without surrendering individual country sovereignty. A political federation comprises states that willingly concede some of their sovereign rights to a federal authority. In a political union states or parties agree to surrender all or part of their sovereign rights to a central authority. It involves the establishment of common institutions and development and implementation of common foreign or defense policies (Biswaro, 2011). Given that the focus of this book is on trade, the rest of the chapter will follow the economists' view of integration.

3.3 Definition and Origins of Regional Trade Agreements

Regional trade agreements (RTAs) seek to promote and enhance trade volumes through the removal of tariff and non-tariff barriers. The roots of modern RTAs could be traced to 1889 when the British Colony of Cape of Good Hope and the Boer Republic of Orange Free State entered into a customs union convention, which was later extended to become the Southern African Customs Union in 1910. (Gerout et al., 2019). However, the need to do something about restrictive trade that had become counter to the free-trade ideals from classical and neoclassical economists did not attract worldwide urgency until the 1930s. Contrary to the promise of free-trade issues of political expediency and broader national welfare goals had produced a mix of quantitative and qualitative measures that were impeding trade. These became especially important when world trade collapsed during the Great

Depression in the 1930s. Though the causes of the depression have been highly debated in the literature (see e.g. Khan, 1946; Pollard, 1962; Saint-Etienne, 1984; Madsen, 2001) declining demand, increased tariffs, and non-tariff trade barriers, increasing bilateral trade and foreign exchange policies have been identified as the main causes. The trigger came, according to Eichengreen and Irwin (2010), in 1928 when the US Federal Reserve decided to tighten monetary policy and France decided to stabilize its currency at a depreciated rate and convert reserves into gold, which drained gold from other countries. Eichengreen and Irwin (2010) pointed out that countries trying to deal with the financial fallout had three options—wage and price deflation to restore balance per the gold parity; trade and payments restrictions to reduce imports and outflow of gold; abandoning the Gold Standard and allowing exchange rate to depreciate. While some countries chose or were forced by the economic and political situation to abandon the Gold Standard, others chose to stick with it albeit in very difficult circumstances due to wage deflation, unemployment, and restriction of trade in order to preserve outflow of gold. Madsen (2001) found that about 41% of the collapse of world trade from 1929 to 1932 was due to discretionary escalation of trade barriers, and 59% due to declining nominal incomes.

Economic historians have attributed the escalation to several factors including the passing of the Hawley-Smoot Tariff Act in June 1930 by the United States, the collapse of the largest bank in Austria, the Creditanstalt, the departure of Great Britain from the Gold Standard in September, 1931, and Britain's Abnormal Importation Act of November, 1931 and the Import Duties Act of February, 1932.

The collapse of the Austrian bank and the departure of Great Britain from the Gold Standard and the subsequent devaluation of the sterling unsettled the world financial system, but it was the trade laws that started the protectionist policies. The Hawley-Smoot Act raised the average tariff by 20% (Eichengreen & Irwin, 2010). The British Abnormal Importation Act granted trade authorities the discretion to impose higher duties on selected goods, while the Import Duties of 1932 increased across-the-board tariffs by 10% of goods (Eichengreen & Irwin, 2010). These invited worldwide retribution against both the United States and Great Britain. Between 1929 and 1932, the world's macro tariff rate, which is defined as Import Duties divided by import value, doubled. Non-tariff rates were imposed at the same time. The gains from world trade in the 1920s were lost by the first 4 years of the depression. Trade volumes from 1930 to 1932 contracted by 6% and further by 3% from 1933 to 1936 due to increasing trade barriers (Madsen, 2001). In a study of 12 European countries, Friedman (1974) showed that about 90% of European countries raised non-tariff barriers from 1931 to 1934. France imposed quotas on about 50 items in 1931, increasing them to 1110 in 1932, with other European countries following suit. Madsen (2001) also found that world trade expanded throughout the 1920s but came to a halt in 1929 because of trade restrictions and declining income. Specifically, he showed that world trade declined by 13% due to declining income, 8% due to discretionary tariff increases, 7% due to discretionary non-tariff barriers, and 5% due to deflation-induced tariff increases. However, by the end of World War II, many nations had seen the devastating impact of extreme use of trade restrictions.

The United States advocated for the need for multinational cooperation to liberalize trade (Gounder & Chand Prasad, 2011). In 1947 the General Agreement on Tariff and Trade (GATT) was signed by the 23 countries that convened at Bretton Woods, New Hampshire, United States. GATT came into effect on January 1, 1948. In 1958, six European countries, Belgium, France, Italy, Luxembourg, The Netherlands, and West Germany, formed the European Economic Community (EEC).

In the meantime, as it has been well documented, the original intent for GATT to transition into an International Trade Organization (ITO), did not happen. Instead, GATT held a series of talks or rounds aimed at the reduction of tariffs among members. It was the last of these rounds—the Uruguay Rounds which began in 1986 that led to the establishment of the World Trade Organization (WTO), on January 1, 1995. Both GATT and WTO have provisions for formation of RTAs under special circumstances. Major growth of RTAs however did not occur until 1980s, but it was in the 2000s that the number of RTAs exploded. By 1980 GATT had received 45 notifications of RTAs of which 42 were in force. By March 2022, WTO had received 577 RTA notifications, of which 353 were in force.

3.4 The Conventional Theory of Regional Trade Agreements

The theory of regional trade agreement has been traditionally built around two questions. The first is whether RTAs increase or decrease trade and raise/lower welfare. The second is whether RTAs serve as building blocks or stumbling blocks to multilateral trade liberalization. Related to these two questions have also been the questions of the rationale and effectiveness of RTAs. We review these questions and their answers, beginning with the rationale for RTAs.

3.4.1 *Rationale for Regional Trade Agreements*

The classical reason for RTAs was articulated by Johnson (1954) when he stated that in the absence of trade agreements, nations would impose tariffs on each other leading to trade wars that would benefit no one. Such an action could start with nations that are large enough to affect the prices of the goods they import imposing tariffs on those imports to improve their terms of trade. This would cause other large nations of similar influence to impose retaliatory tariffs leading to cancellation of benefits of each other. To avoid this, countries would enter into trade liberalization agreements that would be of mutual benefit. Today, RTAs also enhance market access; help countries to get around the uncertainty and long and arduous nature of WTO process that involves more than 160 countries, and deal with a host of trade issues including tariffs, subsidies, and agricultural commodities. RTAs offer faster ways to achieve national trade goals (Pearson, 2015).

3.4.2 Are RTAs Trade Creators or Trade Diverters?

Addressing the first question, Viner (1950) argued that the answer to the above question depended on the balance between trade creation effects and trade-diversion effects. RTAs were beneficial if trade creation outweighed trade-diversion (Viner, 1950; Gounder & Chand Prasad, 2011). Balassa (1961) stated that trade creation was a move toward a free-trade position because it involved a shift from high-cost to low-cost sources of supply. In contrast, trade diversion shifted purchases from lower-cost producers to higher-cost producers, thus acting in the opposite direction.

Closely related to whether RTAs are trade creators or trade diverters has been the question of what counts for effective RTAs. To this, RTA theory has identified several factors including complementarity and competitive rivalry, size, propinquity, and transportation cost. Before the 1950s, protectionists viewed complementarity among members of RTAs (e.g., customs unions) as a boon toward economic autarkic policies, while free-trade advocates saw that rivalry among RTA members would promote free trade. However, Viner (1950) differed from this general view. Viner (1950) saw complementarity and rivalry in terms of similarities and dissimilarities in the range of products of the countries planning to enter into the agreement. Thus, rivalry or competitiveness refers to overlap in the production of a range of goods while complementarity refers to substantial differences in the goods produced. On this basis, Viner concluded that competitive economies would benefit more in an RTA from production efficiency if unit costs of production varied widely. In contrast, complementary economies participating in an RTA would face negative production effects (Balassa, 1961). This of course raised a lot of controversy among subsequent researchers due to definition problems (Balassa, 1961). For example, Meade (1951) saw complementarity and rivalry as differences in comparative cost. Economies were complementary if they showed wide disparities in production cost of the same commodity, and competitive if it was the opposite. In this case, complementarity would be beneficial if the countries were producing the same commodity before the agreement, and a disadvantage if only one country was producing the commodity but the agreement left out the least cost producer (Balassa, 1961). As Balassa (1961) pointed out definition of complementarity and rivalry based on comparative advantage was problematic not only because it was based on constant cost and zero transportation, but also, because they did not distinguish between the range of products available and the unit cost of production.

There are two main views regarding the impact of size on the efficiency of RTAs. On the one hand, there is the view that RTAs that cover a large number of countries will see positive production effects (Viner, 1950; Meade, 1955; Tinbergen, 1959). These proponents argue that all things being equal, larger RTAs enhance division of labor potential, which in turn increases production. On the other hand, there is the view that RTAs covering a small number of countries will see positive production effects (Duncan, 1950; Hawtrey, 1944; Ropke, 1959). These proponents argue that larger countries have the tendency to move toward autarky than smaller countries. However, as Balassa (1961) points out how do we measure the size of RTAs? Market size appears to be the obvious measure but how do we measure it? Some authors suggest geographic extent, but that does not give a full picture of the market size given that vast geographic areas may be uninhabited. Some authors have used population size to measure market size but large population size does not necessarily translate to effective demand. As a result, gross national product has been used to measure market size. If that is accepted, then the proposition is that the larger the size of the RTA, the greater the benefits to the world as a whole; the greater the increase in the market the greater the benefits (Balassa, 1961).

Originally, the role of space and distance was ignored in international trade and RTA theories, and so were propinquity and transportation costs. Thus, Viner (1950) did not think congruity or proximity had enough economic impact on customs union to be given attention. However, Balassa (1961) argued that the economic benefits of a customs union and for that matter RTA is contingent upon its ability to establish continuity for commodity flows that are hindered by national borders. Apart from this, propinquity and proximity have several advantages. First, neighboring countries have shorter distances to travel. Second, neighboring countries are more likely to have similar tastes and it is a lot easier to establish distribution outlets in them. Third, neighboring countries may have a common history and awareness and for that reason potential for developing common economic policies is high. Propinquity also has a major impact on transportation cost, which does not vary only with distance but also with the mode of transportation. Here the practice has been using economic instead of geographic distance, which is defined in terms of cost instead of mileage. In general, the shorter the economic distance, the greater the potential for economic interaction between, and the greater the benefits. Low transportation cost associated with short economic distances will increase the positive production effects, and cause less trade diversion (Balassa 1961).

Subsequent research has looked at various aspects of Viner's (1950) and Balassa's (1961) works, some confirming them, and some disputing them. The factors that have been emphasized in recent literature for effective RTAs include geographic proximity (Krugman, 1991; Hummels, 2007; Leamer & Storper, 2001) similarity in political institutions, (Bandelj, 2002; Bliss & Russett, 1998; Mansfield et al., 2000; Milner & Kubota, 2005), shared cultural traditions (Agarwal, 1994; Bandelj, 2002; Rauch, 1999) and legal and judicial architectures of agreements (Duina, 2016).

Central to these is the concept of "natural trading partners." The new economic geography calls the transaction costs related to geographic, political, and cultural distance "natural trade costs." Countries that exhibit geographic, political, and cultural homophily are considered "natural trading partners," which is also referred to as the "natural regionalism" thesis. These countries also have higher trade volumes between and among them prior to becoming members of the same RTA. As a result, some researchers have found that trade diversion tends to be less among natural trade partners, and for that reason, RTAs should be beneficial to natural trading partners (Wonnacott & Lutz, 1989; Krugman, 1991; Summers, 1991; Frankel et al., 1995; Gounder & Chand Prasad, 2011, etc.).

However, Panagariya (1996) and Bhagwati and Panagariya (1996) have countered that a high volume of initial trade may be due to prior agreements between the countries more than them being natural trade partners and that the high volume of initial trade can be a major loss to a member country of the RTA. In addition, Bhagwati and Panagariya (1996) counter that a country is better off entering an RTA with a distant country than a regional or neighboring country when the countries are the same. In his work on Pacific Island countries (PIC) exports to Australia, Gani (2009) found a negative correlation between volume of trade and distance, and that telecommunication infrastructure was the most important factor explaining trade between PICs and Australia. Apart from this, Gounder and Chand Prasad (2011) point out that there is a definition problem about what is key trading partner or natural trading partner. For example, following Grounder and Chand Prasad (2011)'s illustration of trade between Fiji and Australia, Country A, a developing country, may consider Country B, a developed country, as its key or natural trading partner, but Country B may not see Country A in the same light. So, what constitutes a natural trading partner depends on which country's perspective we are looking at.

Baier and Bergstrand (2004) found that governments/countries will form an FTA: (1). the closer the distance between the two countries; (2) the more remote the pair of continental trade partners is removed from the rest of the world; (3) the larger and more similar in economic size of the partners; (4) the greater the difference between the capital-labor ratio between the partners; (5) the smaller the difference in the capital-labor ratios of the two countries compared to the rest of the world.

Drawing on political science alliance theories, Kandogan and Hiller (2018) argued that the probability of countries entering an RTA is higher if the countries have ties through prior alliances or membership in international governmental organizations. Such ties formalized through rules and regulations through international institutions increase familiarity, good relationships, reduce uncertainty, and build trust between and among countries making it possible for them to enter an RTA.

Pearson (2015) argued that an effective free trade agreement (FTA) is the one in which economic benefits generated for citizens outweigh such costs as reduced output, increased unemployment, and loss of skills and human capital in the import-competing sectors of the economy. Based on the fact that some FTAs have been successful in generating more benefits than costs while others have done the opposite, Pearson (2015) urges that policymakers need to have a good idea about whether a potential partner country will be good or not before conducting feasibility studies.

The goal of RTAs is to facilitate and increase trade within the RTA (Chacha, 2014). The main tool for making this possible is the rules of origin (RoO), which is a set of guidelines by which products should be given preferential access to the RTA's market. They make sure that third countries do not benefit from the treatment RTA members grant each other as part of the agreement. The implementation of RoOs is crucial to whether or not RTAs would live up to their promise. They are negotiated not only at governmental levels but also at sector level within member countries in a given RTA. Where they are strong, such industries and sectors can use their economic and political clout to negotiate rules that are beneficial to them (Chacha, 2014). RoOs can also be used to restrict preferential treatment in RTAs, and for that reason, they can unintentionally become detrimental to free trade. Other authors who have noted the complexity of RoOs include Brenton and Manchin (2003) and Manchin and Pelkmans-Balaoing (2007).

3.4.3 Are RTAs Building Blocks or Stumbling Blocks to Multilateral Trade Agreements?

Bhagwati (1991) argued that the proliferation of RTAs was not serving as a stepping block toward multilateral trade integration, but rather serving as a stumbling block toward integration. In particular, the proliferation has led to the "spaghetti bowl" effect, whereby overlapping membership in multiple RTAs in a region, complicates matters and makes trade more chaotic among member countries (Bhagwati, 2008).

First is the ambiguity about what constitutes place of origin of an imported or a manufactured product. If Country A imports and also makes input parts of a finished product it manufactures, how do we find out how much of the inputs went into the manufactured item? Overlapping membership also results in lack of consistency of trade rules of a given country that belongs to more than one RTA. Second, they are detrimental to the objectives of RTAs. Third, overlapping membership leads to more rules that can lead to interpretation difficulties.

In addition, RTAs differ in their RoOs, and this could complicate implementation since a country belonging to more than one RTA may have to implement two different sets of rules in its trading activities. This could also lead to friction in policy. For example, Chacha (2014) reports that COMESA and SADC in Africa are two RTAs that have a high level of overlapping memberships, yet these two have distinct RoOs that are incompatible. These issues become more complicated by the fact that members of overlapping RTAs also have to conduct trade with nonmembers. In a study of 20 RTAs from developing countries, Chacha (2014) found that the share of trade among members of RTAs declined and that this decline was associated with members engaging in overlapping membership. This was mostly due to multiple RoOs that impeded the flow of goods within the RTAs, due in turn to the amount of time it took to navigate the different rules. In the Economic Community of West African States (ECOWAS) Chacha (2014) found that intra-RTA trade was 10% in 1996, when only one member had overlapping RTA membership. In 1997, intra-RTA trade declined by 0.18% when four members had overlapping membership. In addition, he also found that larger RTAs create more trade than smaller RTAs. Using preferential trade agreements (PTA) as an example, Limao (2007) shows that PTAs can serve as a stumbling block to multilateral trade because they raise tariffs for those not part of the PTA.

In contrast, Wei and Frankel (1996) argued that RTAs could form a stepping stone to multilateral trade liberalization because of their ability to diffuse initial opposition to global free trade. They assert that global free trade may not be feasible initially because of strong opposition. However, regional blocs could divide this initial opposition at a regional level, allowing regional trade agreements to form. Over time a majority consensus is formed in favor of regional trade agreement paving the way for further integration.

Basing themselves on Bhagwati's (1991, 1993) work, Nomura et al. (2016) take a fresh look at the question. They start with three main observations about recent RTAs. First, the majority of them are bilateral trade agreements. Second, most of them are free-trade agreements (FTAs). Third, more of these recent FTAs have been between dissimilar countries than in the past when they were more between similar countries. Against this background, Nomura et al. (2016) examined the question of whether FTAs were building blocks or stumbling blocks to multilateral free trade (MFT). They distinguished between two ways whereby a bilateral RTA“” could become an MFT. The first was an expanding regime, whereby the two members of an existing bilateral agreement accept a third member into the group. In contrast, an overlapping regime is when one member of the group forms an RTA with a third member creating a hub-spoke system, which can eventually lead to MFT. Assuming that a bilateral agreement has already been formed by two symmetric countries, Nomura et al. (2016, p. 6), outlined four main conclusions:

(i) A bilateral FTA becomes a stumbling block for MFT through overlapping regimes, while it acts as a building block for MFT through an expanding regime when market sizes of member and nonmember countries are quite similar.
(ii) When the market size of nonmember countries is smaller than that of member countries, then overlapping regimes lead to MFT, while expanding regimes may or may not.
(iii) If the nonmember country of the original FTA is large, then the expanding regime may not achieve MFT, while the overlapping regime cannot.
(iv) When the market size of the nonmember country is quite large as compared with member countries, MFT never arises through overlapping regimes, expanding regimes, or negotiation of a multilateral trade agreement (MTA).

In a recent work, Zhou (2020) tested several of these ideas, including the two main questions of whether RTAs really promote trade and whether proliferation of RTAs leads to fragmentation. Zhou (2020) tests three hypotheses. First, RTAs increase trade more for countries that are geographically close than for countries that are distant from one another. Second, RTAs increase trade more for countries that are politically similar than countries that are politically different. Third, RTAs increase trade for countries that are culturally similar to countries that are culturally different. Zhou (2020) argues that geographic, political, and cultural proximity is important for promoting trade in RTAs. RTAs work better if countries are proximate along these dimensions. In addition, the efficacy of RTAs is also affected by the countries' status within the overall world system. The effect of RTAs between core countries is more than the effect of RTAs between peripheral countries. Zhou (2020) notes that RTAs remove trade barriers among a group of countries, a process referred to as negative integration. However, there is more to RTAs that go beyond removal of trade and non-trade barriers.

Basing himself on the work of economic sociologists Zhou (2020) argues that there is a whole lot of institutional framework—including formal and informal norms, rules and perceptions that are needed to make negative integration work. Therefore “It is wishful thinking that opening up markets to each other through RTAs would greatly boost bilateral trade.” (p. 4). Thus, negative integration must be balanced by positive integration, which refers to the rules and regulations established to remove disparities and inequalities among members of an RTA. Its mechanism includes institutions for harmonization of rules, regulations, and laws, standardization, and dispute resolution. Zhou (2020) combines two concepts to expound the structure of modern international trade constraints of RTAs. The first is the principle of homophily—which says that similarity among actors leads to greater ties than dissimilar actors. Thus, people sharing similar experiences and living in similar sociocultural environments are more likely to establish business ties. The second is the world system theory, which classifies the world trade system into three categories—the core dominated by developed countries, the periphery consisting of developing countries, and the semi-periphery consisting of newly industrializing countries (emerging economies). Zhou (2020) applies this to international trade, arguing that international trade is conducted by people and businesses on the ground, but within a highly structured system.

Core countries trade among themselves and also with peripheral and semi-peripheral countries. Peripheral countries trade with a limited number of core countries and less among themselves. Semi-peripheral countries combine features of both core and peripheral countries. Several studies indicate that the differential effects of RTAs on countries vary within this structured pattern. For example, it has been established that the benefits of RTAs are highest among core countries. However, they are less likely to be remunerative for peripheral countries, in spite of the fact that these countries are granted more freedom to form RTAs under GATT. Core, semi-peripheral, and peripheral countries also vary in their capacity or ability to trade. Finally, countries also vary regarding motives. RTAs among less developed countries are likely to be unsuccessful because of limited economic capacity (Bhalla & Bhalla, 1997; Zhou, 2020). The reasons for this include lack of capacity to produce competitive products for exports, and the bandwagon effects of less developed countries in emulating what developed countries do, without giving much thought to the real impact of RTAs. Zhou (2020) points out that this situation is consistent with world society theory, which argues that when some world model becomes legitimized and popularized countries feel obligated to adopt the model without really paying attention to its full implications.

With the remaining two hypotheses, Zhou (2020) found that while RTAs generally promote bilateral trade between countries, RTAs were more effective the wealthier the countries. Thus, RTAs are more effective in promoting trade between two core countries, and between a core country and a semi-peripheral country than between two peripheral countries. Zhou (2020) concludes that countries engaging in RTAs that lack common informal institutions due to geographic, political, and cultural distance must emphasize positive integration more than negative integration. In addition, RTAs within the context of peripheral countries need more attention in order for them to succeed.

3.4.4 RTAs and Developing Countries

There are two main contentions about RTAs in developing countries. The first is that RTAs in developing countries have positive impacts on growth leading to accelerated income convergence (Behar & Cirera-i-Criville, 2013; Fielding &

Shields, 2003; Hammouda et al., 2009; Limao, 2007; Sperlich & Sperlich, 2014, 2017). Fielding and Shields (2003) tested whether the CFA Currency Zone in West Africa augmented the integration. They found a substantial positive impact of the currency zone on integration. Behar and Cirera-i-Criville (2013) investigated whether RTAs raise trade for developing countries and compared the North-South RTAs with South-South RTAs. They found that although developing countries may not be natural trading partners, and may have problems with the implementation of RTAs/FTAs South-South RTAs had a higher impact on trade than North-South RTAs. The impact of RTAs on trade among developing countries was higher.

In contrast, there is a second contention that says that RTAs do not lead to income convergence. Hammouda et al. (2009) showed that despite some progress, regional integration in Africa has not led to income convergence as was to be expected. They attributed this to two sources. The first was weak performance growth and the second was weak intraregional trade and limited movement of resources within Africa's sub-regions. The result is that little progress has been made to integrate Africa's economies. Limao (2007) argued that RTAs among developing countries would hamper growth and result in the "poor-stay-poor" trap (Krugman, 1991; Quah, 1993; Venables, 2003). Venables (2003) distinguished between "extreme" and "intermediate" comparative advantage among members of a customs union. He explained these terms as follows: Take two countries A and B that have abundant unskilled labor relative to the world. If Country A in turn has more unskilled labor relative to Country B, then Country A has an extreme comparative advantage and Country B has an intermediate comparative advantage. If the two countries form a customs union, Country A will begin to ship skilled labor manufactured products to Country B, while Country B will ship unskilled labor products to Country A. From this, the country with the intermediate comparative advantage will be better off in the customs union than the one with extreme comparative advantage. As a result, the formation of a customs union (RTAs) will lead to income convergence for poor countries and income divergence for rich countries. (Venables, 2003).

3.5 Political Economy Perspectives of Trade Agreements

The foregoing discussion provides some good insights into the complex aspects of trade agreements and what drives and hinders their success. However, they tend to be single-targeted in focus, and for that reason, they are not able to explain fully the main reasons why some RTAs succeed and others fail. In contrast, political economy perspectives focus on how and why multiple factors interact to shape regional trade agreements and their effectiveness. In particular, they focus on the distribution and contestation of power and resources in a regional context (Mathieson, 2016).

3.5.1 The Five Lenses of Political Economy Perspectives

Broadly speaking, the political economy framework has used what is referred to as five lenses (Byiers et al., 2015) to analyze the central question of "What are the actors and factors affecting the policy agenda of regional organizations? And what are the drivers and blockers of implementation?" (Vanheukelom et al., 2016, p. iii). The five lenses are structural or foundational factors. Institutional factors, power and interests of different actors and groups in those institutions, sectoral characteristics, and external factors and influences. Structural or foundational factors include hard-to-change geographic, economic, and historic factors that affect the dynamics of the region. Institutional factors include the formal and informal "rules of the game." These are what is actually written down in the books and what actually takes place. The power and interest of actors and groups refer to the various local stakeholders and agencies who matter in the mobilization and implementation of ideas. The sector characteristics refer to the peculiar policy features that apply in the subsector of the economy, for example, agriculture, trade, and industrialization. External factors and influences include all the global forces that impact the affairs of the local economy. These include external trade agreements, external donors, and the motives behind their support. This framework has been used by many researchers (Mathieson, 2016; Kraphol, 2017a, 2017b; Hout & Mohamed Salih, 2019; Aniche, 2021).

3.5.2 Krapohl's Two Logics

Krapohl (2017b) argued that there are two logics of regional integration theory—the European Model or the intraregional logic and the non-European model, or the extra-regional logic. Rooted in neofunctionalism the European model reveals that integration works best when there was a preexisting strong economic interdependence among countries before they formed the integration. The result is that once regional integration has been formed it becomes automatic that the group will advance to more prosperity due to several forms of spillovers. These include economic spillover, whereby integration in one area necessitates integration in other areas; political spillover, whereby political actors shift their loyalties to a new political unit of the integration, and a cultivated spillover, which makes created institutions out of the integration push for further integration. Krapohl (2017b) argued that applying the European integration theories to developing countries is problematic for several reasons. First, developing countries do not have the economic interdependence that existed in Europe, before it formed the European Economic Community (EEC). Second, according to the new regionalism theories, the proliferation of regional integration outside of Europe was due to the end of the Cold War and globalization. The end of the Cold War, allowed countries to seek new alliances in the absence of the East and West rivalry, and globalization forced countries to seek alliances to face global competition. Thus, regional integrations were formed to (1) enhance the countries' transition from import-substitution to export-led industrialization; (2) boost countries' abilities to negotiate with outside entities as a group rather than individual countries; (3) provide an integrated market that would yield economies of scale for member countries; and (4) be a tool for attracting investments both domestic and foreign. Finally, the European model provides an explanation of why countries form integration but it cannot explain why some succeed and some fail.

Krapohl (2017b) argued that the European or intraregional model builds on exploitation of comparative costs and economies of scale through removal of tariff and non-tariff barriers, which in turn leads to increased trade. The non-European or extra-regional logic builds on improving the region's competitiveness within the global market through attraction of foreign investments and gaining access to other regional markets. Where such investments go is determined by the extra-regional actors not the members of the integration. Thus, while there is less rivalry in the first logic, there is more in the second, because extra-regional actors often determine the final destinations of investments in the region. For Krapohl (2017b), developing regions benefit more from extra-regional logics while developed regions benefit more from intraregional logics. In the same vein regional powers in developing countries benefit less from integration than smaller countries.

Krapohl (2017b) showed that both intraregional and extra-regional logics have features that resemble the classic prisoner's dilemma and the battle of the sexes' phenomena of game theory. With respect to intraregional logic, the prisoner's dilemma arises from the fact that at the basic minimum tariff and non-tariff barriers must be removed for integration to work. However, member states are also interested in protecting their domestic economies from competitors. Thus, the best case for a member state is where it is able to protect its domestic market within the trade liberalization of the organization, while the worst will be for it to liberalize trade while all the other members protect their economies. In this case, if all member states seek the best possible actions, a Nash equilibrium will be mutual protectionism, and no intraregional trade liberalization will occur. If the group agrees to cooperate for mutual benefit, it also has to contend with the battle of the sexes, whereby it has to choose from different configurations of harmonized policies that will work for the group since every member state will have preferences as to which policies to adopt. With respect to extra-regional logic, Krapohl (2017b) argued that the game member states play against each other depends on the decision made by the extra-regional actors. On the one hand, if extra-regional actors decide to reward integration, member states of the integration may find themselves waging a battle of the sexes. On the other hand, if extra-regional actors decide to pursue a less consistent strategy in supporting integration member states may find themselves facing a Rambo state situation. This is a situation where a member state receives more preferential treatment from extra-regional actors because of its dominant standing such as size of its economy and market. As a result, such members find that they will be better off being alone than being part of the integration, and therefore choose to defect or become disinterested in the integration.

Against this background, Krapohl (2017b) advances two hypotheses of regional integration in developing countries.

> As long as regional integration is systematically rewarded by extra-regional actors, member states of developing regions cooperate within the battle of the sexes. As soon as regional integration is at odds with important regional privileges, the regional powers of developing countries become regional Rambos with the dominant strategy of defection" (Krapohl, 2017b, pp. 54, 55).

These hypotheses were tested with the Association of South East Asian Nations (ASEAN) (Krapohl, 2017c), the Southern Common Market (MERCUSOR) (Fink & Rempe, 2017; Meissner, 2017), and the Southern African Development Community (SADC) (Muntschick, 2017). Since all these will be discussed in later chapters only summary results are provided here. For ASEAN, Krapohl (2017c) found that no member state was big enough in terms of economy to dominate. Second, the group has been fortunate to have its three largest trading partners nearby and in close proximity. For both MERCUSOR and the SADC, the behavior of the dominant economies, namely Brazil and South Africa, confirmed Krapohl's (2017b) hypotheses. As we will see later, this has significantly hindered the progress of the two regional trade agreements.

3.5.3 Economic and Political Asymmetries

The concept of asymmetry is not new in trade discussions. As mentioned in the last chapter, the WTO (2005) identifies information asymmetry as one of the obstacles to trade. The effects of information asymmetry have been discussed by several researchers (see Chap. 1). However, Hout and Mohamed Salih 2019) provide a much broader perspective on the concept and its implications for Africa's trade. They argue that Africa's political economy is characterized by multiple asymmetries that impact any efforts at regionalism on the continent. These asymmetries include systemic, continental, and sub-regional asymmetries. Systemic asymmetry refers to the unequal relationship between Africa and the major regions of the world. This asymmetry is reflected in Africa's North-South relationship (with its former colonial powers and their appendages of the developed world) and its South-South relations, particularly with the so-called emerging markets of China, India, and Brazil. Thus, while the former created a dependent economy in Africa, the latter is doing the same thing following the same playbook of the former. Thus, while the former has created a false transition of African economies—deindustrialization without any industrial development and a shift to service sector, the latter relations are accentuating the situation and making it worse.

Continental asymmetry and sub-regional asymmetry refer to power differentials that exist at the continental and sub-continental levels. These show themselves through regional hegemons—such as the roles of South Africa, Nigeria, and Kenya in their respective regions. Garzon Pereira (2014) argues that a lot of the transactions between regional hegemons and their weaker regional neighbors revolve around policy convergence, transfer of material resources, and the nature of the institutions that manage the resources. These asymmetries influence the extent to which decision-making authority is transferred to the RTAs and the extent to which regional hegemonies are willing to cooperate with their weak neighbors. Many countries are reluctant to delegate decision-making powers to the RECs.

> Regional asymmetries and presence of large hegemonic states frustrate regional integration both within regions and across the continent. They also make it difficult to achieve consensus because national interests stand in the way of regional policies (p. 76).

Regional hegemonies do not appear to be conducive to cooperation at the sub-regional level. Researchers have cited the role South Africa and Nigeria play in their respective regions—their tendency to dominate but their reluctance to lead outside their domains. Others point to the tendency for regional integration in Africa to become a mechanism for more trade diversion than trade creation due to the limited diversity of African economies (Cadot et al., 1999, p. 216). The Economic Partnerships Agreements (EPAs) with the EU may turn out to be another asymmetry. This has led to fragmentation. The African Common Position for Negotiations of a New Agreement of Cooperation with the European Union is supposed to deal with this but will it do that?

3.5.4 Aniche's Post-Neo-Functionalism

Aniche (2021), criticized existing theories of integration as Eurocentric, Western, and parochial. He pointed out that one major defect of the existing theories of integration is the idea that integration was a linear and gradual process. Aniche asserted that this thinking was faulty because of what happened with Brexit. Apart from this, he pointed out that neo-functionalism assumed that integration of states was an exercise among equals instead of unequal. Pointing to the failure of integration in Africa, Aniche (2021) also attacked the usefulness of current theories of integration especially the neo-functionalist framework for integration. Instead, Aniche (2021) proposed a post neo-functionalist approach to regional integration in Africa. Post-neo-functionalism, according to Aniche (2021) was a combination of neo-nationalism, post-nationalism, and humanism. Neo-nationalism consisted of two parts—political and economic nationalism. While political nationalism called for political integration and unity, economic nationalism called for a partial closure of the economy to outside competition till it was able to stand on its own feet. The humanism aspect argued that integration, once ready to occur, must also be humane, humanistic, people driven or private sector-led.

For Aniche (2021) African countries are not prepared for economic and political integration, due to the myriad of problems they face including rentierism, mono-product economy, primary producing economy, deindustrialization, and internal conflicts. In particular, "the clog in the wheel of Africa integration is that countries that cannot achieve unity and integration at the national level cannot logically pursue integration at the regional level because charity begins at home" (Aniche, 2021, p. 225). Thus, Aniche proposes that economic and political integration should start at the national level and then proceed to the regional level. Apart from this regional economic integration should be preceded by regional security cooperation. Economic integration in Africa should not be at the state level but at the business level, with the state having only a facilitator role. This Aniche hoped would lead to initial inequality among individuals and groups but would eventually trickle down through efficient social policy, and would also reduce the huge gap between Africa and the developed regions.

3.6 Conclusion

The theory of regional trade agreements raises a lot of aspirations and expectations for countries. First, RTAs are supposed to increase trade volumes among member states by removing trade barriers. Second, they are also expected to form building blocks for larger multilateral trade organizations. Third, geographic proximity, similarity in culture and political history among member states should lead to effective RTAs. Fourth, RTAs are also supposed to lead to convergence in economic well-being of member states. These aspirations and expectations are reflected in the aims of the AfCFTA.

However, as many have commented before, Africa is famous for over-achieving in crafting institutions on paper but underachieving in what actually translates from the paper to the ground. More importantly, these expectations and aspirations do not seem to match up with the realities, when one looks at the history of RTAs in Africa. As a result, one is left with many unanswered questions. First, why have Africa's RTAs before the formation of the AfCFTA not led to increased volume of intraregional trade? If geographic proximity, similarity in culture and political history of member states of RTAs should lead to effective RTAs, why has Africa's RTAs not been effective? If RTAs are supposed to lead to income convergence of member states, why has this not occurred in Africa? Given Africa's current trade pattern, how do the interests of extra-regional actors factor into the realization of the goals of the AfCFTA? Will the multiple asymmetries existing on the continent support or hinder the aspirations of the AfCFTA? Finally, if Africa's existing RTAs before the AfCFTA have not been effective in achieving their goals, how can they be good models to guide the AfCFTA? Is Africa not ready for regional economic integration? Will Africa be better off starting with security cooperation before regional economic integration? In the following chapters, we try to answer these questions.

References

Aniche, E. T. (2021). Institutions, inequality, and crisis of developmental regionalism in Africa. In E. T. Aniche & T. Falola (Eds.), *Rethinking institutions. Processes and development in Africa* (pp. 211–238). Rowman & Littlefield.

Agarwal, S. (1994). Socio-cultural distance and the choice of joint ventures: A contingency perspective. *Journal of International Marketing, 2*(2), 63–80.

Baier, S., & Bergstrand, J. (2004). Economic determinants of free trade agreements. *Journal of International Economics, 64*(1), 29–63.

Balassa, B. (1961). *The theory of economic integration*. George Allen and Unwin.

Bandelj, N. (2002). Embedded economies: Social relations as determinants of foreign direct investment in Central and Eastern Europe. *Social Forces, 81*(2), 411–444.

Behar, A., & Cirera-i-Criville, L. (2013). Does it matter who you sign with? Comparing the impacts of North–South and South–South trade agreements on bilateral trade. *Review of International Economics, 21*(4), 765–782.

Bhagwati, J. (1991). *The world trading system at risk*. Princeton University Press.

Bhagwati, J. (1993). Regionalism and multilateralism: An overview. In J. de Melo & A. Panagariya (Eds.), *New dimensions in regional integration* (pp. 22–51). Cambridge University Press.

Bhagwati, J. (2008). *Termites in the trading system: How preferential agreements undermine free trade*. Oxford University Press.

Bhagwati, J., & Panagariya, A. (1996). The theory of preferential trade agreements: Historical evolution and current trends. *American Economic Review, 86*(2), 82–87.

Bhalla, A. S., & Bhalla, P. (1997). *Regional blocs: Building blocks or stumbling blocks*. Palgrave Macmillan Press.

Birch, A. H. (1966). Approaches to the study of federalism. *Political Studies, 14*(1), 15–33.

Biswaro, J. M. (2011). *The quest for regional integration in Africa, Latin America and beyond in the twenty first century: Experience, progress, and prospects*. Fernando Morais.

Bliss, H., & Russett, B. (1998). Democratic trading partners: The liberal connection, 1962–1989. *The Journal of Politics, 60*(4), 1126–1147.

Brenton, P., & Manchin, M. (2003). Making EU trade agreements work: The role of rules of origin. *The World Economy, 26*(5), 755–769.

Byiers, B., Vanheukelom, J., & Kingombe, C. K. M. (2015). *A five lenses framework for analysing the political economy in regional integration* (Discussion Paper No. 178). Center for Development and Policy Management.

Cadot, O., De Melo, J., & Olarreaga, M. (1999). Asymmetric regionalism in sub-Saharan Africa: Where do we stand? In J. E. Stiglitz & P.-A. Muet (Eds.), *Governance, equity, and global markets: The annual bank conference on development economics-Europe* (pp. 215–224). World Bank.

Chacha, M. (2014). Regional integration and the challenge of overlapping memberships on trade. *Journal of International Relations and Development, 17*, 522–544.

De Melo, J., & Panagariya, A. (Eds.). (1993). *New dimensions in regional integration*. Cambridge University Press.

Deutsch, K., Burrell, S., & Kann, R. (1957). *Political community and the North Atlantic area: International organization in the light of historical experience*. Princeton University Press.

Duina, F. (2016). Making sense of the legal and judicial architectures of regional trade agreements worldwide. *Regulation & Governance, 10*, 368–383.

Duncan, G. A. (1950). The small state and international economic equilibrium. *Economia Internazionale, 3*(4), 933–943.

Eichengreen, B., & Irwin, D. A. (2010). The slide to protectionism in the great depression: Who succumbed and why? *The Journal of Economic History, 70*(4), 871–897.

Fielding, D., & Shields, K. (2003). Economic integration in West Africa: Does the CFA make a difference? *Economica, 72*(282), 683–704.

Fink, S., & Rempe, D. (2017). Trade network analysis: Economic structures of EC/EU, ASEAN, MERCOSUR, and SADC. In S. Krapohl (Ed.), *Regional integration in the global south: External influence on economic cooperation in ASEAN, MERCOSUR, and SADC* (pp. 91–113). Palgrave Macmillan.

Frankel, J. A., Stein, E., & Wei, S. (1995). Trading blocs and the Americas: The natural, the unnatural and the supernatural. *Journal of Development Economics, 47*(1), 61–96.

Friedman, P. (1974). *The impact of trade destruction on national incomes*. The University Florida.

Gani, A. (2009). Some aspects of trade between Australia and Pacific Island countries. *The World Economy, 33*(1), 1–18.

Garzon Pereira, J. F. (2014). Hierarchical orders: An analytical framework. *Journal of Policy Modeling, 36S*, S26–S46.

Gerout, G., MacLeod, J., & Desta, M. (2019). The AfCFTA as yet another experiment towards continental integration: Retrospect and prospect. In D. Luke & J. MacLeod (Eds.), *Inclusive trade in Africa: The African continental free trade area in comparative perspective* (pp. 87–119). Routledge.

Gounder, N., & Chand Prasad, B. (2011). Regional trade agreements and the new theory of trade: Implications for trade policy in Pacific Island countries. *Journal of International Trade Law and Policy, 10*(1), 49–63.

Hammouda, H. B., Karingi, S. N., Njuguna, A. E., & Jallab, M. S. (2009). Why doesn't regional integration improve income convergence in Africa? *African Development Review, 21*(2), 291–330.

Haas, E. B. (1958). *The uniting of Europe: Political, social, and economic forces, 1950–57*. Stanford University Press.

Haas, E. B. (1964). *Beyond the nation-state*. Stanford University Press.

Haas, E. B. (1976). Turbulent fields and the theory of regional integration. *International Organization, 30*(2), 173–212.

Hawtrey, R. G. (1944). *Economic destiny*. Longmans, Green & Co..

Hout, W., & Mohamed Salih, M. A. (2019). *A political economy of African regionalisms: An overview of asymmetrical development*. Edward Elgar.

Hummels, D. (2007). Transportation costs and international trade in the second era of globalization. *Journal of Economic Perspectives, 21*(3), 131–154.

Johnson, H. G. (1954). Optimum tariffs and retaliation. *Review of Economic Studies, 21*, 142–153.

Kandogan, Y., & Hiller, J. (2018). Alliances in international governmental organizations, regional trade agreement formation, and multinational enterprise regionalization strategy. *Journal of International Business Studies, 49*, 729–742.

Khan, A. E. (1946). *Great Britain in the world economy*. Sir Isaac Pitman.

Krapohl, S. (2017a). Introduction – Integration theory and the new regionalism. In S. Krapohl (Ed.), *Regional integration in the global south: External influence on economic cooperation in ASEAN, MERCOSUR, and SADC* (pp. 1–29). Palgrave Macmillan.

Krapohl, S. (2017b). Two logics on regional integration and the games regional actors play: A theoretical framework for the analysis of regional economic cooperation and defection. In S. Krapohl (Ed.), *Regional integration in the global south: External influence on economic cooperation in ASEAN, MERCOSUR, and SADC* (pp. 33–62). Palgrave Macmillan.

Krapohl, S. (2017c). ASEAN: Extra-regional cooperation triggers regional integration. In S. Krapohl (Ed.), *Regional integration in the global south: External influence on economic cooperation in ASEAN, MERCOSUR, and SADC* (pp. 115–146). Palgrave Macmillan.

Krugman, P. (1991). *Geography and trade*. MIT Press.

Leamer, E. E., & Storper, M. (2001). The economic geography of the internet age. *Journal of International Business Studies, 32*(4), 641–665.

Limao, N. (2007). Are preferential trade agreements with non-trade objectives a stumbling block for multilateral liberalization? *The Review of Economic Studies, 74*(3), 821–855.

Madsen, J. B. (2001). Trade barriers and the collapse of world trade during the great depression. *Southern Economic Journal, 67*(4), 848–868.

Manchin, M., & Pelkmans-Balaoing, A. O. (2007). *Rules of origin and the web of East Asian free trade agreements.* World Bank policy research working paper 4273.

Mansfield, E. D., Milner, H. V., & Rosendorff, B. P. (2000). Free to trade democracies, autocracies, and international trade. *American Political Science Review, 94*(2), 305–321.

Marchal, A. (1965). The European economic community and the developing countries. *Annals of Public and Cooperative Economics, 36*, 51–60.

Mathieson, C. (2016). *The political economy of regional integration in Africa: The East African Community (EAC).* ECDPM. http://ecdpm.org/peria/eac

Meade, J. E. (1951). The removal of trade barriers: The regional versus universal approach. *Economica, 18*(70), 184–198.

Meade, J. E. (1955). *The theory of customs union.* North Holland Publishing.

Meissner, K. L. (2017). MERCOSUR: The ups and downs of regional integration in South America. In S. Krapohl (Ed.), *Regional integration in the global south: External influence on economic cooperation in ASEAN, MERCOSUR, and SADC* (pp. 147–178). Palgrave Macmillan.

Milner, H. V., & Kubota, K. (2005). Why the move to free trade? Democracy and trade policy in the developing countries. *International Organization, 59*(1), 107–143.

Mitrany, D. (1966). *A working peace system.* Quadrangle Books.

Moravscik, A. (1998). *The choice for Europe: Social purpose and state power from Messina to Maastrich.* Cornell University Press.

Muntschick, J. (2017). SADC: Extra-regional trade relations constrain deeper market integration. In S. Krapohl (Ed.), *Regional integration in the global south: External influence on economic cooperation in ASEAN, MERCOSUR, and SADC* (pp. 179–207). Palgrave Macmillan.

Nomura, R., Ohkawa, T., Okamura, M., & Tawada, M. (2016). Expansion of free trade agreements, overlapping free trade agreements, and market size. In T. Ohkawa, M. Tawada, M. Okamura, & R. Normura (Eds.), *Regional free trade areas and strategic trade policies*. Springer.

Panagariya, A. (1996). The free trade area of the Americas: Good for Latin America? *The World Economy, 19*(5), 485–515.

Pearson, D. (2015). What makes for an effective free trade agreement? Examination of theory and evidence. In H. G. Djajadikerta & Z. Zhang (Eds.), *A new paradigm for international business proceedings of the conference on free trade agreements and regional integration in East Asia, Singapore*.

Perroux, F. (1966). Intégration économique. Qui intègre? Au bénéfice de qui s'opère l'intégration ? *Économie Appliquée, XIX*(3–4), 389–414.

Pollard, S. (1962). *The development of the British economy, 1914–50.* Hodder Arnold.

Quah, D. T. (1993). Empirical cross-section dynamics in economic growth. *European Economic Review, 37*(2–3), 426–434.

Rauch, J. E. (1999). Network versus markets in international trade. *Journal of International Economics, 48*(1), 7–35.

Ropke, W. (1959). *International order and economic integration.* D. Reidel.

Saint-Etienne, C. (1984). *The great depression 1929–1938.* Hoover.

Sperlich, S., & Sperlich, Y. (2017). Growth and convergence in South–South integration areas: An empirical analysis. *Review of International Economics, 25*, 799–830.

Sperlich, Y., & Sperlich, S. (2014). Income development and dispersion in South–South integration areas. *Journal of Economic Integration, 29*(4), 726–758.

Summers, L. (1991). Regionalism and the world trading system. In *Policy implications of trade and currency zones*. Federal Reserve Bank of Kansas City.

Tinbergen, J. (1959). *On the theory of economic integration. Selected papers* (pp. 138–151). North Holland Publishing Company.

Tinbergen, J. (1954). *International economic integration.* Elsevier.

Vanheukelom, J., Byiers, B., Bilal, S., & Woolfrey, S. (2016). *Political economy of regional integration in Africa: What drives and constrains regional organizations* (Synthesis report). ECDPM. http://ecdpm.org/peria/synthesis

Venables, A. J. (2003). Winners and losers from regional integration agreements. *The Economic Journal, 113*(490), 747–767.

Viner, J. (1950). *The customs union issue*. Carnegie Endowment for International Peace.

Wei, S.-J., & Frankel, J. A. (1996). Can regional blocs be stepping stone to global free trade? A political economic analysis. *International Review of Economics and Finance, 5*(4), 339–347.

Wonnacott, P., & Lutz, M. (1989). Is there a case for free trade areas? In J. Schott (Ed.), *Free trade areas and US trade policy* (pp. 59–84). Institute for International Economics.

World Trade Organization (WTO) (2005). *World trade report*. WTO.

Zhou, M. (2020). Differential effectiveness of regional trade agreements, 1958–2012: The conditioning effects from homophily and world-system status. *The Sociological Quarterly*, 1–22.

Chapter 4
The Economic Community of West African States

4.1 Introduction

The purpose of this chapter is to examine the trade patterns of the Economic Community of West African States (ECOWAS). It recognizes that ECOWAS was set up to accomplish other things for the member states. However, given the purpose of the book, the discussion in this chapter here will be strictly limited to trade. The chapter examines a three-part question. What was expected of ECOWAS in terms of intraregional trade? What has been the reality of intraregional trade within the subgroup? What explains the discrepancy between expectation and reality and implications for the African Continental Free Trade Area (AfCFTA)? The chapter is divided into five sections. The first section provides some basic information about the countries of ECOWAS. The second describes the formation of ECOWAS. The third section discusses the rationale and expectations, with particular reference to trade. The fourth section examines the merchandise trade of ECOWAS, with respect to its direction and composition and whether it meets expectations. The fifth section examines the reasons for the gap between the expectations and reality and their implications.

4.2 Some Basic Information About ECOWAS

ECOWAS consists of 15 West African countries (Fig. 4.1). By land area, these countries cover a total of 5,287,328 km^2, about 17.6% of the area of Africa. Together these countries contain a total population of 393,437,138 per the 2019 UN population estimates, about 30% of the total population of Africa. In terms of GDP, UN estimates show that in 2019 the total GDP of ECOWAS was about $693.5 billion, about 27% of Africa's total GDP (Table 4.1).

B. Ofori-Amoah, *The African Continental Free Trade Area*,
https://doi.org/10.1007/978-3-031-59181-5_4

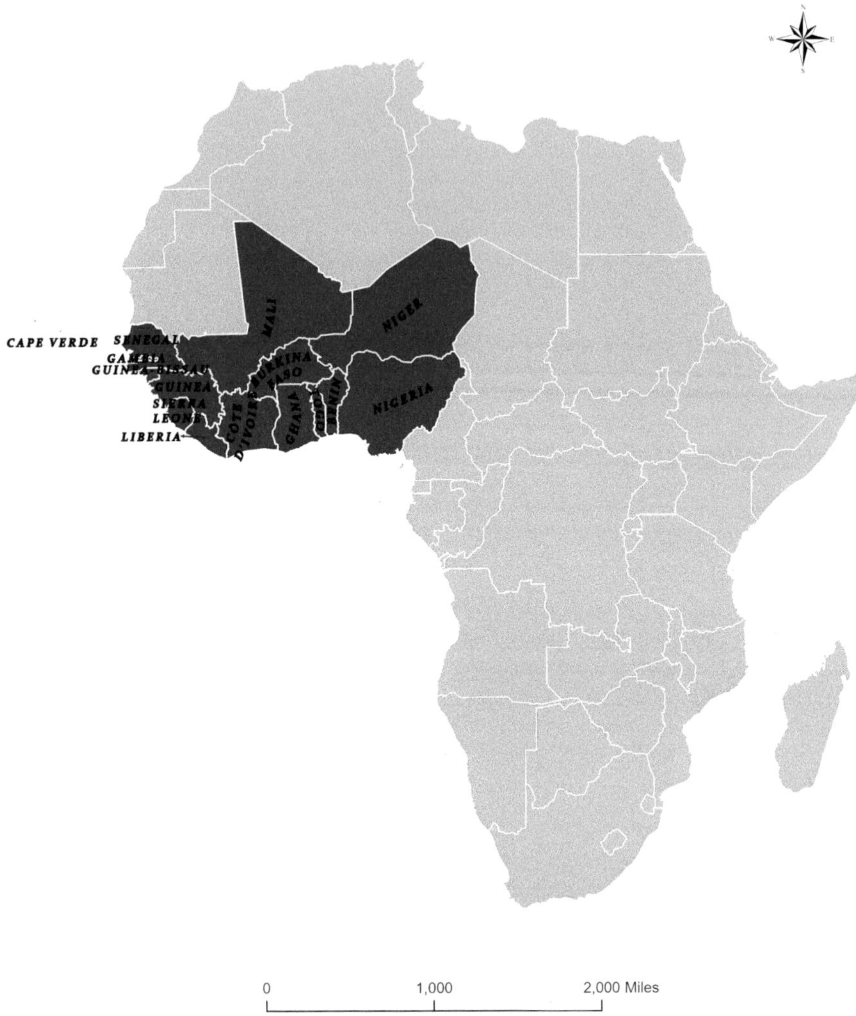

Fig. 4.1 Members of the Economic Community of West African States. (Data source: ICPAC GEOPORTA. The analysis was performed in ArcGIS Pro 3.1.0)

Within the region, however, there are some remarkable asymmetries. Niger, the largest country by land area, accounts for 19% of the total land area of the group. Together with Mali and Nigeria, the top three countries by land area account for 59.3% of the total land area of the group. In terms of population, close to 52% of the total population lives in Nigeria alone, with the remaining 14 countries accounting for 48% of the total population. Nigeria also dwarfs every country of the group in GDP. In 2019, it accounted for 65% of the total GDP of the group. Its GDP of $433.5 billion was about seven times the size of Ghana's, the second country in terms of GDP (Table 4.1). The 15 countries also share colonial histories, but under different colonial administrations that included the British, French, German, and

Table 4.1 ECOWAS by area, population, and Gross Domestic Product (GDP) (US$)—2019

Country	Area (Km^2)	Population	GDP	GDP Per Capita, PPP (US $)
Benin	112,620	12,290,444	14,391,686,633	3426
Burkina Faso	274,200	20,951,639	16,178,162,030	2267
Cabo Verde	475,440	577,031	1,981,845,741	7475
Côte d'Ivoire	322,460	26,147,551	58,539,424,930	5433
Gambia	11,300	2,508,884	1,813,608,280	2320
Ghana	238,540	31,522,290	68,337,537,816	5774
Guinea	245,860	12,877,539	13,442,861,444	2675
Guinea-Bissau	36,120	1,970,457	1,439,638,443	2021
Liberia	111,370	4,985,289	3,319,596,500	1532
Mali	1,024,000	20,567,424	17,280,250,805	2420
Niger	1,186,408	23,443,393	12,916,455,161	1276
Nigeria	923,768	203,304,492	448,120,428,859	5352
Senegal	196,712	16,000,782	23,398,811,424	3510
Sierra Leone	71,740	8,046,829	4,076,578,543	1777
Togo	56,790	8,243,094	7,220,395,248	2211
	5,287,328	393,437,138	692,457,281,855	

Source: Data from United Nations Population Division

Portuguese. Ethnicity of the group is mindboggling. Nigeria, the most populous country of the group and in Africa, has over 250 ethnic groups. While most of the ethnic groups in the region are confined to one country, there are a few that span across several countries. The most widespread of these are the Fulani, who are found in every ECOWAS country except for Cabo Verde, the Hausa, which are found in four countries, and the Mandinka, which are found in ten countries (Ofori-Amoah, 2019). Yet, the region has no lingua franca. The languages of government and business are English, French, and Portuguese. Francophone countries dominate in terms of number of countries, but Anglophone countries dominate in terms of population. In terms of economy, none of the member states can pass as an industrialized economy. Thus, they are all producers of primary commodities—food, agricultural raw materials, fuels, and metals and ores.

4.3 The Formation of ECOWAS

The idea of West African economic integration dates back to the precolonial times. Asante (1986) traces it as far back as 1867 when Africanus Beale Horton talked about "self-government of Western Africa." The idea received more traction during the Pan-African nationalism movement of the early twentieth century. In 1895, the French created French West Africa out of their West African colonies. However, concrete efforts to create such an organization began in the late 1950s. In 1958, Ghana and Guinea created the Union of West African States. In 1959, seven

French-speaking countries—Benin, Côte d'Ivoireote, Mali, Burkina Faso, Mauritania, Niger, and Senegal—formed the Union Douaniere de l'Afrique de l'Ouest (UDAO) to promote free movement of goods and a single tariff on all imported goods (Odhiambo et al., 2016). This group later became the Union Douaniere et Economic de l'Afrique de l'Ouest (UDEAO), but it failed (Edi, 2007).

In the early 1960s, the United Nations Economic Commission for Africa (UNECA) sent a mission to Africa to assess the potential for an economic integration. In 1962, the UNECA decided that it would help African countries to engage in regional cooperation and industrialization. In 1963, the UNECA sent a mission to West Africa, followed by a series of meetings in Niamey, Niger, in 1966, Accra, Ghana, in 1967, and Monrovia, Liberia, in 1968. Several recommendations for economic cooperation in the subregion were made and adopted at the Niamey meeting by 11 Heads of State. Articles of Association for the establishment of an Economic Community were signed by 12 of the 14 members at the Accra meeting. The protocol for establishing the organization was signed at the Monrovia meeting. In addition, the meeting mandated Nigeria and Guinea to study areas of possible cooperation, while Liberia and Senegal were mandated to prepare a draft Treaty and a protocol for a customs union (Asante, 1986). However, very slow progress was made after the Monrovia meeting. A meeting to discuss the report by Nigeria and Guinea failed to convene, and nothing happened until 1972.

The death of President Charles De Gaulle of France and the end of the Nigerian Civil War in 1970, respectively diminished the influence of France in Africa and gave Nigeria the confidence to play a leadership role in the subregion. As Asante (1986) reported, an increasing number of former French colonies—in particular, Benin, Mauritania, and Niger, denounced the agreements with France—the Yaoundé Conventions—as neo-colonists instruments. In 1972, Mauritania unilaterally declared all the agreements null and void. In 1973, the French-speaking countries made another attempt when they created the Economic Community of West Africa (CEAO), but once again, this organization did not survive.

In 1972, President Gnassingbé Eyadema of Togo and President Yakubu Gowon of Nigeria signed an agreement that they hoped would serve as the bedrock for a much bigger organization of West African countries. After that, they set out on a tour to convince their fellow West African heads of state to join them (Asante, 1986; Edi, 2007). In December 1973, all the 15 countries in West Africa that were independent—Benin, Burkina Faso, Côte D'Ivoire, Gambia, Ghana, Guinea, Guinea-Bissau, Liberia, Mali, Mauritania, Niger, Nigeria, Senegal, Sierra Leone, and Togo—met in Lomé, Togo. The meeting called on Nigeria and Togo to prepare detailed proposals for the organization and drew up a timetable for implementation. On May 27 and 28, 1975, the 15 countries met in Lagos, Nigeria, to sign the ECOWAS Treaty. On June 23, the Treaty came into effect when seven countries, Burkina Faso, Côte d'Ivoire, Ghana, Guinea, Liberia, Nigeria, and Togo, ratified the agreement. In 1977, Cape Verde joined the group, but in 1999, Mauritania withdrew on the grounds that its Arab heritage made it difficult to collaborate with the group members (Edi, 2007).

4.4 Aims and Expectations of ECOWAS

Asante (1986) offers three rationales for the creation of ECOWAS. First, many of the early post-independence industrialization efforts were discussed or undertaken in isolation. The countries did not talk to each other and so failed to take advantage of the fact that industrial establishments are interrelated. Second, developed plans followed a similar pattern—disjointed and inward-looking, lacking coordination with external linkages. Third, and most important, the small market sizes of individual countries made it more difficult for industries to compete globally. As a result, many of the industries that were established were small scale, but high cost and economically inefficient to operate. In this case, a larger market would, among other things, allow industries to expand, reduce commodity prices, increase consumption, and make the region more attractive for investment. Against this background, the 1975 ECOWAS Treaty aims were

> To promote co-operation and development in all fields of economic activity particularly in the fields of industry, transport, telecommunications, energy, agriculture, natural resources, commerce, monetary and financial questions and in social and cultural matters for the purpose of raising the standard of living of its peoples, of increasing and maintaining economic stability, of fostering closer relations among its members and of contributing to the progress and development of the African continent (United Nations, 1976, p. 20).

This was to be achieved through

- the elimination as between the member states of customs duties and other charges
- of equivalent effect in respect of the importation and exportation of goods
- the abolition of quantitative and administrative restrictions on trade among the member states
- the establishment of a common customs tariff and a common commercial policy toward third countries
- the abolition as between the member states of the obstacles to the free movement of persons, services, and capital (United Nations, 1976)

In addition, the Treaty also called for the harmonization of agricultural, industrial, and monetary policies as well as implementation of transportation, communication, and other infrastructural facilities. The Treaty also established the following institutions:

(a) the Authority of Heads of State and Government
(b) the Council of Ministers
(c) the Executive Secretariat
(d) the Tribunal of the Community and
(e) the following Technical and Specialized Commissions: the Trade, Customs, Immigration, Monetary and Payments Commission; The Industry, Agriculture and Natural Resources Commission; Transport, Telecommunications and Energy Commission; and the Social and Cultural Affairs Commission (United Nations, 1976, p. 21)

Chapter III of the Treaty, which dealt with Customs and Trade required members to not impose import duties during the first 2 years after the Treaty came into force but progressively reduce tariffs and quantitative restrictions such as quotas over the next 8 years after the two-year period until there will be on tariffs and quantitative restrictions on intraregional trade. In addition, over a period of 15 years after its establishment, the community would become a customs union, at which point there would be no tariffs on member states but a common tariff wall against nonmembers.

The Treaty was revised and signed by all the 15-member states on July 21, 1993, due to problems with the 1975 Treaty in dealing with events in the subregion in the 1980s, in particular with civil wars in Sierra Leone and Liberia, and also due to changing conditions. The revised Treaty expanded the role and competence of the community beyond the narrow confines of economic integration to cooperation in political, legal, and security matters. It added new principles, including nonaggression among members, maintenance of security and stability in peaceful settlements of dispute; promotion, recognition, and protection of human rights; and promotion and consolidation of democratic system of governance (Odhiambo et al., 2016). The Treaty also added new institutions, including Community Parliament Economic and Social Council, Community Court of Justice, and Funds for Cooperation Compensation, and Development. Finally, the revised Treaty considered African Union's (AU) African Economic Community (AEC) goals and objectives, which allowed AU to recognize ECOWAS as a pillar of the AEC (Odhiambo et al., 2016). In summarizing the revised Treaty, Odhiambo et al. (2016, p. 54) noted:

> Overall, the revision of the 1975 ECOWAS Treaty has expanded the focus of the community from the narrow field of economic integration to a wider range of economic, social, security and political issues. Hence, the ECOWAS Commission announced that "ECOWAS is an organization for political and economic integration, quite distinct from what is referred to as 'regional economic communities,' which have restricted their scope of intervention to the common market." Civil society can therefore validly pursue and support non-economic agendas within the ECOWAS framework.

However, Chapter VIII of the treaty, which deals with Cooperation in Trade, Customs, Taxation, Statistics, Money, and Payment, retained most of the articles in the 1975 Treaty, except that the time frame to become a customs union was set at 10 years from January 1, 1990. As before, all quotas, quantitative restrictions, and administrative obstacles to trade would be removed. So, how has ECOWAS enhanced intraregional trade since its establishment? We answer this question by diving into the realities of ECOWAS' trade patterns. In particular, we do this by focusing on ECOWAS' direction of trade and composition of trade.

4.5 Trade of ECOWAS

4.5.1 Direction of Trade

Asante (1986) reported that intraregional trade of ECOWAS in 1977 was very low, less than 3% of both their exports and imports. He also reported that most of the trade of the region was with non-West African countries, with majority of the trade going to Europe, Japan, and the United States in that order. Given that this was only 2 years after the ECOWAS Treaty had been signed, such a low percentage of intraregional trade was excusable. Hess (1991) reported that by the end of the 1980s, intraregional trade had reached 10%. However, available data since that period indicate that not much has changed (Table 4.2). Thus, since 1995, the intraregional export trade within ECOWAS has not risen above 10%.

Trade with the rest of Africa over the same period has not been encouraging either. Indeed, there is lesser trade with the rest of Africa than trade within the group. ECOWAS' export trade within itself plus trade with the rest of Africa constitute less than 20% of its total trade for each of the years in consideration. In contrast, its trade with the rest of the world has ranged from 88.6% in 1995 to 84.8% in 2019. The breakdown of ECOWAS' export trade with the rest of the world is shown in Fig. 4.2. It shows that in 1995, ECOWAS' export trade partners were Europe

Table 4.2 Direction of export trade of ECOWAS, 1995–2019 (Percentage share)

Year	ECOWAS	Africa	ECOWAS + Africa	Rest of the World	Total
1995	9.1	2.3	11.4	88.6	100
2000	9.2	2.9	12.1	87.9	100
2005	9.5	4.4	13.9	86.1	100
2010	7.4	9.0	16.3	83.7	100
2015	9.4	6.6	16.0	84.0	100
2019	8.8	6.4	15.2	84.8	100

Source: Author's calculation based on data from UNCTADStat

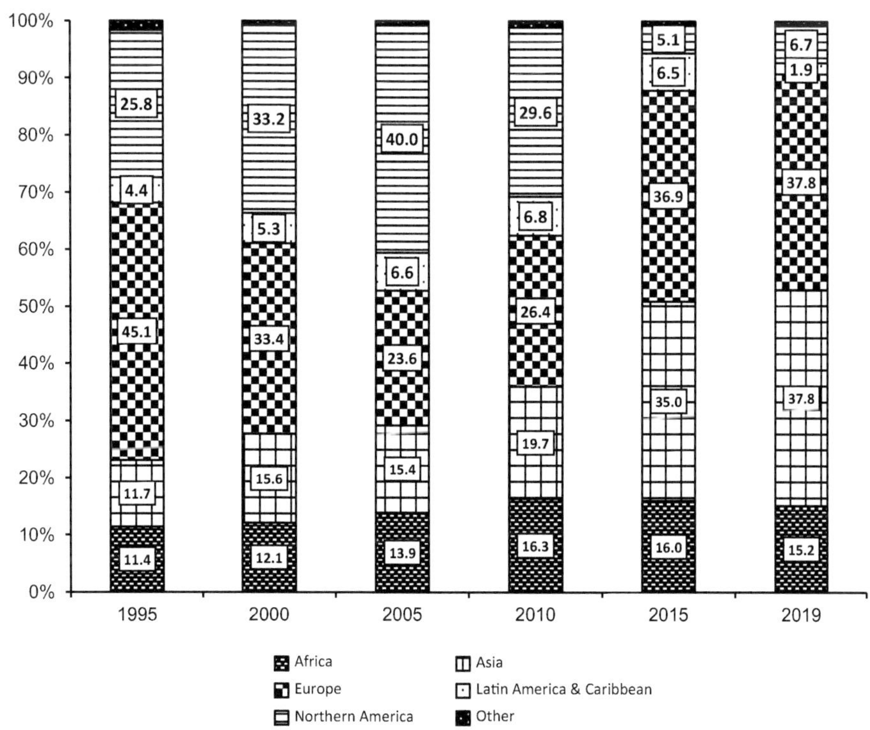

Fig. 4.2 Direction of export trade of ECOWAS, 1995–2019

Table 4.3 Top 20 export markets of ECOWAS, 2001–2019

2001		2005		2010		2015		2019	
Country	%	Country	%	Country	%	Country	%	Country	%
US	28.6	US	41.4	US	27.8	India	13.9	India	12.0
India	8.5	Spain	7.1	India	8.7	NLD	9.4	China	7.5
France	8.1	France	5.4	Brazil	5.4	Spain	5.9	NLD	6.9
Spain	5.3	Brazil	4.3	So. Africa	5.4	France	5.3	SUI	6.6
Italy	4.5	NLD	3.3	NLD	5.2	SUI	4.3	So. Africa	6.4
Brazil	3.9	So. Africa	2.8	France	4.4	So. Africa	4.1	Spain	6.1
NLD	3.7	*C′ d'Ivoire	2.4	Italy	3.2	US	3.9	France	5.0
Germany	3.5	Germany	2.4	Spain	3.1	Brazil	3.7	US	4.3
Indonesia	2.6	Portugal	2.0	Eq. Guinea	2.6	UAE	3.6	*Ghana	4.2
SUI	2.6	Belgium	1.9	Canada	2.6	UK	3.1	UAE	3.6
*Ghana	1.9	SUI	1.8	Belgium	2.4	China	3.0	Italy	2.6
UK	1.8	Italy	1.8	SUI	2.0	*C′ d'Ivoire	2.7	Germany	2.1
Portugal	1.8	Japan	1.7	Portugal	1.8	Italy	2.4	Canada	1.9
So. Africa	1.8	Nigeria	1.7	Botswana	1.8	Germany	2.2	UK	1.9
*Côte d'Ivoire	1.7	Indonesia	1.6	China	1.6	Japan	2.1	*Mali	1.7
Canada	1.4	China	1.3	UK	1.6	**Ghana	1.6	*Côte d'Ivoire	1.7
*Mali	1.1	*Ghana	1.3	*C′ d'Ivoire	1.3	Mali	1.6	Indonesia	1.6
Taiwan	1.0	Cameroon	1.3	*Ghana	1.2	Belgium	1.5	Türkiye	1.6
*Senegal	1.0	UK	1.0	Germany	1.1	Indonesia	1.5	Belgium	1.4
Japan	0.9	Senegal	1.0	Malaysia	1.1	Türkiye	1.1	Malaysia	1.2
Total	85.8	Total	87.4	Total	84.4	Total	77.0	Total	80.5

Source: Author's calculation based on data from International Trade Center Trade Map; *ECOWAS members
NLD Netherlands, *SUI* Switzerland, *CIV* Côte d'Ivoire, *So. Africa* South Africa

(45.1%), Northern America (25.8%), and Asia (11.7%). By 2019, Europe and China were tied as top export trade destinations with Northern America in the distant fourth. Only 15.2% of the export trade occurred within Africa. Table 4.3 shows the top 20 export markets of ECOWAS by country from 2001 to 2019. The table confirms what we have already noted that ECOWAS members trade more with outside entities than among themselves and other African countries. Thus, in 2001, for example, only five out of the 15 member states made the list of the top 20 export markets of the group—Ghana, which ranked 11th; Côte d'Ivoire 15th; Mali 17th; and Senegal 19th. The only other African country in the top 20 list was South Africa, which ranked 14th. The top 20 countries accounted for 85.8% of the total export market of the group. In 2019, only three member states made it to the list—Ghana, which ranked 9th; Mali, which ranked 15th; and Côte d'Ivoire, which ranked 16th (Table 4.3).

Table 4.4 Direction of ECOWAS' import trade, 1995–2019 (percentage share)

	ECOWAS	Rest of Africa	ECOWAS + Africa	Rest of the World	Total
1995	8.4	2.1	10.5	89.5	100
2000	13.5	3.2	13.5	86.5	100
2010	12.5	4.3	16.7	83.3	100
2015	9.0	4.1	13.1	86.9	100
2019	8.7	3.9	12.6	87.4	100

Source: Author's calculation based on data from UNCTADStat

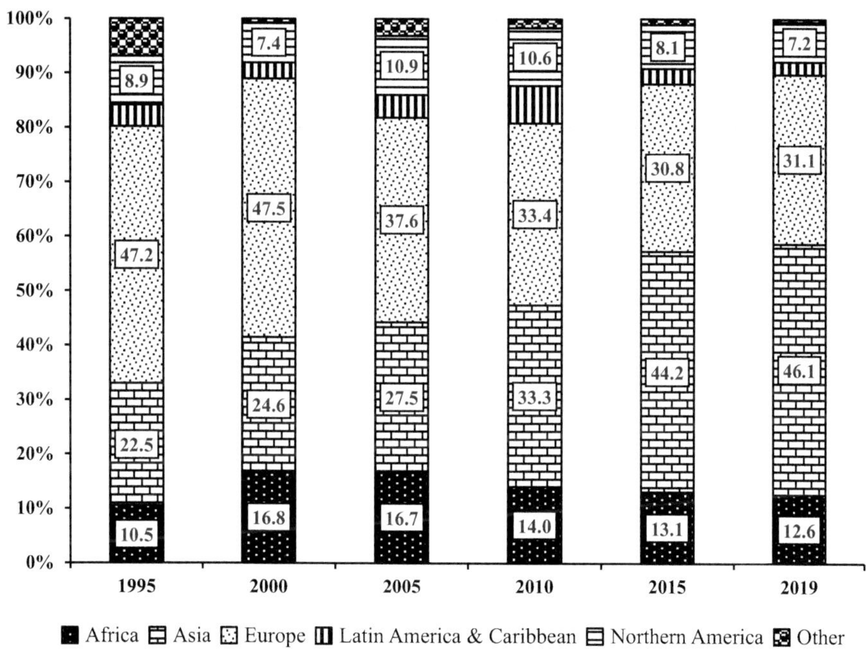

Fig. 4.3 Direction of import trade of ECOWAS, 1995–2019

Import trade has followed a similar pattern. Intraregional import trade reached 13.5% in 2000 but has since declined (Table 4.4). In 2019, it was only 8.7% of total trade. Once again, import trade among ECOWAS members and with the rest of Africa accounted for 10.5% of its total import trade in 1995. In 2019, it was only 12.6% (Table 4.4). In contrast, since 1995, more than 80% of ECOWAS' import trade has occurred with entities outside of Africa.

The breakdown of ECOWAS' import trade is shown in Fig. 4.3. Once again in 1995, ECOWAS imported 47.2% of its goods from Europe, followed by 22.5% from Asia. In 2019, it was 46.1% from Asia and 31.1% from Europe. Africa's share in this trade was 10.5% in 1995 and 12.6% in 2019 (Fig. 4.3). On the import side, only two countries—Nigeria and Côte d'Ivoire—made it to the top 20 import markets of ECOWAS, with South Africa being the only other African country in the list. In 2019, there were only three countries—Nigeria, Côte d'Ivoire, and Senegal (Table 4.5). So, the question is, Why is it that after 44 years

Table 4.5 Top 20 import markets of ECOWAS, 2001–2019

2001		2005		2010		2015		2019	
Country	%	Country	%	Country	%	Country	%	Country	%
France	13.6	France	10.3	China	16.5	China	17.3	China	22.3
UK	7.2	China	7.8	US	10.7	US	6.0	India	7.7
Germany	6.6	South Korea	6.6	France	6.9	France	5.8	US	6.6
US	6.4	US	5.8	So. Korea	6.7	India	5.2	France	4.9
So. Korea	5.5	*Nigeria	5.4	Japan	4.0	Belgium	4.7	NLD	4.7
Japan	5.5	UK	5.3	Singapore	3.7	NLD	4.3	Belgium	3.3
China	4.5	Japan	4.4	India	3.4	So. Korea	3.4	Japan	3.2
*Nigeria	4.5	NLD	4.2	Belgium	3.0	UK	3.3	So. Korea	2.9
NLD	3.8	Germany	3.9	*Nigeria	2.9	Singapore	3.2	Singapore	2.9
Belgium	3.7	*CIV	3.6	Italy	2.8	Germany	2.9	Germany	2.7
*CIV	3.3	Brazil	3.2	UK	2.6	*Nigeria	2.8	UK	2.2
Italy	2.8	India	3.1	ATG	2.5	Japan	2.3	Türkiye	2.1
So. Africa	2.1	Singapore	2.9	UAE	2.3	*CIV	2.2	*Nigeria	2.0
India	2.0	Italy	2.8	Brazil	2.2	Spain	2.2	UAE	2.0
Spain	2.0	Belgium	2.2	NLD	2.2	Italy	2.1	Russia	1.7
Singapore	2.0	So. Africa	2.1	So. Africa	1.6	Thailand	1.9	Italy	1.7
Thailand	1.7	Thailand	1.9	Germany	1.4	So. Africa	1.7	Brazil	1.5
Brazil	1.3	Spain	1.7	*CIV	1.3	Brazil	1.7	Spain	1.5
Norway	1.3	Ghana	1.3	Spain	1.1	UAE	1.4	*CIV	1.5
Russia	1.2	Sweden	1.0	Thailand	1.1	Türkiye	1.3	*Senegal	1.4
Top 20	81.1		79.5		78.7		75.8		78.9

Source: Author's calculation based on data from ITC Trade Map data *ECOWAS members
ATG Antigua and Barbuda, *CIV* Côte d'Ivoire, *NLD* Netherlands, *SUI* Switzerland, *So. Korea* South Korea, *So. Africa* South Africa

since its founding, ECOWAS' export and import trade is still oriented toward outside than inside of Africa?. The answer we argue lies in its composition of trade.

4.5.2 *Composition of Trade*

The composition of ECOWAS' trade has been traditionally dominated by primary commodities. In 1995, primary goods accounted for 92.3% of total export trade. In 2019, they still accounted for 94.2%. Over the same period, manufactured goods accounted for 7.5% in 1995 and 5.7% in 2019 (Table 4.6). In contrast, ECOWAS' import trade was dominated by manufactured goods—67.4% in 1995 and 65.3% in 2019. The breakdown of exports is clear from Table 4.7, which indicates that fuel accounts for over 50% of ECOWAS' export trade. Fuel is followed by food, and pearls and precious stones, with manufactured goods playing very insignificant role.

In contrast, manufactured goods led by machinery and transportation equipment, other manufactures, and chemical products dominate the import trade of ECOWAS (Table 4.8). Since 1995, these have accounted for more than 60% of imports.

Table 4.6 Composition of export and import trade of ECOWAS, 1995–2019

Year	Primary Goods		Manufactured Goods		Unclassified Goods	
	Export	Import	Export	Import	Export	Import
1995	92.3	27.1	7.5	67.4	0.2	5.5
2000	93.2	33.7	5.1	64.2	1.7	2.1
2005	93.3	33.4	6.2	65.6	0.5	1.0
2010	94.3	31.5	5.5	67.5	0.2	1.0
2015	92.5	32.7	7.1	66.2	0.4	1.1
2019	94.2	34.0	5.7	65.3	0.1	0.7

Source: Author's calculation based on data from UNCTADStat

Table 4.7 Export trade of ECOWAS by major commodity groups, 1995–2019

Commodity Group	1995	2000	2005	2010	2015	2019
Food	18.3	11.0	10.5	11.4	16.9	14.0
Agricultural raw materials	9.3	5.0	3.7	2.6	3.5	3.7
Ores and metals	4.8	2.5	2.2	2.2	2.8	4.3
Fuels	54.0	72.4	75.3	73.4	57.7	58.4
Pearls, precious stones and nonmonetary gold	5.9	2.3	1.6	4.7	11.6	13.8
Chemical products	2.8	1.2	1.4	1.3	1.6	1.4
Machinery and transport equipment	1.3	1.5	1.8	1.7	3.0	1.9
Other manufactured goods	3.4	2.4	2.6	2.6	2.5	2.4
Unassigned	0.2	1.7	0.9	0.2	0.3	0.1
	100.0	100.0	100.0	100.0	100.0	100.0

Source: Author's calculation based on UNCTADSTAT

Table 4.8 Import trade of ECOWAS by major commodity groups, 1995–2019

Major Commodity Groups	1995	2000	2005	2010	2015	2019
Food	16.0	16.5	18.4	15.1	15.9	14.9
Agricultural raw materials	1.1	1.4	1.1	1.0	0.9	1.1
Ores and metals	1.2	1.4	1.5	1.3	1.3	1.1
Fuels	8.8	14.4	12.3	14.1	14.5	16.9
Pearls, precious stones & nonmonetary gold	0.0	0.0	0.0	0.1	0.2	0.0
Chemical products	13.3	12.8	11.3	10.8	11.8	11.7
Machinery and transport equipment	30.5	29.8	31.6	34.9	30.7	31.4
Other manufactured goods	23.6	21.5	22.8	21.7	23.7	22.3
Unassigned	5.5	2.1	1.0	1.0	1.0	0.7
Total	100	100	100	100	100	100

Source: Author's calculation based on data from UNCTADSTAT

Table 4.9 Export trade within ECOWAS by major commodity groups, 1995–2019

Commodity Groups	1995	2000	2005	2010	2015	2019
Food	12.1	9.7	10.3	15.7	17.4	16.3
Agricultural raw materials	13.1	4.9	2.7	1.1	0.6	0.5
Ores and metals	4.1	0.8	1.3	1.9	1.1	1.3
Fuels	42.7	61.1	62.5	52.0	45.4	46.7
Pearls, precious stones, and nonmonetary gold	0.0	0.2	0.0	0.5	1.9	1.1
Chemical products	11.1	6.7	6.5	6.2	9.0	7.0
Machinery and transport equipment	3.4	5.0	2.0	10.8	8.7	7.9
Other manufactured goods	13.3	11.1	12.5	11.7	15.8	19.2
Unassigned	0.3	0.4	2.2	0.1	0.1	0.0
Total	100	100	100	100	100	100

Source: Author's Calculation based on UNCTADSTAT

Within ECOWAS, much of the export trade involves fuel, followed by food, and other manufactured goods. Machinery and transportation equipment, which constitute the largest imported items account for a small percentage in the list of exports (Table 4.9). Fuels is again dominant in the import trade. However, over the past decade, there has been a little increase in manufactured goods as percentage of imports. In 1995, other manufactured goods were only 13% of exports and 14% of imports. In 2019, they were 19% of exports and 20% of imports (Tables 4.9 and 4.10).

Finally, ECOWAS' trade with Africa was no different from the intra-ECOWAS trade. Fuel was the most important item in both the export and import trade. Other manufactured goods and food items ranked the distant second the third most important trade items (Tables 4.11 and 4.12).

Table 4.10 Import trade within ECOWAS by major commodity groups, 1995–2019

Commodity Groups	1995	2000	2005	2010	2015	2019
Food	10.0	10.3	10.2	14.0	15.6	17.1
Agricultural raw materials	1.9	3.1	2.3	0.9	0.6	0.6
Ores and metals	1.4	0.8	1.6	1.4	0.8	0.6
Fuels	59.1	63.3	62.5	54.0	46.4	46.0
Pearls, precious stones, and nonmonetary gold	0.0	0.1	0.0	0.5	2.0	0.0
Chemical products	10.0	6.6	8.0	5.1	8.0	7.4
Machinery and transport equipment	2.7	4.8	3.2	13.5	11.3	8.3
Other manufactured goods	14.4	10.6	10.6	10.4	15.3	20.0
Unassigned	0.3	0.4	1.6	0.0	0.1	0.0
Total	100	100	100	100	100	100

Source: Author's calculation based on UNCTADSTAT data

Table 4.11 ECOWAS export trade with Africa, 1995–2019 by major commodity groups

Major Commodity Groups	1995	2000	2005	2010	2015	2019
Food	14.0	10.9	9.2	9.4	13.2	11.9
Agricultural raw materials	14.8	5.5	2.6	0.9	0.9	1.0
Ores and metals	4.1	1.8	1.1	1.2	0.9	0.9
Fuels	39.1	59.3	62.8	60.1	52.6	55.5
Pearls, precious stones, and nonmonetary gold	0.0	2.2	5.1	11.5	5.8	5.9
Chemical products	11.1	5.8	5.4	3.4	5.9	4.8
Machinery and transport equipment	3.4	4.4	2.2	6.7	9.4	7.8
Other manufactured goods	13.2	9.8	10.1	6.8	10.7	12.2
Unassigned	0.3	0.4	1.6	0.1	0.5	0.0
	100	100	100	100	100	100

Source: Author's calculations based on UNCTADSTAT data

Table 4.12 ECOWAS import trade with Africa, 1995–2019

Year	1995	2000	2005	2010	2015	2019
Food	13.3	12.7	14.0	15.7	17.4	18.7
Agricultural raw materials	1.9	2.9	1.9	1.2	0.9	1.1
Ores and metals	2.0	1.3	2.7	2.1	1.1	1.1
Fuels	52.8	54.0	51.1	38.4	33.7	33.6
Pearls, precious stones, and nonmonetary gold	0.0	0.1	0.0	0.3	1.3	0.0
Chemical products	10.2	8.1	9.6	8.5	12.0	11.0
Machinery and transport equipment	3.7	6.9	6.3	18.7	17.3	11.8
Other manufactured goods	15.4	13.0	13.0	14.9	16.1	22.8
Unassigned	0.7	1.1	1.3	0.1	0.1	0.0
	100	100	100	100	100	100

Source: Author's calculation based on UNCTADSTAT data

4.6 Explanations of ECOWAS Intraregional Trade Performance

ECOWAS was established to enhance the capacity of member states in intraregional trade through the removal of tariff and nontariff barriers and free movement of people across the subregion. Yet, most research work that has looked at the performance of the community comes to the same conclusion. It has failed to promote intraregional trade (Asante, 1986; Okolo, 1989; Okolo & Wright, 1990; Gambari, 1991; Bundu, 1997; Jebuni, 1999; Edi, 2007). Thus, Iyoha (1984) noted that in 1979, 5 years after the ECOWAS Treaty came into force, intraregional export trade of the community was just 3% of the community's total export, while intraregional import trade was 5.8% of the total import trade. This meant that 97% of export trade and 94.2% of import trade occurred outside the region. After 35 years, share of ECOWAS' trade with Africa is still very low. It was 8.8% in exports and 6.4% in imports in 2019.

This was attributed to several reasons, including (1) the failure of ECOWAS member states to reduce their dependence on the industrialized countries; (2) the continuous export of primary products; (3) the inability of political leaders to manage their economic and political differences that made ECOWAS a low priority; (4) crucial lack of infrastructure especially transportation and communication; (5) political instability brought by many military coups and governments; and (6) the economic crises of the 1980s and 1990s (Asante, 1986; Okolo & Wright, 1990; Edi, 2007).

Kuffour (2006) also identified several reasons why ECOWAS' trade liberalization goals of promoting intraregional goals failed. First, trade tax constituted a major source of government revenue. This made it difficult for countries to comply with the trade liberalization policy of gradual reduction of tariffs until they are completely gone. Second, there were many French-owned firms operating in several of the former French colonies, especially Senegal and Côte d'Ivoire. Ghana and Nigeria were concerned that trade liberalization policies would benefit those French-owned firms and harm their own infant industry firms. Third, there were not sufficient funds to support the trade liberalization policies. Given that trade tax was a major source of government revenue for member states, it was decided to set up a fund that could be used to support member states who lost revenue due to the liberalization policy. However, the funds were short because only three countries—Nigeria, Mali, and Burkina Faso—paid their dues. To make matters worse, the Secretariat did not have any power to enforce the terms of the Treaty. Overlapping membership and continued affiliations with former colonial powers also complicated matters. For example, the French-speaking countries still belonged to the West African Monetary and Economic Union (UEMOA), which was also aiming at becoming a customs union. This created a problem of loyalty when it came to membership. Finally, there were no clear mandates of the authorities of the community, and decisions of the community were not binding.

In its assessment of regional integration in Africa, the United Nations Economic Commission for Africa (2010, p. 13) said

> ECOWAS faces persistent barriers to trade, despite having signed cross-border trading provisions. A number of state employees deliberately continue to violate such provisions. A large percentage of trade in the region is small in scale or informal and is often sustained by price variability from country to country. In the past, such activities among traders were viewed as smuggling, which prompted their unfair treatment by security agencies. The treaty's effect on the free movement of persons also presents problems, namely harassment, multiple roadblocks, illegal barriers and reduced road.

These are all valid reasons for the low level of intraregional trade within ECOWAS. However, some of these reasons can hinder trade in general. For example, poor road and communication networks has not stopped land-locked countries in ECOWAS from exporting and importing from outside Africa. They still have to import and transport their commodities over poor transportation and communication network in the interior. Bureaucratic red tape and corrupt practices still present problems for external imports and exports as they do for within-group trade. The case of trade tax is a tough one because that is the very essence of forming a free trade area—to reduce tariffs so as to increase the volume of trade among members, which will then generate more revenue to offset the loss of trade tax. This becomes even more problematic in a customs union where there is a common tariff. However, the main reason why intraregional trade in ECOWAS is so low is due to lack of complementarities and competitiveness of the economies of member states of ECOWAS. Borrowing from the principles of spatial interaction, complementarity refers to demand and supply relationships between places. In this regard, the absence of complementarity is due to the fact that member states of ECOWAS are mostly producers of primary products and consumers of manufactured products. With no country or member state that is industrialized, it is very easy to understand why ECOWAS member states trade mostly with outsiders than among themselves. The economies of member states are not competitive in the markets of the products that are in high demand in the member states. Intraregional in ECOWAS will not rise to expectations unless its member state embarks on industrialization.

4.7 Conclusion

Established in 1975, ECOWAS was expected to enhance intraregional trade among members. However, after decades of its formation, it has been identified as one of the building blocks of the AfCFTA. Examination of its trade shows little change since its formation. ECOWAS trades more with nonmember states than its own members, and that most of its export trade are primary products and import trade are manufactured goods. This has been attributed to several reasons, including dependence on industrialized countries, the low content of manufactured goods in member states' product mix, poor transportation and communication infrastructure, and lack of political will. While all these are valid reasons, we argue that the most important of these reasons is the lack of competitiveness of ECOWAS' economies, which in turn is due to lack of vibrant industrial sectors in the economies of member states. It is true that the new ECOWAS Treaty expanded its activities beyond trade, and ECOWAS leaders can brag about expanding the Treaty beyond its original narrow confines of trade. However, this is not a case where the expansion of activities followed from ECOWAS being a success in its original mission, which was trade. So, if it has not succeeded in its original mission, what guarantees that it will in its expanded mission. Apart from this, how is ECOWAS going to fulfill its expanded mission with its weak economies? The lack of a vibrant manufacturing sector is the Achilles heel of the economies of the ECOWAS' member states, and until that changes, it is going to be difficult to achieve the goals of any trade area agreements and beyond.

References

Asante, S. K. B. (1986). *The political economy of regionalism in Africa: A decade of the Economic Community of West African States (ECOWAS)*. Praeger Publishers.

Bundu, A. (1997). ECOWAS and the future of regional integration in West Africa. In R. Lavergne (Ed.), *Regional integration and cooperation in West Africa: A multidimensional perspective*. Africa World Press, Inc.

Edi, E. M. (2007). *Globalization and politics in the economic community of West African States*. Carolina Academic Press.

Gambari, I. A. (1991). *Political and comparative dimensions of regional integration: The case of ECOWAS*. Humanities Press.

Hess, R. (1991). *Report on study on constraints to trade, payments and investment flows in ECOWAS* (Report prepared for ECOWAS). Imani Development Ltd.

Iyoha, M. A. (1984). Economic development and trade theories: Relevance and implications for ECOWAS. In A. Orimalade & R. E. Ubogu (Eds.), *Trade and development in Economic Community of West African States (ECOWAS)*. Vikas Publishing House Ltd..

Jebuni, C. D. (1999). The role of ECOWAS in trade liberalization. In Z. Igbal (Ed.), *Trade reform and regional integration in Africa* (pp. 489–506). International Monetary Fund.

Kuffour, K. O. (2006). *The institutional transformation of the Economic Community of West African States*. Ashgate.

Odhiambo, M., Chitiga, R., & Ebobrah, S. (2016). *The civil society guide to regional economic communities in Africa*. Odhiambo et al.

Okolo, J. E. (1989). Obstacles to increased intra-ECOWAS trade. *International Journal, 44*(1), 171–214.

Okolo, J. E., & Wright, S. (Eds.). (1990). *West African regional cooperation and development*. Westview Press.

Ofori-Amoah, B. (2019). *Africa's geography: Dynamics of place, cultures, and economies*. Wiley & Sons.

United Nations Economic Commission for Africa. (2010). *Assessing regional integration in Africa; Enhancing intra-African trade*. United Nations Commission for Africa.

United Nations Organization. (1976). *Treaty of the economic community of West African States*.

Chapter 5
The Economic Community of Central African States

5.1 Introduction

The Economic Community of Central African States (ECCAS) was recognized by the African Union (AU) as one of the building blocks for the African Continental Free Trade Area (AfCFTA). In this chapter, we examine the state of ECCAS' trade with particular reference to how it has enhanced intraregional trade and the potential of it becoming a building block for the AfCFTA. The chapter is in five sections. The first section provides some basic information and characteristics of the ECCAS. The second section provides an overview of the formation of the ECCAS, and the third section is about its aims and expectations. The fourth section discusses ECCAS trade, and the fifth section the reasons for the trade performance. The chapter concludes with implications for AfCFTA.

5.2 Some Basic Facts About the ECCAS

The ECCAS consists of ten countries located in central portion of Africa. These are Angola, Burundi, Cameroon, Central African Republic, Congo Republic, Democratic Republic of Congo (DRC), Equatorial Guinea, Gabon, Sao Tome, and Principe (Fig. 5.1). By land area, these 10 countries cover a total of 6,169,601Km^2, about 20.4% of Africa's total land area. The estimated population of 190,834,938 in 2019 constituted 14.4% of Africa's total population. The estimated gross domestic product (GDP) of \$218.3 billion in 2019 was about 8.8% of its gross domestic product (Table 5.1).

All the countries share colonial histories. DRC was a former colony of Belgium, Angola, and Sao Tome and Principe were Portuguese colonies, while the remaining seven were former French colonies. Like most other countries in Africa, they are all

B. Ofori-Amoah, *The African Continental Free Trade Area*,
https://doi.org/10.1007/978-3-031-59181-5_5

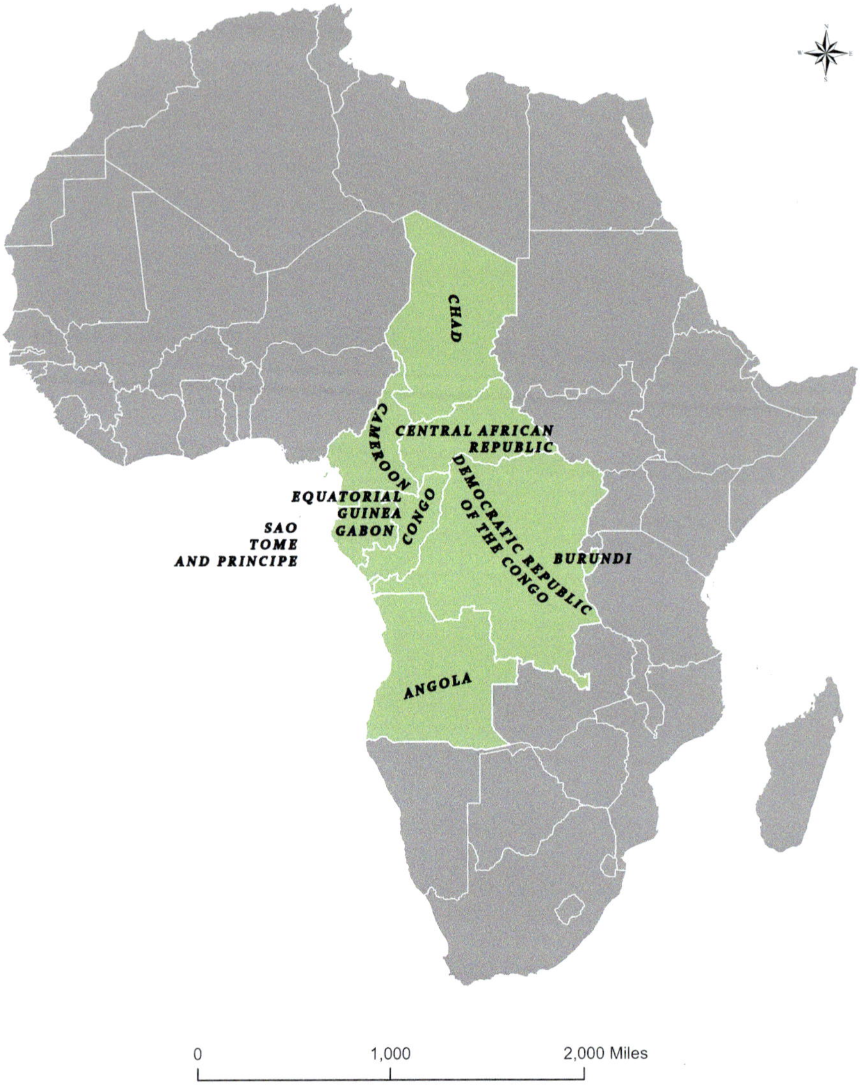

Fig. 5.1 Members of the Economic Community of Central African States. (Data source: ICPAC GEOPORTA. The analysis was performed in ArcGIS Pro 3.1.0)

multiethnic. Beyond these, the region has some asymmetric characteristics. DRC dominates the group in terms of its geographic area and population. It accounts for 38% of the total group area and 47% of its population. Indeed, about 77.6% of the population in the group live in the three countries of DRC, Angola, and Cameroon (Table 5.1). There is also a remarkable asymmetry in terms of distribution of natural resources. Angola, Equatorial Guinea, and Gabon have rich oil fields. DRC is a powerhouse of precious stones and metals—with large deposits of diamonds, cobalt, zinc, and copper. The DRC is also home to most of Africa's equatorial rain forest

Table 5.1 ECCAS members by area, population, GDP, and GDP per capita PPP, 2019

Country	Area (Km^2)	Population	Gross domestic product (US$)	GDP per capita, PPP (US $)
Angola	1,246,700	32,353,588	69,309,104,807	6995
Burundi	27,830	11,874,838	2,581,268,126	783
Cameroon	4030	25,782,341	39,670,977,333	3901
Central African Rep	622,980	5,209,325	2,221,301,401	986
Chad	1,284,000	16,126,866	11,314,951,343	1646
Congo Dem. Rep	2,345,410	89,906,891	51,775,830,726	1144
Congo Republic	342,000	5,570,733	12,750,338,736	3987
Equatorial Guinea	28,050	1,553,031	11,364,134,109	19,385
Gabon	267,670	2,242,786	16,874,405,840	15,577
Sao Tome and Principe	1001	214,599	427,425,040	4174
	6,169,671	190,834,998	218,289,737,459	

Source: United Nations Population Division

and houses the Congo, Africa's largest river basin, its second longest river, and a juggernaut of hydroelectric power potential. At the same time, there are relatively less endowed countries such as Chad, Congo Republic, and Burundi. The three largest economies per GDP, Angola, DRC, and Cameroon, account for 73.3% of the total GDP of the group. All the countries are multiethnic, with some of them spread across national borders, yet there is no lingua franca. The language of government business is French and Portuguese.

5.3 The Formation of the ECCAS

The ECCAS was established in 1983. It was part of the OAU's Lagos Plan of Action (LPA) of 1980. The ECCAS was preceded by several regional organizations in Central Africa (Union of Internationational Association, 2020). In June 1959, four prime ministers from four previous colonies—Central African Republic, Chad, Congo, and Gabon—signed an agreement to form a customs union called Union Douanière Equatoriale (UDE) or Equatorial Customs Union (ECU) (Nono, 2013). Cameroon joined the UDE in 1961. On December 8, 1964, the Heads of State of the Central African Republic, Chad, Congo, and Gabon signed the Brazzaville Treaty, which created the Union Douanière et Économique de l'Afrique Centrale (UDEAC) or Central African Customs and Economic Union (CACEU) (Ropivia, 1999). In April 1968, Central African Republic and Chad left the UDEAC to join Zaire (DRC) to form the Union des Etats de la Afrique Centrale (UEAC) or Union of Central African States (UCAS), but this was very short-lived as Central African Republic rejoined the UDEAC in December that same year. In September 1976, another group of countries, including Burundi, Rwanda, and Zaire signed an agreement to re-establish the economic links they had during the colonial period, and to promote security. The agreement created the Communauté Économique des Pays des Grand Lacs (CEPGL) or the Economic Community of Great Lakes Countries (ECGLC) (ICG, 2011; Meyer, 2011). In December, 1981, a conference of Heads of State from UAEC and CEPGL in Libreville, Gabon, adopted a recommendation to form ECCAS within the framework of the OAU Lagos Plan of Action and the Final Act of Lagos. The ECCAS Treaty was adopted on October 18, 1983, and came into force on December 18, 1984. The founding members included Angola, Burundi, Cameroon, Central African Republic, Chad, Congo Republic, Rwanda, Sao Tome and Principe, and Zaire (Congo Democratic Republic). Two additional members, Gabon and Equatorial Guinea, have since joined (Fig. 5.1). Among its main institutions were the Conference of Heads of State and Government, the Council of Ministers, the Court of Justice, the General Secretariat, the Consultative Committee, and other technical committees that might be needed.

However, the ECCAS "remained stillborn" (Pourtier, 1999) during its first 15 years due to a cycle of widespread violence and political leaders who were more interested in personal gains than regional goals. It was not until 1998 when the membership decided to revive the regional trade agreement (RTA) (Meyer, 2008, 2011; Palmateer & Clark, 2018; Lemarchand, 2016). This revival led to establishment of four new institutions that were all geared more toward security than trade. Among these were the Council for Peace and Security of Central Africa (COFAX), the Commission for Defense and Security (CDS), an early warning system (MARAC), and the Force Multinationale en Centrafrique (FOMUC) (Meyer, 2008).

5.4 Aims and Expectations of the ECCAS

The aims of the ECCAS as spelled out in Article 4 of the ECCAS' Treaty were to promote and enhance harmonious cooperation and balanced self-maintaining development in all fields of economic, social, political, and scientific activities to collective autonomy (UNECA, 1983). It also was charged with raising the standard of living of the people and promoting peace, security, and stability within the subregion. Specific objectives include (1) elimination of customs duties and all other equivalent taxes on the import and export of merchandise among member states; (2) abolish quantitative restrictions and other hindrances to trade; (3) establish a commercial policy with respect to third countries; (4) progressively eliminate obstacles to free circulation of persons, goods, services, capital, and right of establishment; (5) harmonize national policies so as to promote common activities, notably in the areas of industry, transport and communications, energy, agriculture, natural resources, trade, currency and finance, human resources, tourism, education and culture, and science and technology; (6) create a cooperation and development fund; accelerate development of member states either land-locked, partially islands, semi-enclosed, and/or in the category of least developed countries , economic stability (UNECA, 1983).

Article 6 of the treaty sets up a three-stage process for achieving these aims over a 12-year period, with each stage lasting for 4 years. The first stage would be devoted to stabilizing the fiscal conditions of member states and studies to determine the timetable for progressive removal of tariff and non-tariff barriers and for adoption of a common external tariff. The second stage was the creation of a free trade area, while the third stage was creation of a customs union. The community bound itself to the ideal that it would change to the next stage only when the aims allotted to a stage have been achieved. As a result, the community is expected to achieve these goals in a period not less than 10 years and not more than 20 years. How much of this has occurred in reality?

5.5 ECCAS Trade

Previous assessments of the performance of the ECCAS indicate that hardly has anything been achieved at all regarding especially its trading goals (Myer, 2008; Palmateer & Clark, 2018; Garlinska-Bielawska & Janicka, 2018, Inançli & Addi, 2019). For example, we have already noted the observations by Palmateer and Clark's (2018) assessment of ECCAS. In addition, Inançli and Addi (2019) found that the formation of ECCAS neither led to trade creation nor trade diversion between 2006 and 2016. The result is that very little of its original goals were achieved. The revival of the ECCAS, however, tilted the orientation of the group toward the additional goal of regional security, but this did not change the ineffectiveness of the group (Meyer, 2008). Thus, the ECCAS is generally considered one of the poorest of Africa's RTAs (UNCTAD, 2013; Palmateer & Clark, 2018).

5.5.1 *Direction of ECCAS Trade*

Recent data show that not much has changed. For example, in 1995, only 1.5% of ECCAS' trade occurred within itself. In 2019, it was still 1.6%, after reaching 3.2% in 2015 (Table 5.2). Trade with Africa has not been impressive either, except that in 2015, it rose to 11.4%, only to decline after that to 7.6% in 2019. The trend is the

Table 5.2 Direction of export trade of the ECCAS, 1995–2019

	ECCAS	Africa	ECCAS and Africa	Rest of the World	Total
1995	1.4	1.7	3.1	96.9	100
2000	0.9	2.3	3.2	96.8	100
2005	1.0	2.7	3.7	96.3	100
2010	2.2	3.6	5.8	94.2	100
2015	3.2	11.4	14.6	85.4	100
2019	1.6	7.6	9.2	90.8	100

Source: Author's calculation from UNCTADStat data

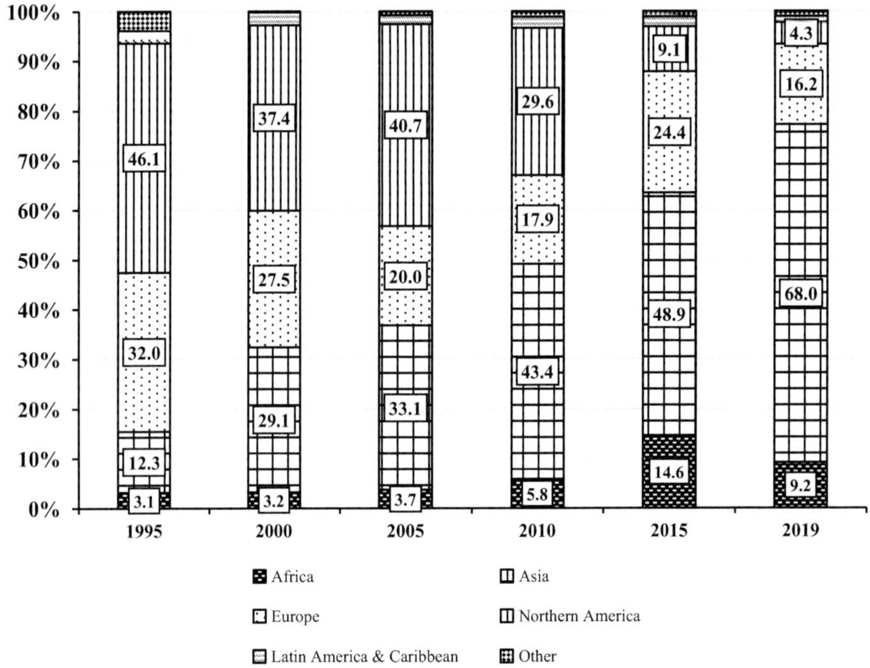

Fig. 5.2 Direction of export trade of ECCAS, 1995–2019

same with total intra-African export trade—from 3.1% in 1995 to 9.2% in 2019. In contrast, over 90% of the group's export trade has been conducted with entities outside of Africa. In 1995, it was 96.9%. It went down to 85% in 2015, but in 2019 went back up to 90.8%.

The breakdown of the destination of ECCAS export is provided in Fig. 5.2. The chart shows a dramatic shift in export destination of the ECCAS from Northern America and Europe toward Asia. In 1995, Asia accounted for only 12.3% of ECCA export trade. In 2019, 68% of total exports went to Asia. At the same time, the share of Northern America and Europe respectively dropped from 46% and 32% in 1995 to 4.3% and 16.2% in 2019.

Import trade has followed a similar pattern. In 1995, only 3.2% of ECCAS trade was within itself. This rose to 5.7% in 2010 but fell back to 2.8% in 2019. Import trade from Africa showed an improvement over the export trade—ranging from 12.7% in 1995 to 17.7% in 2019, with a peak number of 27% in 2010. However, import trade with countries outside of Africa is still substantially higher, more than 70% of total trade during the period of consideration (Table 5.3).

Figure 5.3 shows the import trade of ECCAS from 1995 to 2019, which shows that most of ECCAS' import trade in 2019 was with Asia (37.8%) and Europe (33.4%). Once again, the chart shows a shift away from Europe toward Asia, while Northern America has held steady over the period. Table 5.4 shows the top 20 export markets of ECCAS in selected years from 2001 to 2019. In 2001, the top 20 export

Table 5.3 Direction of import trade of ECCAS, 1995–2019

Year	ECCAS	Africa	ECCAS and Africa	Rest of the world	Total
1995	3.2	9.6	12.7	87.3	100
2000	2.5	18.5	21.0	79.0	100
2015	3.0	19.3	22.2	77.8	100
2010	5.7	21.3	27.0	73.0	100
2015	3.7	12.5	16.2	83.8	100
2019	2.8	14.9	17.7	82.3	100

Source: Author's calculation from UNCTADStat data

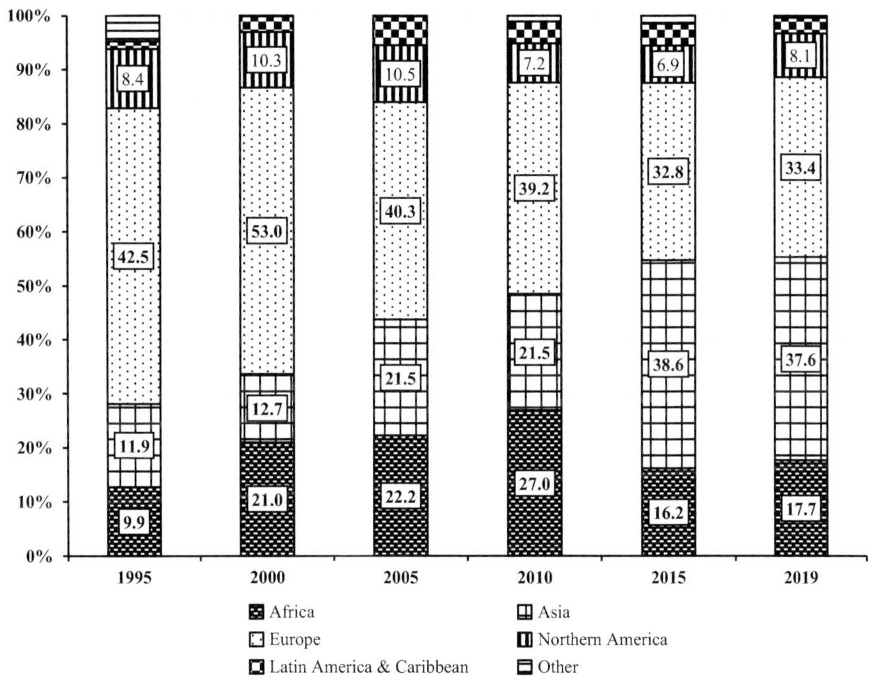

Fig. 5.3 Direction of import trade of ECCAS, 1995–2019

markets of ECCAS accounted for 93.4% of the total trade of the group. Of these, only three African countries made the list, one from ECCAS (Cameroon) and the other two from outside of the group (Ghana and South Africa (Table 5.4), In 2010 and 2015, the number of African countries in the top 20 trading partner list increased to five and six respectively, but while three of the countries in 2010 were ECCAS member states only one was ECCAS member in 2015. In 2019, four African countries made the top 20 export market list, but only one was a member of ECCAS (Table 5.4).

On the import side, the number of ECCAS members that made the top 20 markets was similar to the export numbers—two in 2001, one in 2005, three in 2010, two in 2015, and one in 2019 (Table 5.5). However, the number of African countries

Table 5.4 Top 20 export markets of ECCA in selected years from 2001 to 2019

2001		2005		2010		2015		2019	
Country	%	Country	%	Country	%	Country	%	Country	%
US	15.1	US	27.0	US	19.9	China	13.1	China	31.0
Taiwan	12.5	China	21.0	China	18.3	S. Africa	12.7	S. Africa	11.1
Belgium	11.9	Spain	7.4	Spain	5.9	Tanzania	6.5	India	7.4
Spain	11.7	Taiwan	6.9	France	5.3	US	6.0	UAE	6.4
China	10.7	France	4.5	Italy	5.0	Spain	5.6	Tanzania	5.2
Italy	7.4	Belgium	4.0	NLD	4.6	India	5.0	NLD	3.4
S. Korea	5.2	Italy	3.9	Zambia	4.3	NLD	3.4	Singapore	3.2
France	4.2	NLD	2.6	Taiwan	3.6	S. Korea	3.4	US	3.1
Germany	2.8	Portugal	2.5	S. Korea	3.3	Togo	3.1	Spain	3.0
NLD	2.8	S. Korea	2.4	*Angola	3.1	*Angola	2.8	Zambia	2.8
Norway	1.7	Canada	2.3	Canada	2.4	Australia	2.8	Italy	2.0
Finland	1.3	UK	1.9	Brazil	2.4	Italy	2.7	Finland	1.6
Brazil	1.2	Brazil	1.8	Portugal	1.7	Portugal	2.6	Belgium	1.6
Canada	1.1	TTO	1.5	Belgium	1.5	France	2.5	Mozambique	1.5
Portugal	1.1	Japan	1.2	*Gabon	1.3	Zambia	1.9	Viet Nam	1.3
UK	0.6	Germany	0.9	Australia	1.3	Namibia	1.8	Portugal	1.2
Thailand	0.6	Finland	0.6	Nigeria	1.2	UAE	1.7	France	1.2
*Cameroon	0.6	*Cameroon	0.4	Japan	1.2	UK	1.7	Congo DR	1.2
Kenya	0.5	S. Africa	0.4	India	1.2	Brazil	1.7	Malaysia	0.9
Japan	0.5	Ghana	0.3	Chad	1.2	Switzerland	1.6	Germany	0.9
Total	93.4	Total	93.4	Total	88.9	Total	82.4	Total	89.9

Source: Author's Calculation from UNCTADStat data
NLD Netherlands, *TTO* Trinidad and Tobago *ECCAS members

Table 5.5 Top 20 import markets of ECCAS in selected years from 2001 to 2019

2001		2005		2010		2015		2019	
Country	%	Country	%	Country	%	Country	%	Country	%
France	18.2	France	14.2	Nigeria	18.2	China	13.5	China	21.3
US	10.6	Nigeria	9.0	China	9.6	France	6.4	US	12.0
Belgium	7.3	US	8.1	France	9.0	US	6.3	France	6.2
Nigeria	5.7	Belgium	6.2	S. Africa	5.3	S. Africa	6.1	S. Africa	4.8
Italy	4.7	Italy	5.3	Belgium	3.9	Singapore	4.7	India	4.3
Germany	4.6	S. Africa	5.1	US	3.8	India	4.0	UAE	4.2
S. Africa	4.1	China	4.6	*Angola	3.0	Gabon	3.7	Nigeria	3.9
Eswatini	3.5	Germany	3.1	*Cameroon	2.9	Spain	2.7	Belgium	3.6
UK	2.9	NLD	2.8	UK	2.7	UAE	2.7	Gabon	2.1
NLD	2.8	Kenya	2.6	Italy	2.2	S. Korea	2.5	Türkiye	1.9
Japan	2.8	Côte d'Ivoire	2.4	Côte d'Ivoire	2.2	Germany	2.5	Germany	1.8
China	2.6	UK	2.4	NLD	2.2	NLD	2.5	Tanzania	1.7
Spain	1.9	Spain	2.2	Singapore	2.2	Nigeria	2.4	Zambia	1.7
*Cameroon	1.6	India	2.2	Germany	2.0	Japan	2.4	S. Arabia	1.7
Kenya	1.6	Japan	1.9	Spain	2.0	Italy	2.4	Italy	1.7
India	1.5	Brazil	1.6	*Equat. Guinea	1.8	Belgium	2.3	Spain	1.6
Côte d'Ivoire	1.4	Uganda	1.6	Uganda	1.6	Vanuatu	1.9	Kenya	1.6
S. Arabia	1.4	UAE	1.5	Zambia	1.6	Norway	1.8	Russia	1.5
Zambia	0.9	Zambia	1.4	Japan	1.6	UK	1.6	Thailand	1.5
Hong Kong	0.9	Tanzania	1.3	Kenya	1.4	*Angola	1.6	NLD	1.4
*Equat. Guinea	0.9	*Cameroon	1.2	India	1.3	Thailand	1.5	UK	1.2
Total	81.9	Total	80.6	Total	80.6	Total	75.5	Total	81.8

Source: Author's calculations from UNCTADStat data
NLD Netherlands, *Equat. Guinea* Equatorial Guinea, *S. Africa* South Africa; *ECCEAS members

in the top 20 import markets of ECCAS was much higher than that of Economic Community of West African States (ECOWAS). Indeed, in both 2001 and 2005, there were eight African countries that made the list, and these accounted for 18.1% of total import trade of the group in 2001 and 24.6% of total import trade in 2005 (Table 5.5). In 2010, there were nine African countries in the top 20 import market list, accounting for 38% of total import trade that year. The numbers were lower in 2015 and 2019—four and six, respectively, but they were still higher than those of ECOWAS. An interesting question here is that the ECCAS might be seen as the weakest of the RTAs recognized by the AU, but in terms of intraregional trade, it seems to be doing relatively better than other RTAs that are deemed stronger and more successful. In spite of the fact there are more African countries in ECCAS' top 20 export and import markets the trade volume is still relatively low compared to the volume of trade it conducts outside Africa. So, an additional question here is: why have both export and import trade been more oriented toward outside of Africa, and how can this trade pattern become a founding block for the AfCFTA? We answer this question by examining the composition of trade of the ECCAS.

5.5.2 *Composition of ECCAS' Trade*

The composition of trade of ECCAS members explains to a large extent the ECCAS' direction of trade. Traditionally, primary goods have accounted for more than 90% of the total trade of ECCAS, except in 2015, when it was slightly below 90%. In contrast, manufactured goods have dominated the import trade of ECCAS. In 1995, it was 69.2% of its total imports. In 2019, it was 73.8% (Table 5.6).

Breaking these broad categories into component parts, Table 5.7 provides details of the major trade goods. With the export trade, the dominant product has been fuels, accounting for more than 60%. Next to fuel were ores and metals. Manufactured goods played a very insignificant role in the export trade of ECCAS.

With respect to import trade, machinery, and transportation equipment as well as other manufactured goods dominated the import sector, followed by food (Table 5.8).

Table 5.6 Composition of ECCAS' trade, 1995–2019

	Primary goods		Manufactured goods		Unclassified	
Year	Export	Import	Export	Import	Export	Import
1995	97.2	29.6	2.7	69.2	0.2	1.1
2000	97.3	32.8	2.7	65.1	0.7	2.1
2005	97.5	29.3	2.4	69.4	0.2	1.4
2010	96.6	34.2	3.2	65.1	0.2	0.8
2015	89.2	22.1	10.4	73.8	0.5	4.1
2019	93.7	30.8	6.2	68.8	0.1	0.5

Source: Author's calculation from UNCTADStat data

Table 5.7 Composition of export trade of ECCAS, 1995–2019

Trade item	1995	2005	2010	2015	2019
Food	7.9	1.6	1.5	2.1	2.1
Agricultural raw materials	13.3	3.6	2.0	2.9	3.8
Ores and metals	6.7	2.8	5.1	13.0	17.5
Fuels	66.1	86.3	86.5	70.4	69.0
Pearls, precious stones, and nonmonetary gold	3.2	3.1	1.6	0.8	1.4
Chemical products	0.3	0.7	0.5	2.4	3.9
Machinery and transport equipment	0.6	0.7	1.9	6.4	1.2
Other manufactured goods	1.7	1.0	0.8	1.5	1.1
Unassigned	0.2	0.2	0.2	0.5	0.1

Source: Author's calculation from UNCTADStat data

Table 5.8 Composition of import trade of ECCAS, 1995–2019

Trade item	1995	2000	2005	2010	2015	2019
Food	19.9	21.2	18.6	15.3	13.9	18.7
Agricultural raw materials	1.9	1.4	1.1	1.0	0.9	1.3
Ores and metals	1.3	1.3	1.2	0.9	1.0	1.8
Fuels	6.5	8.8	8.2	16.9	6.3	8.6
Pearls, precious stones, and nonmonetary gold	0.0	0.1	0.1	0.0	0.0	0.4
Chemical products	9.8	9.3	7.6	7.1	8.3	12.1
Machinery and transport equipment	33.5	33.9	40.1	36.0	41.0	31.3
Other manufactured goods	25.9	21.9	21.7	21.9	24.4	25.3
Unassigned	1.1	2.1	1.4	0.8	4.1	0.5

Source: Author's calculation from UNCTADStat data

Within ECCAS, trade among members has not been encouraging, with the exception of food and fuel. The percentage shares look good with fuels and food and is understandable given that there are good food and oil producers in the group. However, it is not clear why the percentage shares of machinery and equipment jumped to 55.8% in 2010 and 58.2% in 2015, given that no country in the group produced machinery and transportation equipment (Table 5.9). Could this be a data issue, third-country exports or both?

In terms of imports, fuel, machinery, and transportation equipment, and food have been the most important commodities of trade within the ECCAS (Table 5.10). In 1995, other manufacturers accounted for 29.9%; in 2019, it accounted for 21.9%. Fuel accounted for only 18% of ECCAS' intraregional import trade. In 2019, it was 25.1%. Machinery and transportation equipment constituted only 8.3% of intraregional import trade; in 2019, it was 25.6%. Once again this could be third-country re-imports since no member state produced these items.

Finally, in trade with Africa, ECCAS shows strength again in the trade in primary goods. Given its fuel and other mineral wealth, the ECCAS has been particularly engaged in intra-African trade with respect to ores, metals, and fuel in its export trade with Africa. Perhaps related to the oil production, the ECCAS has also shown

Table 5.9 Composition of export trade within the ECCAS

Trade item	1995	2000	2005	2010	2015	2019
Food	32.6	26.8	23.9	7.3	9.0	21.0
Agricultural raw materials	5.7	0.6	2.2	0.2	1.6	0.9
Ores and metals	4.2	3.9	2.4	0.4	0.5	3.4
Fuels	14.5	48.9	44.1	25.9	17.4	31.0
Pearls, precious stones, and nonmonetary gold	0.0	0.0	0.1	0.0	0.0	1.9
Chemical products	6.1	3.2	4.4	2.5	3.2	6.6
Machinery and transport equipment	9.8	2.9	7.4	55.8	58.2	18.8
Other manufactured goods	26.9	13.7	15.4	7.9	10.0	16.4
Unassigned	0.1	0.1	0.0	0.0	0.0	0.0

Source: Author's Calculation from UNCTADStat data

Table 5.10 Composition of import trade within the ECCAS, 1995–2019

Trade item	1995	2000	2005	2010	2015	2019
Food	29.0	21.0	25.4	8.0	12.9	21.9
Agricultural raw materials	4.2	0.6	1.8	0.2	1.1	1.0
Ores and metals	4.7	3.9	2.6	0.4	0.6	3.4
Fuels	18.0	52.5	45.6	21.1	28.0	25.1
Pearls, precious stones, and nonmonetary gold	0.0	0.0	0.1	0.0	0.0	2.6
Chemical products	5.8	3.5	3.9	1.9	3.3	5.6
Machinery and transport equipment	8.3	3.0	6.7	62.0	44.7	25.6
Other manufactured goods	29.9	15.4	13.9	6.4	8.8	14.9
Unassigned	0.1	0.1	0.0	0.0	0.6	0.0

Source: Author's Calculations from UNCTADStat data

an upward trend in the trade of chemical products. There was an uptick in machinery and transportation equipment but declined in 2019 (Table 5.11). With respect to import trade with Africa, manufactured goods, fuel, and food still dominate (Table 5.12).

5.6 Explanation for the Trade Performance of ECCAS

The reasons for the low trade performance on ECCAS have been well discussed in the literature (Pourtier, 1999; Lemarchand, 2016; Palmateer & Clark, 2018; Nguenkwe & Tchitchoua, 2019). Palmateer and Clark (2018) identified several reasons for this. First, trade patterns before the creation of ECCAS were strongly dominated by former colonial powers. Intraregional trade was very minimal and those that occurred were mostly in the informal sector. This entrenched pattern of trade continued in the post-ECCAS period and was, in fact, exacerbated by the arrival of China in the region, which changed the old established pattern but only in its direction. Thus, China gradually replaced Europe and the USA as the leading trade

Table 5.11 Composition of ECCAS' export trade with Africa

Trade item	2005	2010	2015	2019	2020	2021
Food	9.3	4.4	3.0	5.7	6.3	5.9
Agricultural raw materials	5.2	2.4	1.4	1.5	1.8	2.3
Ores and metals	9.2	10.3	33.3	48.0	41.4	30.2
Fuels	49.2	49.0	19.9	13.6	15.0	14.5
Pearls, precious stones and nonmonetary gold	0.3	0.1	0.0	4.5	4.1	5.7
Chemical products	2.2	4.5	11.4	21.6	21.8	33.3
Machinery and transport equipment	9.6	23.1	27.6	5.3	8.9	9.3
Other manufactured goods	14.7	6.2	3.5	3.8	4.2	3.6
Unassigned	0.3	0.0	0.0	0.0	0.0	0.0

Source: Authors calculations from UNCTADStat data

Table 5.12 ECCAS import trade with Africa

Trade item	1995	2000	2005	2010	2015	2019
Food	30.8	26.1	22.7	12.8	18.3	18.6
Agricultural raw materials	1.5	0.7	0.9	0.5	0.6	0.7
Ores and metals	5.5	3.6	2.3	1.2	2.2	3.0
Fuels	24.6	34.1	32.5	42.8	19.3	20.6
Pearls, precious stones, and nonmonetary gold	0.1	0.1	0.3	0.2	0.1	9.7
Chemical products	10.4	7.9	8.2	6.1	10.4	14.8
Machinery and transport equipment	6.4	9.7	12.3	23.7	27.8	20.1
Other manufactured goods	20.4	17.7	20.9	12.7	20.0	20.3
Unassigned	0.0	0.0	0.0	0.0	0.0	0.0

Source: Author's calculation from UNCTADStat data

patterner of ECCAS member states. Third, the recurrent political strife that occurred in ECCAS countries throughout the 1990s made matters worse. These included the civil wars in Angola, Burundi, Congo DR, Congo Republic, and Rwanda, and political instability in Central African Republic and Chad. These conflicts divided the member states making it difficult to implement any treaties that had been signed. In addition, there were also some significant geographic barriers due to the poor state of transportation and communication infrastructure in the region. Fifth, as a result of all the political and social unrests that occurred in the ECCAS countries, when the membership decided to revive the group in 1998, regional security became a top priority even though the original trade intent was retained. Given the interest and support of the international community in security matters this new focus became an opportunity for political leaders of ECCAS to exploit the situation for their individual and personal goals. Palmateer and Clark (2018) provide several examples in which the leaders of Gabon, Central African Republic, Chad, Congo DR, and Congo Republic used these external security support sources to strengthen their internal regimes. Under such conditions, it is not surprising that intra-group trade did not see much progress in ECCAS. On top of all these, the member states of ECCAS are known among the African countries with the most multiple RTAs memberships. In particular, four of the countries—Burundi, DRC, Rwanda, and Uganda belong to no less than five other RTAs, which include the East African Community (EAC), the Common Market of Eastern and Southern Africa (COMESA), the International Conference on the Great Lakes Region (ICGLR) and the Economic Community of the Great Lakes States (CEPGL) (Lemarchand, 2016).

Another explanation refers to the lack of a regional hegemon in Central Africa due to the catastrophic failure of DRC as a natural hegemon (Lemarchand, 2016), which in turn is due to "a multiplicity of regional groupings, internal political instability, economic challenges, and the neo-colonial hand of France" (Nkumbe & Njie, 2021, p. 32). For Nguenkwe and Tchitchoua (2019), the low intraregional trade performance of the ECCAS could be attributed to poor economic infrastructure, especially road network, ICT, custom, and regulatory environmental indicators.

All these are valid factors, but the fact is ECCAS members still engage in trade with outside partners more than they do among themselves. The question is do these factors affect ECCAS internal trade more than its external trade? Is ECCA's external trade more and stronger than its internal trade because of the obstacles listed above or because of necessity and need? We would argue that it is much more of the latter reason because without any substantial industrial capacity to produce the manufactured goods they so much need, ECCAS members have no choice but to trade more with external partners for the manufactured goods they so much need.

5.7 Conclusion

The ECCAS was established as regional trade agreement with a view to enhancing trade among its members. However, as a result of a cycle of violence, civil wars, and political instability, the ECCAS was moribund for 15 years. When both international and domestic entities became concerned about this situation, the pressure that was brought to bear upon the group to resuscitate itself caused it to move toward security and stability concerns even though it did not drop its original trade mission. This reorientation toward security and stability became exploited by governments that were themselves previously insecure to perpetuate their own dictatorial rules and power to the detriment of economic well-being and trade improvement of their countries. The result is that the ECCAS remains the weakest of the RTAs that have been recognized by the AU. Granted, it is hard to trade when there is so much social, political, and economic unrest, but in the absence of these disturbances, the ECCAS was not going to be the powerhouse as far as its intraregional trade was concerned, because of lack of competitiveness of the economies. Thus, with most of its exports being primary products and imports being manufactured products, ECCAS members would still trade with outsiders for the goods they need with what they were able to produce. That is, the lack of strong manufacturing content in the production capacities of member states would still push the ECCAS to beckon outside of Africa for manufactured products.

References

Garlinska-Bielawska, J., & Janicka, M. (2018). Fragile States in African economic communities as exemplified by the economic and monetary community of Central Africa (CEMAC) – Investment issues. *Politeja, 5*(56), 231–246.

Inançli, S., & Addi, H. M. (2019). Trade creation and trade diversion effects in the economic community of Central African States. *African Development Review, 31*(3), 307–317.

International Crisis Group [ICG]. (2011). *Implementing peace and security architecture: Central Africa*. Africa Report No. 181, November.

Lemarchand, R. (2016). Region-building in Central Africa. In D. H. Levine & D. Nagar (Eds.), *Region-building in Africa: Political and economic challenges* (pp. 231–244). Pelgrave Macmillan.

Meyer, A. (2008). *Regional integration and security in Central Africa: Assessment and perspectives 10 years after the revival* (Egmont Papers (25)). Academia Press.

Meyer, A. (2011). *Peace and security cooperation in Central Africa: Developments, challenges and prospects* (Discussion paper). Nordiska Afrikainstitutet.

Nguenkwe, R. B., & Tchitchoua, J. (2019). Intraregional trade facilitation: A comparative analysis between ECCAS and ECOWAS. *The Turkish Economic Review, 6*(4), 294–312.

Nkumbe, E. R., & Njie, M. J. (2021). Explaining the absence of a regional Hegemon in the Central African sub-region. *Central European Journal of International and Security Studies, 15*(4), 32–47.

Nono, G. M. (2013). Regional integration and free movement in Central Africa. *Regions & Cohesion, 3*(3), 123–140.

Palmateer, G., & Clark, J. F. (2018). The uses (and abuses) of the economic community of Central African States: The hidden functions of regional economic community membership for African regimes. In J. Warner & T. M. Shaw (Eds.), *African foreign policies in international institutions, contemporary African political economy* (pp. 127–149). Palgrave Macmillan.

Pourtier, R. (1999). The renovation of UDEAC: Sense & nonsense in Central African integration. In D. C. Bach (Ed.), *Regionalisation in Africa: Integration & disintegration* (pp. 129–138). Indiana University Press.

Ropivia, M.-L. (1999). Failing institutions & shattered space: What regional integration in Central Africa? In D. C. Bach (Ed.), *Regionalisation in Africa: Integration & disintegration* (pp. 125–127). Indiana University Press.

UNCTAD. (2013). *Economic development in Africa report intra-African trade: Unlocking private sector dynamism*. United Nations Conference on Trade and Development.

Union of International Associations. (2020). *Economic Community of Central African States (ECCAS) yearbook of international associations*. https://uia.org/s/or/en/1100007392

United Nations Economic Commission for Africa (UNECA). (1983). *Treaty for the establishment of the Economic Community of Central African States*. UNECA.

Chapter 6
The Southern African Development Community

6.1 Introduction

The Southern African Development Community (SADC) is often held as the most exemplary group of what a trade agreement could be. It has been held out as a successful regional integration and many observers have commented on its activities. In this chapter, we examine the SADC, with particular reference to its trade and the extent to which its past and present trade patterns can help move AfCFTA to its goal. The chapter is in six sections. The first section presents some basic facts about the SADC region. The second section reviews the major events leading to the formation of the SADC. The third section discusses the goals and expectations of the SADC. The fourth section presents data to examine the trade performance of the SADC. The fifth section discusses the reasons for the SADC trade performance, and the last section summarizes with conclusions.

6.2 Some Basic Information About the SADC

SADC is made up of 16 countries (Fig. 6.1). With a total land area of 9,954,407 km^2 the SADC takes 33% of the land area of the continent of Africa. In 2019, the SADC was home to an estimated 361,174,564 people, about 22.7% of the total population of Africa (Table 6.1). Its gross domestic product (GDP) of $705.4 billion in 2019 was 28% of Africa's total gross domestic product in 2019. Like most countries in Africa, the countries all share a common history as being former colonies of Europe. However, there are extreme asymmetries. There are countries that are geographically very large—such as Democratic Republic of Congo (DRC), South Africa, and Angola compared to a bunch of small island countries such as the Comoros, Seychelles, and Mauritius. In terms of population, there are five countries—DRC,

B. Ofori-Amoah, *The African Continental Free Trade Area*,
https://doi.org/10.1007/978-3-031-59181-5_6

Fig. 6.1 Member States of the Southern African Development Community. (Data source: ICPAC GEOPORTA. The analysis was performed in ArcGIS Pro 3.1.0)

South Africa, Angola, Mozambique, and Tanzania, with populations of more than 30 million each, while there are four countries that have less than 2 million people—Comoros, Eswatini, Mauritius, and Seychelles. Like ECOWAS, the economies of the SADC countries are dwarfed by one country, which is South Africa, in terms of GDP. Thus, the 2019 estimated \$387.9 billion of South Africa's gross domestic product accounted for 55% of the total gross domestic product of the SADC region. Angola, the second largest economy in the region has a gross domestic product that is only 17% that of South Africa.

Table 6.1 Some basic facts about the SADC

Country	Area (Km^2)	Population	GDP (US$)	GDP per capita, PPP (US $)
Angola	1,246,700	32,353,588	69,309,104,807	6995
Botswana	600,370	2,499,702	16,695,925,027	17,097
Comoros	2170	790,986	1,195,019,559	3188
Congo DR	2,345,410	89,906,891	51,775,830,726	1144
Eswatini	17,360	1,169,613	4,466,066,557	9018
Lesotho	30,350	2,225,702	2,451,257,579	2768
Madagascar	587,041	27,533,134	14,191,911,512	1687
Malawi	118,480	18,867,337	11,025,370,769	1602
Mauritius	1860	1,296,279	14,045,808,843	23,835
Mozambique	801,590	30,285,595	15,390,031,040	1336
Namibia	823,144	2,446,645	12,543,203,411	10,223
Seychelles	71,740	104,373	1,684,228,529	30,605
South Africa	1,219,912	58,087,055	387,934,574,098	14,289
Tanzania	945,090	59,872,579	61,136,873,692	2773
Zambia	752,610	18,380,477	23,308,667,781	3617
Zimbabwe	390,580	15,354,608	19,284,289,739	2408
Total	9,954,407	361,174,564	706,438,163,669	

Source: United Nations Population Division

Other asymmetries occur in the distribution of natural resources, especially mineral deposits. The SADC is the most mineralized zone of Africa, containing its largest diamond fields, gold fields, cobalt, zinc, copper, and Africa's only major coalfield. The region leads the world in the production of these minerals in addition to other strategic minerals such as vanadium, palladium, and tantalite. However, these minerals are unevenly distributed. The overwhelming bulk of them are located in a few countries in the region. These are South Africa, DRC, Zambia, and Botswana.

6.3 The Formation of the SADC

The SADC originated from the Southern African Development Coordination Conference (SADCC), which was established on April 1, 1980, by the Frontline States (FLS), a group of countries that bound together to fight apartheid in South Africa (Anglin, 1983; SADC, 1993). The group included Angola, Botswana, Lesotho, Mozambique, Tanzania, Zambia, and Zimbabwe. The goal of the SADCC was to reduce dependence of the member countries on apartheid South Africa and to create genuine and equitable economic integration through forging links and mobilization of resources of member states. Thus, original members of SADCC were Angola, Botswana, Lesotho, Malawi, Mozambique, Swaziland (Eswatini), Tanzania, Zambia, and Zimbabwe, with Namibia joining in 1990 (SADC, 1993; Mufune, 1993; Mlambo, 2020).

Discussion for the formation of the SADCC began in 1977. Through the effort of Sir Seretse Khama, President of Botswana, a meeting of the FLS Foreign Ministers in Gaborone, Botswana, in May 1979, called upon the Ministers of Economic Development to consider the matter. In July 1979, the Ministers of Economic Development met in Arusha, Tanzania, and established the SADCC (Nsekela, 1981). In April 1980, the meeting of the Heads of State of the Frontline States in Lusaka, Zambia, adopted the Lusaka Declaration: "Southern Africa: Towards Economic Liberation," launching the SADCC. The SADCC was established on five principles, namely (1) sovereign equality of member states; (2) solidarity, peace, and security; (3) human rights, democracy, and rule of law; (4) equity, balance, and mutual benefit; and (5) peaceful settlement of disputes (Odhiambo et al., 2016). The primary goal of the SADCC was to reduce dependence on apartheid South Africa, forge links to develop a full integration, and mobilize resources to implement state and regional policies (Abegunrin, 1984–85).

Based on the experience of other regional integrations in Africa, the SADCC wanted to minimize administrative costs, so it opted for a decentralized system of administration. Each member state was assigned a sector of the economy and that became the member state's responsibility. Thus, the energy sector was assigned to Angola, forestry, wildlife, and fisheries to Malawi, industrial development to Tanzania, and minerals and mining to Zambia (Muntschick, 2018; Odhiambo et al., 2016). Decision-making was based on consensus. Critics charged that the decentralized approach subjected some of the organization's projects to national interests instead of the region as a whole. However, as Muntschick (2018) reports, the SADCC was quite successful in mobilizing funds for its projects, but most of it came from external sources, and this made the group more externally dependent.

The fall of the Berlin Wall in 1989, Namibia's independence in 1990, and the beginning of negotiations to end apartheid in South Africa in 1990 brought the SADCC to a watershed moment. In two short years, the reasons for its existence evaporated and it was time to self-reflect as to what it was going to be. At its 1991 summit, the SADCC Heads of State directed the Council of Ministers to work on options and strategies for economic cooperation in a post-apartheid era (Ramutsindela, 2007). At its 1992 summit in Windhoek, Namibia, the member states of the SADCC signed the Southern African Development Community (SADC) Treaty that transformed SADCC to SADC, on August 17. After that, the membership of the group grew to include South Africa in 1994, Mauritius in 1995, the DRC and Seychelles in 1997, and Madagascar in 2005. Seychelles withdrew its membership in 2004 but rejoined in 2008.

6.4 Aims and Expectations of the SADC

The SADC aimed at evolving through the traditional phases of economic integration—it established a free trade area in 2008 that would become a customs union in 2010, a common market in 2015, an economic union in 2016, and a monetary union in 2018 (Fink & Rempe, 2017).

The objectives of the SADC were as follows: (1) to promote development, poverty reduction, and economic growth through regional integration; (2) to consolidate, defend and maintain democracy, peace, security, and stability; (3) to promote common political values and institutions that are democratic, legitimate and effective; (4) to strengthen links among the people of the region; and (5) to mobilize regional and international private and public resources for the development of the region (SADC, 1993).

Unlike its predecessor, the SADC opted for a centralized system of administration. It set up 21-sector coordinating unit under four directorates—food, agriculture, and natural resources; infrastructure and services; social and human development and special programs; and trade, industry, finance, and investment. Among its core institutions include the Summit of Heads of State and Government; the Summit of the Organ on Politics, Defense, and Security; SADC Tribunal; SADC Council of Ministers, Sector and Cluster Ministerial Committees; Standing Committee of Senior Officials; SADC Secretariat, the SADC National Committees, and the SADC Parliamentary Forum (SADC, 1993).

At the time of its formation, the SADC was expected to increase intraregional trade given a number of small countries that were rich in natural resources and South Africa's industrial economy, which served as the natural hub for the group. The establishment of the SADC-Free Trade Area (SADC-FTA) led to some improvements in intraregional trade—rising from 6.8% in 1996 to 15.7 in 2012. South Africa was the most important market of the group and was the top market for three of the SADC members—Malawi, Mozambique, and Zimbabwe in 2008, but intraregional trade was mostly among neighboring countries. However, after establishing its free trade area in 2008, the SADC failed to achieve its goal of becoming a customs union in 2010 and does not seem to be able to ever achieve that goal (Muntschick, 2018). So, how has the SADC performed with respect to trade, and how does that performance inform the prospects of the SADC as a foundation block for the AfCFTA?

6.5 Trade of SADC

6.5.1 Direction of SADC Trade

Table 6.2 summarizes the direction of trade of the SADC group. The formation of the SADC free trade area has increased intraregional trade. For example, in 1995 intraregional export trade was 13.7% of total trade (Table 6.2). In 2019, it increased to about 21%. However, SADC export trade with the rest of Africa has remained very low over the same period—2.6% in 1995 and only 3.9% in 2019. Thus, while the SADC's trade within Africa has risen from 12.4% in 1995 to 23.7% in 2019, it is still low compared to the trade it conducts outside of Africa. The result is that more than 70% of SADC's export trade goes outside of Africa.

Table 6.2 Percent share of export trade of SADC, 1995–2019

Year	SADC	Africa	SADC and Africa	Rest of World	Total Trade
1995	13.7	2.6	16.3	83.7	100
2000	13.0	2.2	15.2	84.8	100
2005	10.9	2.9	13.8	86.2	100
2010	17.8	2.8	20.6	79.4	100
2015	23.7	2.9	26.6	73.4	100
2019	20.7	3.1	23.9	76.1	100

Source: Author's calculation based on UNCTADStat data

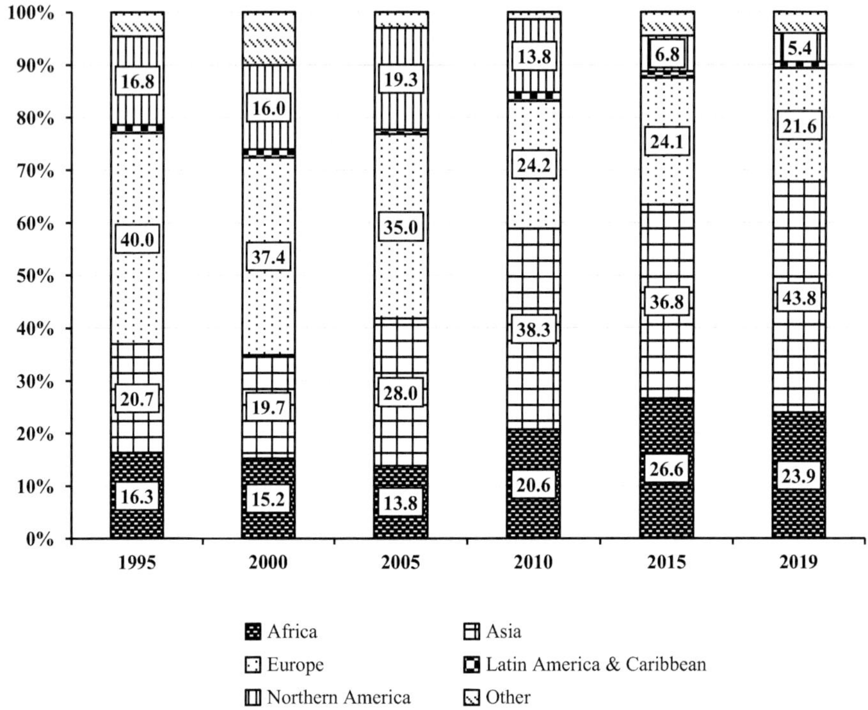

Fig. 6.2 Direction export trade of SADC, 1995–2019. Source: UNCTADStat

The breakdown of SADC's export trade by destination is given in Fig. 6.2, which shows dramatic changes in the direction of export trade of the SADC, over the 24-year period from 1995 to 2019. Thus, in 1995, Europe accounted for 40% of SADC's export trade, followed by Asia (20.7%), Northern America (16.8%) and Africa (16.3%). In 2019, after 24 years, the destination of SADC's export trade flipped, with Asia constituting 43.8%, Africa 23.9%, Europe 21.6%, and Northern America only 5.4%. While Africa's proportion of the trade has increased only slightly from 16% to 24%, trading partners outside of Africa still account for 76% of the export trade of SADC.

Table 6.3 shows the top 20 export markets of the SADC from 2001 to 2019. It shows that the number of member states making the top 20 list increased from four in 2001 to seven in both 2015 and 2019, but they accounted for much less than the export markets outside of Africa. Thus, in 2001, SADC accounted for 10.5% out of the 82% due to the top 20 markets. The equivalent percentages for the rest of the period were 14.1% out of 80.1% in 2010, 20.1% out of 74.7% in 2015, and 18.4% out of 76.5% in 2019. Indeed, no African country outside of the SADC made the top 20 export markets in the period under consideration.

Import trade has followed a similar pattern. In 1995 intraregional import trade was 10.6% of total trade (Table 6.4). In 2019, it increased to about 20%. However, SADC trade with the rest of Africa has remained very low over the same period—1.8% in 1995 and only 3.9% in 2019. Thus, while the SADC's trade within Africa rose from 12.4% in 1995 to 23.7% in 2019, it is still low compared to the trade it conducts externally to Africa. The result is that more than 75% of SADC's import trade occurs outside of Africa.

Figure 6.3 shows the major sources of SADC's import trade. In 1995, 39.6% of SADC's imports were from Europe, followed by 30.7% from Asia, and 12.4% from

Table 6.3 Top 20 export markets of SADC in selected years from 2001 to 2019

2001		2005		2010		2015		2019	
Country	%	Country	%	Country	%	Country	%	Country	%
US	16.8	UK	14.5	China	19.8	China	17.6	China	21.4
UK	15.1	US	9.4	US	10.8	*S. Africa	7.4	S. Africa	6.5
Germany	5.8	Japan	7.7	India	5.0	India	5.3	India	5.9
Japan	5.5	NLD	5.4	*S. Africa	4.7	US	5.3	US	4.8
*S. Africa	5.0	Germany	5.4	UK	4.7	SUI	3.7	Germany	4.4
Belgium	4.9	*S. Africa	4.7	Japan	3.9	Germany	3.4	UAE	3.6
France	4.8	Belgium	4.1	SUI	3.7	UK	3.1	UK	3.1
NLD	3.1	Switzerland	3.3	Germany	3.5	*Botswana	3.0	Belgium	3.0
China	2.8	China	3.0	Canada	2.9	*Namibia	3.0	*Botswana	2.7
*MOZ	2.4	France	2.8	NLD	2.7	Japan	2.8	Japan	2.7
Italy	2.2	Australia	2.7	*Botswana	2.5	NLD	2.6	*MOZ	2.6
Spain	2.1	Spain	2.5	France	2.5	Belgium	2.5	SUI	2.5
Taiwan	2.0	Italy	2.2	*Namibia	2.3	Spain	2.3	NLD	2.1
*Zimbabwe	1.7	*Zimbabwe	2.1	Taiwan	2.2	UAE	2.2	*Namibia	2.1
S. Korea	1.6	India	1.9	*Zambia	1.9	France	2.0	*Zambia	1.9
*Zambia	1.4	*MOZ	1.7	Belgium	1.6	*Zambia	1.9	Spain	1.6
SUI	1.3	*Zambia	1.5	Spain	1.5	Italy	1.7	Singapore	1.5
Israel	1.2	Israel	1.4	*Zimbabwe	1.5	*MOZ	1.7	*Congo, DR	1.3
India	1.1	S. Korea	1.3	Italy	1.4	*Tanzania	1.6	France	1.3
Australia	1.0	UAE	1.3	*MOZ	1.2	*Zimbabwe	1.5	*Tanzania	1.3
Top 20 Total	82	Total	79.1	Total	80.1	Total	74.7	Total	76.5

Source: Author's calculation based on ITC trade map data

MOZ Mozambique, *SUI* Switzerland, *NLD* The Netherlands, *S. Africa* South Africa; *SADC members

Table 6.4 Percent share of import trade of the SADC, 1995–2019

Year	SADC	Africa	SADC & Africa	Rest of the world	Total trade
1995	10.6	1.8	12.4	87.6	100
2000	21.2	1.3	22.6	77.4	100
2005	18.1	1.8	19.9	80.1	100
2010	20.5	3.5	24.0	76.0	100
2015	20.7	3.7	24.4	75.6	100
2019	19.9	3.9	23.7	76.3	100

Source: Author's calculation with UNCTADStat data

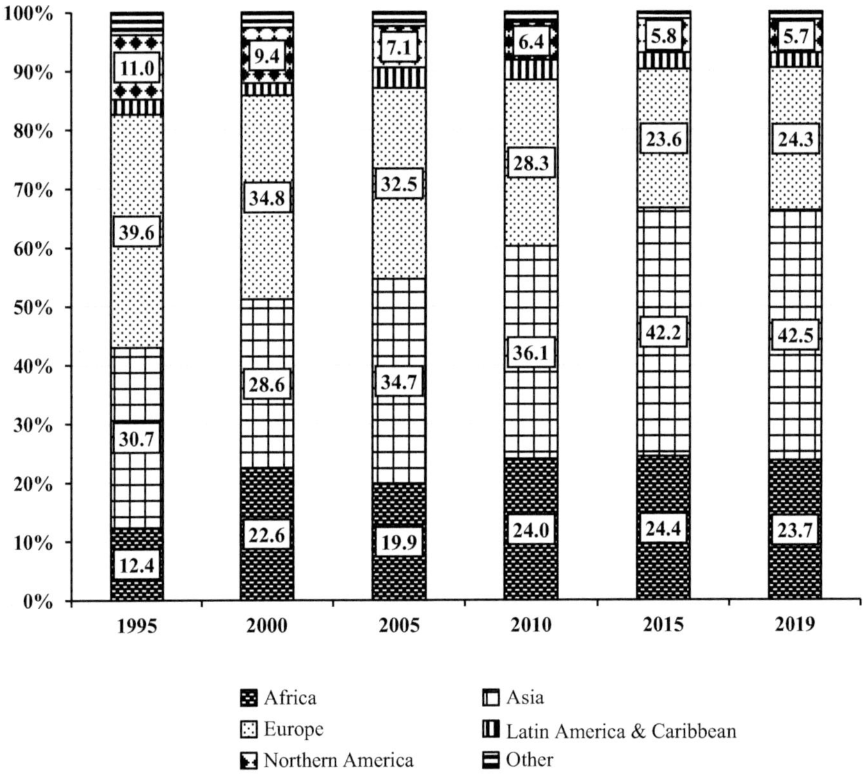

Fig. 6.3 Direction of import trade of SADC, 1995–2019

Africa. In 2005, Asia overtook Europe as the leading source of imports for the SADC. By 2019, 42.5% of imports were coming from Asia, compared to Europe's 24.3%. Imports from Africa increased over the period but appear to have stagnated at 24% since 2010.

Table 6.5 shows the top 20 import markets of the SADC group in selected years from 2001 through 2019. The number of SADC members that made the top 20 import market is very small. It was one each in 2001, 2005, and 2015 and two each in 2010 and 2019. The one country was South Africa, while the two in 2010 and

Table 6.5 Top 20 import markets of SADC in selected years from 2001 to 2019

2001		2005		2010		2015		2019	
Country	%	Country	%	Country	%	Country	%	Country	%
*S Africa	15.8	*S. Africa	13.2	*S. Africa	13.7	China	14.7	China	16.2
Germany	9.6	Germany	9.7	China	11.2	*S. Africa	13.5	*S. Africa	11.3
US	8.8	China	7.5	Germany	6.8	Germany	6.3	Germany	5.9
UK	6.6	US	6.3	US	6.1	US	5.1	US	5.8
Japan	4.9	Japan	5.2	India	4.0	S. Arabia	5.1	India	5.5
S. Arabia	4.3	UK	4.6	Japan	3.8	India	5.1	UAE	4.1
France	3.8	France	4.1	UK	3.6	Japan	2.8	France	3.3
China	3.5	S. Arabia	3.9	NLD	3.1	Singapore	2.6	Japan	2.7
Italy	3.0	Iran	2.6	France	3.1	UK	2.5	S. Arabia	2.6
S. Korea	2.8	India	2.4	S. Arabia	2.3	UAE	2.3	UK	2.6
Iran	2.4	Italy	2.3	Iran	2.1	France	2.1	Nigeria	2.1
Australia	2.2	Brazil	2.1	UA E	2.0	Italy	1.8	Thailand	2.0
Brazil	2.0	S. Korea	1.9	Portugal	1.9	Nigeria	1.7	Italy	1.9
NLD	1.7	Belgium	1.9	Belgium	1.8	Thailand	1.6	Singapore	1.6
Belgium	1.6	Portugal	1.8	Italy	1.8	NLD	1.4	Belgium	1.5
India	1.5	NLD	1.7	Brazil	1.7	S. Korea	1.4	Portugal	1.4
Taiwan	1.5	Australia	1.6	Nigeria	1.6	Portugal	1.4	Spain	1.4
Portugal	1.4	Spain	1.4	S. Korea	1.5	Belgium	1.4	*Zambia	1.3
SUI	1.4	UAE	1.3	Thailand	1.5	Spain	1.3	S. Korea	1.2
Spain	1.1	Thailand	1.3	*Angola	1.3	Brazil	1.2	Brazil	1.1
Total	79.9	Total	76.7	Total	74.8	Total	75.2	Total	75.4

Source: Author's calculation based on ITC trade map data
SUI Switzerland, *S. Arabia* Saudi Arabia, *NLD* Netherlands;
*SADC members

2019 were South Africa and Angola, and South Africa and Zambia, respectively. The only other African country that made the list was Nigeria in 2010, 2015, and 2019 (Table 6.5). So, we ask the same question as to why the SADC trade is mostly outside oriented? In particular, why does the SADC have more of its members in its top 20 export markets than its top 20 import markets? As before, we investigate by looking at the composition of trade of the SADC.

6.5.2 Composition of Trade of the SADC

The SADC shares the common characteristics of the other regional groupings we have considered so far in this book. In 1995, SADC export trade consisted of 63% primary goods and 35.5% of manufactured goods (Table 6.6). In 2019, the percentage share of primary goods had increased to 72.7%, while that for manufactured goods had dropped to 26.9%. Looking at import trade, the percentage share of primary goods rose from 24.9% to 33%, while the share of manufactured goods fell from 68.7% in 1995 to 62.3% in 2019.

Table 6.6 Composition of trade in the SADC, 1995–2019 (Percentage shares)

	Primary Goods		Manufactured Goods		Unclassified Goods	
Year	Export	Import	Export	Import	Export	Import
1995	63.3	24.9	34.5	68.7	2.1	6.3
2000	57.4	27.6	33.9	66.4	8.6	6
2005	68.1	26.1	31.5	67.6	0.4	6.3
2010	73.3	31.9	26.2	64.0	0.3	4.6
2015	70.9	30.8	28.8	64.1	0.3	4.1
2019	72.7	33.1	26.9	62.3	0.4	4.6

Source: Author's calculation from UNCTADStat data

Table 6.7 Composition of SADC's export trade (Percentage shares)

Commodity	1995	2000	2005	2010	2015	2019
Food	15.0	12.3	9.0	8.9	11.0	10.6
Agricultural raw materials	3.6	3.6	2.3	1.7	1.8	1.5
Ores and metals	16.9	8.8	16.1	21.8	22.1	25.6
Fuels	15.8	21.5	30.8	35.8	25.8	25.1
Pearls, precious stones, and NMG	12.1	11.3	10.0	5.2	10.2	9.7
Chemical products	5.3	5.2	5.2	4.6	5.8	6.1
Machinery and transport equipment	11.7	10.8	11.5	10.1	12.6	11.6
Other manufactured goods	17.5	17.9	14.8	11.6	10.5	9.2
Unassigned	2.1	8.6	0.4	0.4	0.3	0.4
Total	100	100	100	100	100	100

Source: Author's calculation based on UNCTADStat data

At the commodity level, the bulk of SADC's exports in general consisted of food (15.8%), ores and metals, precious metals (16.8%), food (15%), and other manufactured goods (11.7%) in 1995. In 2019, the dominant exports were still ore and metals (25.6%), fuel (25%), machinery and transportation equipment (11.6%),and food (10.6%) (Table 6.7). The composition of import trade of the SADC has remained mostly unchanged with very few variations. In 1995, the top import trade goods were machinery and transportation equipment (36.3%), other manufactures (21.6%), fuel (11.4%), chemical products (10.8%), and food (8.6%). In 2019, it was the same, although some of the percentage shares had changed. For example, machinery and equipment accounted for 27.5%, other manufactures 21.8%, chemical products 14.4%, fuels 12.4%, and food 12.1% (Table 6.8).

So far, we have examined composition of SADC's global trade, but what about its local and regional trade? As already indicated, SADC's intraregional trade as well as trade with Africa is relatively small compared to its trade with the rest of the world (Table 6.9).

Export trade within SADC shows declining percentage shares in its total output. The leading export commodities in intraregional trade in 1995 all saw declines over the period of 1995 to 2019. For example, food accounted for 20.3% in 1995. In 2019, it accounted for just 16.3%. Similarly, other manufactured goods which

Table 6.8 Composition of SADC's import trade (Percentage shares)

Commodity	1995	2000	2005	2010	2015	2019
Food	8.6	9.5	9.1	10.9	10.3	10.6
Agricultural raw materials	1.6	1.5	1.1	1.0	1.0	1.1
Ores and metals	2.0	2.5	2.3	2.4	3.2	4.0
Fuels	11.4	12.8	12.5	16.8	14.5	15.4
Pearls, precious stones, and NMG	1.4	1.3	1.2	0.9	1.9	2.1
Chemical products	10.8	10.9	10.1	10.7	11.3	12.3
Machinery and transport equipment	36.3	34.0	36.4	32.3	31.9	28.8
Other manufactured goods	21.6	21.5	21.1	20.9	21.0	21.2
Unassigned	6.3	6.0	6.3	4.1	5.1	4.6
Total	100	100	100	100	100	100

Source: Author's calculation based on UNCTADStat data
NMG nonmonetary gold

Table 6.9 Composition of export trade within SADC (Percentage shares)

Commodity	1995	2000	2005	2010	2015	2019
Food	20.3	21.4	17.3	18.0	16.5	16.3
Agricultural raw materials	1.7	4.2	2.9	1.2	1.3	1.2
Ores and metals	2.9	6.1	7.4	6.1	12.0	15.8
Fuels	11.4	12.1	14.8	16.4	12.2	11.6
Pearls, precious stones, and NGM	0.7	1.2	6.1	2.6	9.4	6.8
Chemical products	12.5	12.5	11.1	11.3	13.0	14.1
Machinery and transport equipment	22.8	18.7	16.8	20.5	17.5	16.1
Other manufactured goods	26.3	23.2	23.4	23.6	18.0	18.2
Unassigned	1.3	0.4	0.2	0.2	0.2	0.1
	100	100	100	100	100	100

Author's calculation based on UNCTADStat data

accounted for 26.3% in 1995, constituted 18.2% in 2019. Machinery and transportation equipment also went from 22.8% in 1995 to 16.1% in 2019. The only exceptions were ores and metals, and chemicals. Ores and metals accounted for 2.9% in 1995, but in 2019, their share was 15.8%. Similarly, chemical products rose slightly from 12.5 to 14.1%. This trend of declining intraregional trade shares is disturbing because it shows intraregional trade being substituted by increasing extraregional trade.

Import trade inside the group is shown in Table 6.10. From the Table 6.10, we can see the most dramatic increase in imported intraregional commodity trade occurred in fuels and ores and metals. For example, fuels went from just 15.8% of total trade in 1995 to 25.1% in 2019. Similarly, ores and metals went from 16.9% of total trade in 1995 to 25.6% in 2019 (Table 6.10). In contrast, imports of chemical products increased only slightly, while food, machinery and transportation equipment, and agricultural raw material all saw declining shares in intraregional trade.

Table 6.10 Composition of import trade within SADC (Percentage shares)

Commodity	1995	2000	2005	2010	2015	2019
Food	15.0	12.3	9.0	8.9	11.0	10.6
Agricultural raw materials	3.6	3.6	2.3	1.7	1.8	1.5
Ores and metals	16.9	8.8	16.1	21.8	22.1	25.6
Fuels	15.8	21.5	30.8	35.8	25.8	25.1
Pearls, precious stones, and NMG	12.1	11.3	10.0	5.2	10.2	9.7
Chemical products	5.3	5.2	5.2	4.6	5.8	6.1
Machinery and transport equipment	11.7	10.8	11.5	10.1	12.6	11.6
Other manufactured goods	17.5	17.9	14.8	11.6	10.5	9.2
Unassigned	2.1	8.6	0.4	0.4	0.3	0.4
	100	100	100	100	100	100

Source: Author's calculation from UNCTADStat data

Table 6.11 SADC's export trade with Africa (Percentage shares)

Commodity	1995	2000	2005	2010	2015	2019
Food	20.5	21.6	16.6	17.9	16.7	17.5
Agricultural raw materials	1.8	3.9	2.5	1.2	1.3	1.3
Ores and metals	3.0	5.8	7.5	6.1	11.0	14.3
Fuels	11.3	11.5	14.1	15.1	12.2	11.2
Pearls, precious stones, and NMG	0.6	1.1	4.8	2.3	8.3	6.4
Chemical products	14.1	13.1	11.7	11.6	13.3	13.8
Machinery and transport equipment	22.1	19.1	17.3	21.0	18.6	16.2
Other manufactured goods	25.5	23.5	25.3	24.5	18.5	19.2
Unassigned	1.2	0.4	0.2	0.3	0.2	0.1
	100	100	100	100	100	100

Source: Author's calculation based on UNCTADStat data

Finally, the composition of SADC's trade with Africa is provided in Tables 6.11 and 6.12. Table 6.11 shows that SADC's export trade with Africa involved mostly food and manufactured goods. However, with the exception of ores, metals, and fuel, all the other commodities show a downward trend in their percentage shares. For example, in 1995, food export was 20.5% of SADC's Africa export trade. In 2019, it was down to 17.5%. In the same way, machinery and transportation equipment was 20.1% of total export trade to Africa. In 2019, it was down to 16.3%. Other manufactured goods followed the same trend (Table 6.11).

The import trade followed similar trends. Food imports declined from 21.4% in 1995 to 15.9% in 2019. The same goes for manufactured goods, except for chemical imports that increased over the period. Ores and metals import trade with Africa also increased slightly over the period, while fuels held steady throughout the period. The declining percentage shares could be due to large and small base effects that usually affect percentages. However, it could also be a sign that member states are relying more on trading partners that are outside of Africa. In the broader scheme of things, we have shown that SADC states, like other African countries, trade less

Table 6.12 Composition of SADC's import trade with Africa (Percentage shares)

Commodity	1995	2000	2005	2010	2015	2019
Food	21.4	17.6	16.7	17.4	16.0	15.9
Agricultural raw materials	3.1	2.0	1.6	1.2	1.2	1.2
Ores and metals	2.8	4.1	5.7	4.4	6.4	8.7
Fuels	15.1	15.2	16.9	23.0	21.5	23.1
Pearls, precious stones, and NMG	0.1	0.1	2.6	0.5	4.9	4.3
Chemical products	8.5	11.0	11.5	11.3	11.0	11.5
Machinery and transport equipment	20.0	24.6	20.3	20.4	20.3	16.6
Other manufactured goods	27.2	24.5	24.0	21.3	18.3	18.5
Unassigned	1.8	0.8	0.7	0.5	0.4	0.1
	100	100	100	100	100	100

Source: Author's calculations from UNCTADStat data

among themselves than outside entities. Granted, there is nothing wrong with that, but when the fate of the AfCFTA is built on the assumption that entities such as the SADC will form a basis for Africa's integration project, it leaves much to be desired.

6.6 Explanations for SADC's Performance in Intraregional Trade

The SADC is perhaps the most studied of all the regional trade agreements in Africa. As a result, the reasons are many and so are the perspectives. In their analysis of SADC's trade network, Fink and Rempe (2017, p. 105) described a network that is marked by "extremely few and asymmetrical trade ties within the region and high interdependence with extraregional partners." The few internal ties that exist are with South Africa, which serves as the regional hub. However, they also noted that most of South Africa's trade was extraregional, so while its support for intraregional trade was crucial, its main economic interests were outside, which made SADC's situation precarious.

Muntschick (2017) examined the ups and downs of the SADC to find out whether Krapohl's (2017) hypotheses applied. Muntschick (2017) argued that two asymmetrical economic relationships faced the SADC countries at its formation—one was external and the other was internal. The external asymmetry derived from the strong dominance of the EU in the economies of the SADC countries due to the latter's inability to sever their colonial ties. The result was that the EU was still the leading trading partner and the source of most of the development aid for about half of the member countries, followed by the US. The internal asymmetry was the dominant position South Africa occupied in the economies of the region in terms of trade and investment flows. However, intraregional trade was very low. South Africa's major trading partners were outside of the SADC and only a small number of SADC countries had South Africa as the top destination or source of their export and import trade respectively. The volume of SADC's intraregional trade was far outweighed by the volume of its extrarational trade. There were also differences in the negotiation for the SADC-FTA. It is reported that member countries had different schedules for trade liberalization process—time schedule for liberalization, different goods to be targeted, and special agreement on sensitive products. The countries with less developed economies wanted to protect their economies against South Africa's exports. In turn South Africa wanted a quick and comprehensive trade liberalization to enable it to export.

Another sticking point was the rules of origin of commodities. This was needed to avoid a situation whereby nonmembers of SADC could ship through another member country to compete with domestically produced goods. It was easy to define the rules of origin for agricultural products, but not so for manufacturing products because of multiple sources of product inputs.

The SADC-Free Trade Area (SADC-FTA) was successfully established in 2008, and the plan was to establish SADC-Customs Union (SADC-CU) by 2010. However, this did not occur because of several reasons. First was the influence of the EU as the most important trading partner and development aid donor of the SADC. So, on the one hand, it had supported the SADC through its development aid and also a part of its effort to export its model of development through integration. On the other hand, the idea of the SADC-Customs Union (SADC-CU) ran counter to the EU's external trade policy. So, when it came to SADC-CU negotiations, EU became an obstacle.

In terms of external trade, the most important change was the increasing importance of China, but the EU was still dominant. The Lomé Convention, an Economic Partnership Agreement (EPA) between the EU and its former colonies in Africa, the Caribbean, and the Pacific (ACP) regions, had to be replaced by a new agreement that was not in violation of the World Trade Organization rules. The Cotonou Agreement, which replaced it, called for new negotiated agreements that were based on reciprocity. South Africa, the regional power, already had an agreement with the EU, which gave it a privileged position and did not need a new EPA, like its smaller regional partners. However, South Africa did not see any incentive to provide leadership for the SADC group in negotiation for a new EPA. Given EU's dominant position in the economies of SADC member states, it was able to dictate what it wanted to the SADC members. Thus, the EU demanded that reciprocity agreements be implemented as soon as possible. It also put pressure on SADC members through its development aid and aid for trade policies. Second, SADC members did not negotiate with the EU as a group due to their diverse interests. Instead, they split into four different groups as follows: (Muntschick, 2017, p. 196).

- SADC-EPA Group – Angola, Botswana, Lesotho, Mozambique, Swaziland, and South Africa.
- ESA (Eastern and Southern Africa)-EPA group – Madagascar, Malawi, Mauritius, Seychelles, Zambia, and Zimbabwe.
- EAC (East African Community)-EPA group – Tanzania.
- CEMAC (Economic and Monetary Community of Central Africa)-EPA group – DRC.

Out of the SADC-EPA group, only Botswana, Lesotho, Mozambique, and Swaziland signed an interim agreement. Namibia rejected on the grounds that it wanted to trade more with African countries. When South Africa later joined the group, it also refused to sign the agreement. The ESA-EPA group members all signed the interim agreement in 2008, and the EAC-EPA Tanzania signed in 2007. A permanent agreement was signed between the SADC-EPA and the EU in 2016, but this was only with the South African Customs Union (SACU) member states and Mozambique, but not with other SADC member states. Thus, as reported by Muntschick (2018), if all the permanent agreements are signed, the SADC will consist of three groups with varying external trade regimes with the EU. This will make a SADC-CU, as envisaged originally impossible, since such a move will conflict with the EPA agreements. The irony is that the EPAs are not in conflict with SADC-FTA because, in a free trade area, member states do not have common trade laws against nonmembers, but each retains its own trade laws. The result is that an organization that was aimed at bringing members closer over time is rather stalled on the first phase of that long-term goal with no hope of getting to the ultimate goal.

The important question is why is the EU still dominant in the economies of the SADC member states? Why do South Africa's trade interests lie outside the continent and not inside it? Europe is still dominant in the economies of African countries because of the failure of African countries to achieve economic independence. Such economic independence does not lie in just possession of natural resources, but in the ability to add value to the resource that will command decent prices on the world market than products that are priced by the consumer instead of the supplier. Basically, it comes down to an industrialized economy and all the technological changes that come with it. South Africa is the only industrialized country in the SADC, but South Africa is not able to produce everything that it needs. The bad news for the other SADC member states is that South Africa is also blessed with a host of minerals, some of which are not only strategic but also do not occur anywhere else on the continent. So, its choices are clear, especially when one considers the fact that trade links are also associated with investment capital. The situation even becomes more uncertain when one thinks about the next move to make AfCFTA a customs union, because, at that level, it will require competitive economies among African countries to present a common front and break the strength of external influences' "divide and rule" tactics. The issue is not only South Africa. Each of the member states has its own trading partners that have been forged out of the colonial relationship and neocolonial mechanisms such as international aid and aid for trade. Will the members of the SADC forgo those ties and survive without being able to replace their former markets with new ones?

6.7 Conclusion

The SADC has been one of the more successful regional trade agreements in Africa. The ten countries that make up its membership are diverse in their sizes, ethnic makeup as well as their economies. Most of them are small countries endowed with a few natural resources, mostly minerals. However, there are several asymmetries within the group, the most obvious one being South Africa, which accounts for more than 50% of the economic production of the entire group. It is also the only industrialized economy of the group and endowed with a wide range of mineral wealth. At the time of the formation of the SADC, there were high hopes for the group because of South Africa's position. It was thought that South Africa was going to be hub that will propel the group from a free trade area through a customs union, a common market and much more. The establishment of the free trade area did raise the level of intraregional trade, but it has not been enough to break the fact that SADC conducts most of its import and export trade with entities outside of Africa. The challenge for the AfCFTA is that SADC has been selected by the African Union as one of founding blocks that will eventually coalesce to form the AfCFTA, yet its intraregional trade is less than its extraregional trade. South Africa has taken much of the blame for why the SADC has not worked out the way it was intended. However, every member state has a part to play by transforming their economies toward industrialization and weaning themselves from the dependence of external agents—Europe and the United States then, and China now. Without deliberate effort to industrialize their economies, it will be difficult to turn the extraregional trade that now exists in the SADC into intraregional trade.

References

Abegunrin, L. (1984–85). Southern African Development Coordination Conference (SADCC): Towards regional integration of Southern Africa for Liberation. *A Current Bibliography on African Affairs, 17*(4), 363–384.

Anglin, D. G. (1983). Economic liberation and regional cooperation in Southern Africa: SADCC and PTA. *International Organization, 37*(4), 681–711.

Fink, S., & Rempe, D. (2017). Trade network analyses. In S. Krapohl (Ed.), *Regional integration in the global south* (International political economy series) (pp. 91–111). Palgrave Macmillan.

Krapohl, S. (Ed.), (2017). *Regional integration in the global south: External influence on economic cooperation in ASEAN, MERCOSUR, and SADC*. Pelgrave Macmillan.

Mlambo, D. N. (2020). The quest for post-colonial regional integration: Examining the Southern African Development Community (SADC) in Southern Africa post-1992. *Journal of African Foreign Affairs, 7*(1), 23–48.

Mufune, P. (1993). The future of Southern African Development Coordination Conference (SADCC). *Pula: Botswana Journal of African Studies, 7*(1), 14–34.

Muntschick, J. (2017). SADC. In S. Krapohl (Ed.), *Regional integration in the global south* (International political economy series). Palgrave Macmillan.

Muntschick, J. (2018). *The Southern African Development Community (SADC) and the European Union (EU)*. Palgrave Macmillan.

Nsekela, A. J. (Ed.). (1981). *Southern Africa: Toward economic liberation*. Rex Collings.

Odhiambo, M., Ebobrah, S., & Chitiga, R. (2016). *Civil society guide to regional economic communities in Africa*. African Minds, on behalf of the Open Society Foundations.

Ramutsindela, M. (2007). *Transfrontier conservation in Africa: At the confluence of capital, politics, and nature*. CABI.

SADC. (1993). *Towards the Southern African development community: A declaration by the Heads of State or Government of Southern African States*. SADC Secretariat.

Chapter 7
The Community of Sahel-Saharan States

7.1 Introduction

The Community of the Sahel-Saharan States (CEN-SAD in French) is the largest trading bloc in Africa. In this chapter, we examine the trade pattern of this bloc to see the extent to which it can serve as a foundation for the new AfCFTA. We will do this in six sections. The first section will provide some basic facts about the group. The second section will discuss the formation of the group. The third section will outline the aims and expectations of the group. The fourth section will examine the trade of CEN-SAD with the particular reference to direction and composition of trade. In section five, we will discuss the reasons for CEN-SAD's trade performance and its implications for the AfCFTA, in section six.

7.2 Some Basic Facts About CEN-SAD

The CEN-SAD boasts of 29 members (Fig. 7.1). By land area, these countries cover 13,375,916 Km^2, which is about 44% of Africa's land area (Table 7.1). With an estimated total population of 617,592,898 in 2019, CEN-SAD accounted for 47% of Africa's total population in 2019. The total gross domestic product (GDP) of the group in 2019 was estimated at US$1.3 trillion, which was about 51% of Africa's total GDP in that year. Like other regions of the continent, the asymmetry within the member states is remarkable. About 50% of the total population of CEN-SAD live in two countries—Nigeria and Egypt. If we add Morocco, the third most populous state of the group, the three countries account for 56% of the people in the group, leaving 44% of the population in the remaining 26 countries. The GDP generated by the 29 countries shows more disparities. In 2019, about 51% of the total GDP was due to just two countries—Nigeria and Egypt. Including Morocco, the three

B. Ofori-Amoah, *The African Continental Free Trade Area*,
https://doi.org/10.1007/978-3-031-59181-5_7

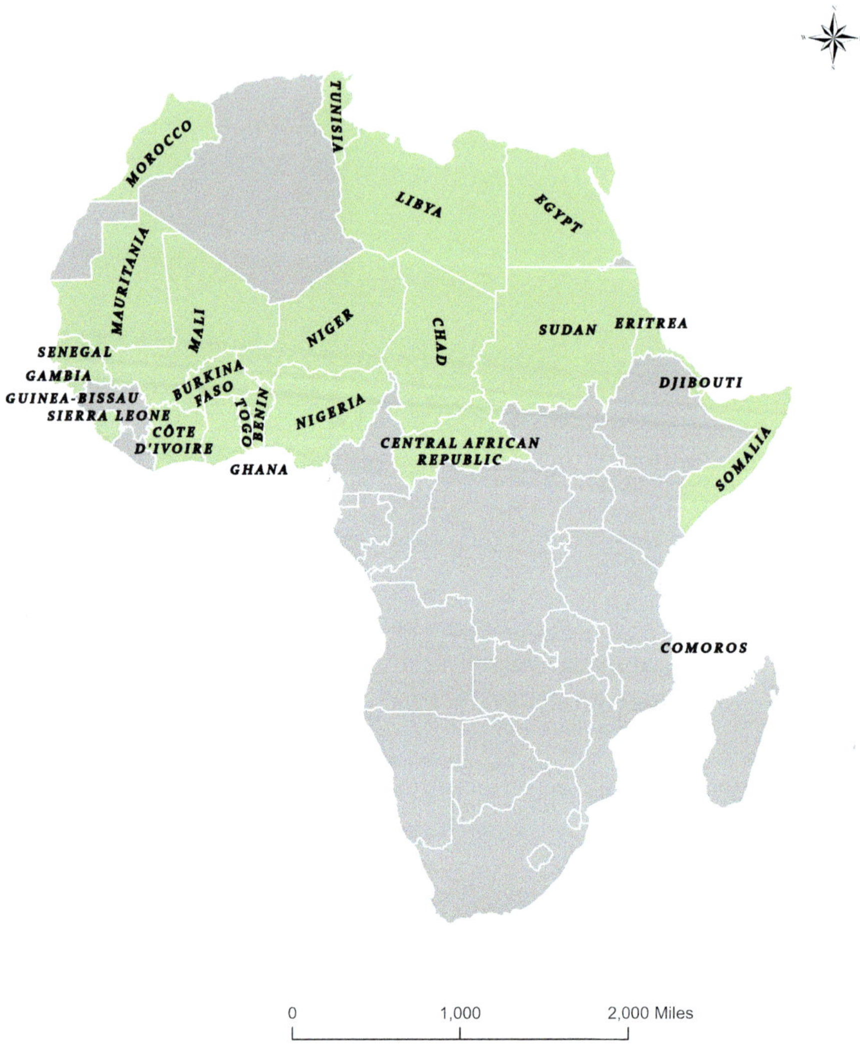

Fig. 7.1 Members of the Community of Sahel-Saharan States. (Data source: ICPAC GEOPORTA. The analysis was performed in ArcGIS Pro 3.1.0)

countries generated 69% of the total GDP of the group in 2019. Libya had the highest GDP per capita purchasing power parity, US$22,764, while Central African Republic had the lowest, US$986. The physical environmental diversity of the region is also wide, with biome types ranging from the equatorial rainforest and savanna woodland to the Sahel, hot desert, and the Mediterranean. As a result, these countries also show a wide range of natural resource endowments, including rich oil fields of Nigeria and Libya, the world's largest deposits of phosphates (in Morocco), and bauxite (in Guinea) and a number of countries with substantial gold reserves. Agricultural products include cotton, rice, sorghum, cocoa, and olives. All the

Table 7.1 Member states of CEN-SAD by area, population, GDP, and GDP per capita, 2019

Country	Area (Km^2)	Population	GDP (US$)	GDP Per Capita, PPP (US $)
Benin	112,620	12,290,444	14,391,686,633	3426.05
Burkina Faso	274,200	20,951,639	16,178,162,030	2267.32
Cent. African Rep.	622,980	5,209,325	2,221,301,401	985.99
Chad	1,284,000	16,126,866	11,314,951,343	1646.29
Comoros	2170	790,986	1,195,019,559	3188.08
Côte d'Ivoire	322,460	26,147,551	58,539,424,930	5432.55
Djibouti	22,000	1,073,994	3,088,853,639	5482.01
Egypt	1,001,450	105,618,671	303,080,865,604	12,259.72
Eritrea	121,320	3,498,818	–	–
Gambia	11,300	2,508,884	1,813,608,280	2320.31
Ghana	238,540	31,522,290	68,337,537,816	5773.86
Guinea-Bissau	36,120	1,970,457	1,439,638,443	2021.14
Libya	1,759,540	6,569,088	69,252,306,372	22,764.48
Mali	1,024,000	20,567,424	17,280,250,805	2419.69
Mauritania	1,030,700	4,383,849	7,889,655,284	5569.54
Morocco	446,550	36,304,408	119,870,439,114	7865.26
Niger	1,186,408	23,443,393	12,916,455,161	1276.05
Nigeria	923,768	203,304,492	448,120,428,859	5352.24
Senegal	196,712	16,000,782	23,398,811,424	3510.42
Sierra Leone	71,740	8,046,829	4,076,578,543	1777.16
Somalia	637,660	15,981,301	6,476,674,592	1236.52
Sudan	1,886,068	43,232,093	32,338,079,165	4349.71
Tunisia	163,610	12,049,314	41,772,900,763	11,902.86
Total	13,375,916	617,592,898	1,264,993,629,758	

Source: United Nations Population Division

countries within the group share a common heritage of being former colonies of European countries—France, Britain, and Portugal.

7.3 The Formation of CEN-SAD

CEN-SAD was established on February 8, 1998, after a meeting of Heads of States of six African countries in Tripoli, Libya. The six countries were Burkina Faso, Chad, Libya, Mali, Niger, and Sudan (NEPAD, 2015). It was founded at the initiation of former President Muammar al Ghaddafi of Libya. The countries that formed the group had a common economic problem of drought, size, landlocked status, and economic structure, with Libya having the technological, financial, and political will to address those problems (Oxford Analytica, 2008). It became a regional economic community in 2000, having been recognized by the Organization of African

Unity's Conference of Heads of States and Government in Lomé, Togo (NEPAD, 2015).

The group expanded in 1999–2009 to incorporate all contiguous states in the Horn of Africa, and Central and West Africa that were drought affected. Central African Republic, Eritrea, and Nigeria joined in 1999; Djibouti, Gambia, and Senegal in 2000; Egypt, Morocco, Somalia, and Tunisia in 2001; Benin and Togo in 2002; Côte d'Ivoire and Liberia in 2004; Ghana, Sao Tome and Principe, and Sierra Leone in 2005; Comoros, Guinea, and Guinea-Bissau in 2007; Mauritania in 2008; and Cabo Verde in 2009. By that time, CEN-SAD's membership had reached 29, making it the largest trading bloc in Africa.

CEN-SAD became an African Union regional economic community in 2006 (NEPAD 2015). The major institutions of CEN-SAD include the Conference of Leaders and Heads of State, the Executive Council, the General Secretariat, the Sahel-Saharan Investment and Trade Bank, and the Economic, Social, and Cultural Council (Akonor, 2009). Since its inception, CEN-SAD has been headquartered in Tripoli, Libya, but in 2019, the headquarters moved to N'Djamena, Chad.

7.4 Aims of CEN-SAD

CEN-SAD's main goals include

- Economic union, but not within any defined territory (monetary union is implicit only)
- Freedom of trade, as well as free movement of peoples, capital, and so on
- Investment and trade promotion in the Sahel area, especially in agriculture
- Improvement of transport and telecommunications links across the Sahara
- Harmonization of political, employer, and employment rights for all CEN-SAD citizens, educational and cultural policies

Two consecutive crises, the Libyan Crisis of 2011 and the Malian Crisis of 2012, impacted CEN-SAD in a major way causing a pause in many of the group's activities, as states already dealing with drought had to fight insurgence, drug trafficking, and refugees. In 2013, the CEN-SAD Treaty was revised to give it a new mission, which is collective security and sustainable development. Article 3 of the new Treaty "aims specifically to (1) preserve and consolidate peace, security, and stability; (2) promoting political dialogue and fighting cross-border organized crime and its related activities such as drug, human beings, and arms trafficking, money laundering, and terrorism; (3) fight against desertification, drought, and climate change through the conservation of natural resources and research and development of renewable energy; (4) cooperate in economic, trade, scientific and socio-cultural cooperation, infrastructure development as well as the promotion of free movement of people, goods and services "(NEPAD, 2015).

The revised Treaty also added three new bodies to CEN-SAD's institutional structure. These were the Permanent Peace and Security Council, the Permanent

Council in Charge of Sustainable Development, and the Committee of Ambassadors and Permanent Representatives. Kenya, Liberia, Sao Tome and Principe, and Cabo Verde did not sign the 2013 revised Treaty, so they are no longer CEN-SAD members.

NEPAD (2015) reported that CEN-SAD has implemented several projects, including the Great Green Wall of the Sahel-Sahara initiative, the Regional Food Security Program, and Initiatives in Transport, Infrastructure, Mines, and Energy. At the same time, it identified several areas for improvement, such as lack of capacity to manage many of its program areas.

7.5 CEN-SAD Trade

7.5.1 Direction of Trade of CEN-SAD

Most of the trade conducted by CEN-SAD members occurred outside of the group instead of inside the group (Table 7.2). CEN-SAD was formed in 1998 so the 1995 data is an estimate based on the member countries traded among themselves before CEN-SAD was formed. At that time, the data shows that only 8% of export trade conducted by the member countries occurred among them. An additional 1.5% occurred with Africa, bringing the group's intra-African trade to 9.6%, while 90.4% outside of Africa. Over the years, export trade among CEN-SAD members declined slightly from 8%, while export trade with the rest of Africa increased slightly (Table 7.2). In 2019, export trade within CEN-SAD accounted for 7.1%, that within Africa was 12.5%, and the rest of the world was 87.5%.

Figure 7.2 shows the direction of CEN-SAD's export trade by major regions of the world. Europe continues to be the leading destination of export trade of CEN-SAD. In 1995, it accounted for 57.8% of all export trade of CEN-SAD. Since then, the percentage of export trade with Europe has declined, and in 2019, it was down to 45.2%. At the same time, the share of Asia increased from 2.5% in 1995 to 32.8% in 2019. Export trade to Northern America rose from 13.5 in 1995 to 21.6% in 2005 but then started declining. In 2019, it was down to just 6.6%.

Table 7.2 Direction of export trade of CEN-SAD, 1995–2019 (Percentage share)

Year	CEN-SAD	Rest of Africa	CEN-SAD & Africa	Rest of World	Total
1995	8.0	1.5	9.6	90.4	100
2000	7.2	1.9	9.1	90.9	100
2005	6.5	2.6	9.2	90.8	100
2010	5.8	5.4	11.1	88.9	100
2015	7.9	5.2	13.1	86.9	100
2019	7.1	7.1	12.5	87.5	100

Source: Author's calculation based on UNCTADStat data

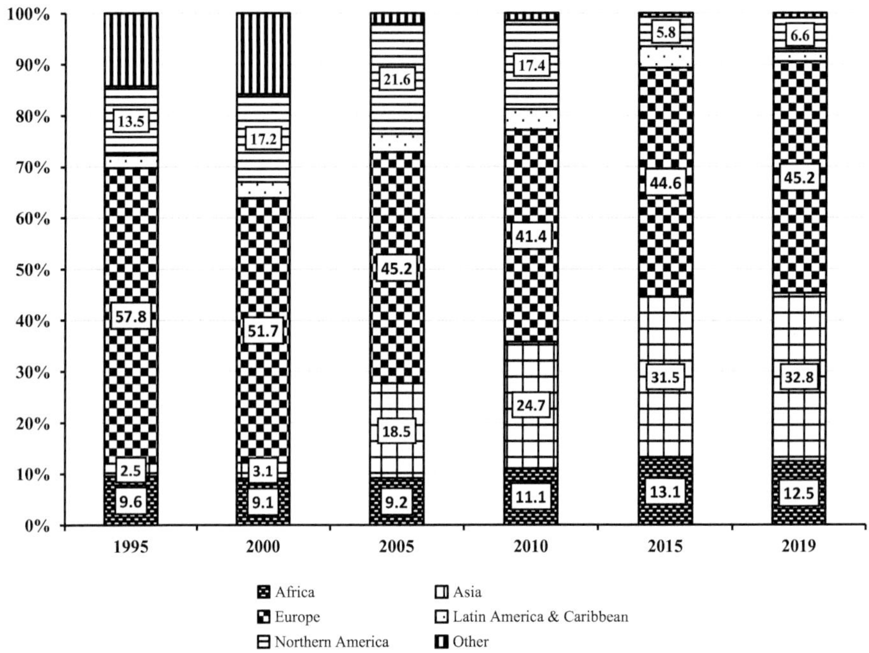

Fig. 7.2 Direction of export trade of CEN-SAD by major world regions, 1995–2019

Table 7.3 shows the breakdown of the top 20 export markets of CEN-SAD, which shows that only two members of CEN-SAD, Ghana and Côte d'Ivoire made the top 20 export markets in 2001. In 2005, it was Côte d'Ivoire and Nigeria. In 2010, it was only Libya, while Ghana and Cote d'Ivoire made the list in both 2015 and 2019. South Africa is the only other African country that made the list over the entire period of consideration, while Equatorial Guinea made it in 2010.

Import trade has followed a similar trend. In 1995, before the formation of CEN-SAD, 5.8% of the total import trade of the member states occurred among themselves (Table 7.4). Trade with Africa was just 7.5%, while the remaining 92.5% was with the rest of the world. After the formation of CEN-SAD, intra-group trade rose a little bit, reaching 7% in 2005 before dropping to 5.5% in 2019. The percentage of CEN-SAD's import trade occurring in Africa reached 10% in 2005 but dropped to 8% in 2019. At the same time, CEN-SAD's trade with rest of the world never dropped below 90% except in 2005, when it was 89.9%.

Figure 7.3 shows the sources of CEN-SAD's import trade by major regions of the world. In 1995, Europe was the source of 52.4% of CEN-SAD's imports, followed by Asia with 19.1% and Northern America with 10%. Since then, Europe's dominance in the import trade started to decline, while Asia's continued to grow. By 2019, Asia had overtaken Europe as the leading source of import trade for CEN-SAD, controlling 41.6% and Europe controlling 39.7%. Northern America's role as import source had declined to only 6.8%.

Table 7.3 Top 20 export markets of CEN-SAD in selected years from 2001–2019

2001		2005		2010		2015		2019	
Country	%	Country	%	Country	%	Country	%	Country	%
US	15.2	US	23.3	US	16.3	India	9.0	Spain	8.7
Italy	15.1	Italy	12.4	Italy	11.3	France	8.8	France	8.4
France	13.1	France	9.6	France	9.1	Spain	7.2	Italy	8.3
Spain	8.7	Spain	8.3	China	6.9	Italy	7.2	China	8.1
Germany	6.7	Germany	5.7	India	5.8	NLD	6.3	India	7.3
India	5.2	China	4.2	Spain	5.4	China	4.9	NLD	4.5
UK	3.0	NLD	2.7	NLD	3.8	US	4.3	US	4.2
NLD	3.0	Brazil	2.3	Brazil	3.2	UAE	4.0	UAE	4.1
China	2.4	Türkiye	2.1	S. Africa	2.9	UK	3.0	SUI	3.6
SUI	2.3	UK	2.0	Germany	2.2	Germany	2.8	S. Africa	3.2
Brazil	2.2	SUI	1.8	UK	2.0	SUI	2.7	Germany	2.8
Türkiye	1.9	Portugal	1.5	Belgium	1.8	Canada	2.4	UK	2.3
Belgium	1.5	S. Africa	1.4	SUI	1.5	Brazil	2.4	Türkiye	2.2
Japan	1.2	Japan	1.4	Canada	1.5	S. Africa	2.3	*Ghana	2.1
Portugal	1.2	Belgium	1.3	Eqt. Guinea	1.3	Saudi Arabia	2.0	Canada	1.5
Indonesia	1.1	India	1.2	UAE	1.3	Türkiye	2.0	Belgium	1.2
*Ghana	0.9	*CIV	1.2	Portugal	1.3	Japan	1.5	Saudi Arabia	1.2
S. Africa	0.9	Indonesia	0.9	Türkiye	1.0	Belgium	1.4	Brazil	1.0
*CIV	0.9	*Nigeria	0.8	Greece	0.9	*CIV	1.0	*CIV	1.0
Greece	0.9	Greece	0.8	*Libya	0.9	*Ghana	0.9	Indonesia	0.9
Total	87.1	Total	84.9	Total	80.3	Total	76.1	Total	76.7

Source: Author's calculation based on UNCTADStat data
CIV Côte d'Ivoire, *S. Africa* South Africa, *NLD* Netherlands, *SUI* Switzerland; *CEN-SAD members

Table 7.4 Direction of import trade of CEN-SAD, 1995–2019 (Percentage shares)

Year	CEN-SAD	Rest of Africa	CEN-SAD + Africa	Rest of the world	Total
1995	5.8	1.7	7.5	92.5	100
2000	6.8	2.1	9.0	91.0	100
2005	7.0	3.1	10.1	89.9	100
2010	6.0	3.0	8.9	91.1	100
2015	5.5	2.9	8.4	91.6	100
2019	5.5	2.5	8.0	92.0	100

Author's calculation based on UNCTADStat data

From Table 7.5, only two CEN-SAD members, Nigeria and Cote d'Ivoire made the top 20 import markets in 2001 and 2005. In 2010 and 2015, only Nigeria made the top 20 import markets list, while in 2019, it was only Egypt. As it was the export list, only two non-CEN-SAD African countries made the top 20 import market list. They were South Africa in 2001 and Algeria in 2010. The question once again is, Why does the largest trading bloc in Africa with 47% of the continent's population

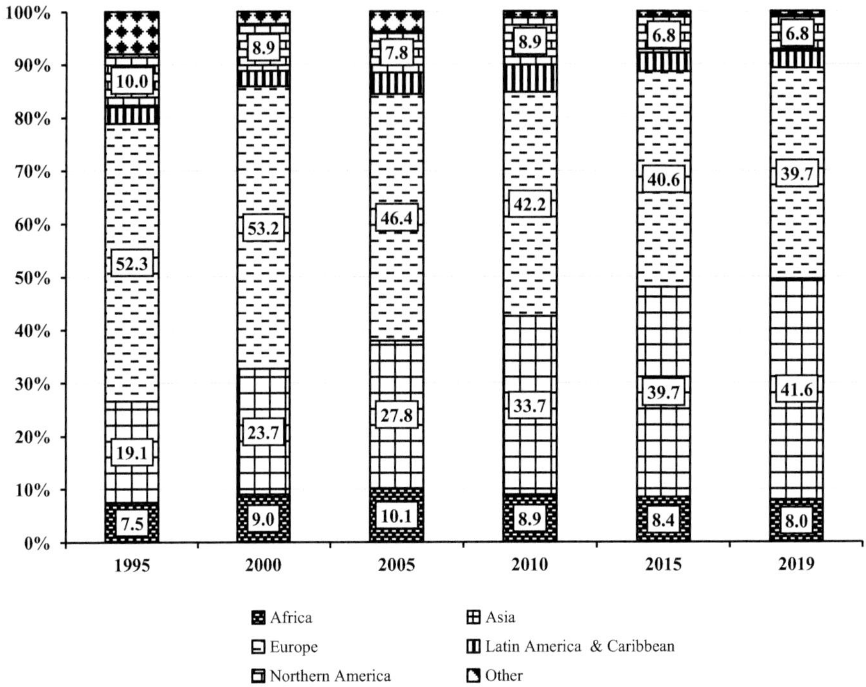

Fig. 7.3 Direction import trade of CEN-SAD by major regions of the world, 1995–2019

and 51% of its total GDP trade less with itself and fellow African countries than the rest of the world? As before, we argue that it is because of the composition of its trade.

7.5.2 Composition of CEN-SAD Trade

Like other regions, CEN-SAD is essentially an exporter of primary commodities and importer of manufactured goods (Table 7.6). More than 70% of exports of CEN-SAD are primary goods, while manufactured goods have been no more than 27% over the period under consideration.

The breakdown of the export trade shows fuel as the leading export commodity followed by food, other manufactured goods, and pearls, precious stones, and non-monetary gold (Table 7.7).

On the import trade side, machinery and transportation equipment leads the list of imported commodities, followed by other manufactured goods, food, fuels, and chemical products (Table 7.8).

Table 7.5 Top 20 import markets of CEN-SDAD in selected years from 2001 to 2019

2001		2005		2010		2015		2019	
Country	%	Country	%	Country	%	Country	%	Country	%
France	13.7	France	11.6	China	11.3	China	14.4	China	16.9
Italy	8.1	Italy	7.2	US	8.8	France	7.1	US	6.3
Germany	7.4	China	6.7	France	8.8	US	5.7	France	6.0
US	7.2	Germany	5.3	Italy	6.0	Germany	5.0	India	5.3
UK	5.5	US	5.1	Germany	4.8	Italy	4.9	Spain	4.6
Spain	3.7	UK	4.1	Spain	3.1	Spain	4.4	Italy	4.4
China	3.6	Spain	3.7	India	3.0	India	3.7	Türkiye	4.3
Belgium	2.9	Sau. Arabia	2.8	Sau. Arabia	2.8	Türkiye	3.6	Germany	4.1
NLD	2.8	Russia	2.8	Türkiye	2.7	Russia	2.8	UAE	3.4
Japan	2.7	NLD	2.8	UK	2.6	UAE	2.7	NLD	2.9
Sau. Arabia	2.7	Brazil	2.6	S. Korea	2.6	Belgium	2.7	Russia	2.8
Russia	1.9	Japan	2.4	Japan	2.5	NLD	2.6	Sau. Arabia	2.8
S. Korea	1.9	India	2.4	Brazil	2.5	UK	2.3	Belgium	2.2
*Nigeria	1.8	*Nigeria	2.2	Belgium	2.2	S. Korea	2.3	UK	2.0
India	1.7	S. Korea	2.0	UAE	2.2	Brazil	2.2	Brazil	1.9
Brazil	1.6	Belgium	1.9	Russia	2.2	Sau. Arabia	2.2	S. Korea	1.7
*CIV	1.3	Türkiye	1.9	NLD	1.9	Japan	1.7	Ukraine	1.4
Australia	1.2	UAE	1.8	*Nigeria	1.3	Ukraine	1.6	Japan	1.3
SUI	1.2	Ukraine	1.5	Ukraine	1.3	Thailand	1.5	*Egypt	1.0
S. Africa	1.1	*CIV	1.4	Algeria	1.2	*Nigeria	1.1	Thailand	1.0
Total	74.2	Total	72.3	Total	73.7	Total	74.4	Total	76.2

Source: Author's calculation based on UNCTADStat data
CIV Côte d'Ivoire, *Sau. Arabia* Saudi Arabia, *NLD* Netherlands, *SUI* Switzerland; *CEN-SAD members

Table 7.6 Composition of trade of CEN-SAD, 1995–2019 (Percentage)

Year	Primary Goods		Manufactured Goods		Unclassified Goods	
	Export	Import	Export	Import	Export	Import
1995	74.7	30.4	25.1	64.6	0.2	5
2000	77.5	32.6	21.1	64.8	1.4	2.5
2005	80.9	32	17.5	64.5	1.6	3.5
2010	82.4	33.6	17.2	65.1	1.6	1.3
2015	72.8	33.7	26.6	65.8	0.6	0.5
2019	75.2	35.1	24.6	63.8	0.2	1.1

Source: Author's calculation based on UNCTADStat data

Table 7.7 Composition of export trade of CEN-SAD, 1995–2019 (Percentage)

	1995	2000	2005	2010	2015	2019
Food	16.1	10.7	8.8	9.7	17.2	14.7
Agricultural raw materials	6.3	3.4	2.5	1.8	2.5	2.5
Ores and metals	3.5	2.4	2.1	2.8	3.5	3.3
Fuels	47.4	59.9	66.7	64.1	42.0	46.1
Pearls, precious stones, and NMG	1.4	1.1	0.8	4.1	7.6	8.6
Chemical products	6.4	4.2	3.4	4.3	5.8	5.9
Machinery and transport equipment	2.6	3.6	4.0	4.6	9.9	8.9
Other manufactured goods	16.1	13.3	10.1	8.3	11.0	9.8
Unassigned	0.2	1.4	1.6	0.3	0.6	0.2
Total	100	100	100	100	100	100

Source: Author's calculation based on UNCTADStat data

Table 7.8 Composition of import trade of CEN-SAD, 1995–2019 (Percentage)

	1995	2000	2005	2010	2015	2019
Food	18.2	16.8	15.1	15.3	16.4	16.2
Agricultural raw materials	3.4	2.5	2.0	1.8	1.5	1.5
Ores and metals	2.1	2.0	2.4	2.6	2.3	2.7
Fuels	6.7	11.3	12.4	13.7	13.3	14.7
Pearls, precious stones, and NMG	0.1	0.1	0.1	0.1	0.2	0.1
Chemical products	11.3	10.7	10.3	10.3	11.6	11.8
Machinery and transport equipment	27.7	29.4	29.8	31.8	29.7	29.5
Other manufactured goods	25.6	24.7	24.4	23.0	24.5	22.6
Unassigned	5.0	2.5	3.5	1.3	0.5	1.1
	100	100	100	100	100	100

Source: Author's calculation based on UNCTADStat data

Table 7.9 Composition of export trade with members, 1995–2019 (Percentage share)

Year	1995	2000	2005	2010	2015	2019
Food	14.0	14.4	13.8	21.2	23.7	21.4
Agricultural raw materials	9.9	4.7	2.9	1.8	1.4	1.3
Ores and metals	2.9	1.1	1.8	2.9	1.7	1.6
Fuels	35.8	48.2	50.8	34.9	29.9	33.7
Pearls, precious stones, and NMG	0.0	0.1	0.0	0.3	0.1	0.0
Chemical products	11.9	10.5	9.8	9.8	11.8	11.9
Machinery and transport equipment	3.9	4.8	3.6	11.0	11.8	8.7
Other manufactured goods	21.2	15.7	17.1	17.8	19.5	21.4
Unassigned	0.3	0.6	0.2	0.2	0.2	0.0
	100	100	100	100	100	100

Source: Author's calculation based on UNCTADStat data

Composition of CEN-SAD trade within itself and with the rest of African countries mirrors this general trend. Tables 7.9 and 7.10 show overwhelming dominance of fuel exports and imports, respectively, among members of the group. It is the same with the export and import trade with Africa (Tables 7.11 and 7.12).

7.5.3 Explanation of the Trade Performance of CEN-SAD

Two previous evaluations of capacity of CEN-SAD as a regional economic community in 2006 and 2008 (ACBF, 2008) concluded that there were substantial gaps between CEN-SAD's capacity and stated goals. In particular, the reports found that several senior administrative positions needed for proper functioning of the group were vacant. It was the hope that a revised Treaty signed in 2010 would bring a change. However, as we have seen, changes in trading relations have been slow. In a recent study on the flow of foreign direct investments (FDI) to the group,

Table 7.10 Composition of import trade with members, 1995–2019 (Percentage share)

Commodity	1995	2000	2005	2010	2015	2019
Food	14.0	15.6	15.3	20.8	22.8	23.6
Agricultural raw materials	4.0	3.6	2.5	1.5	1.2	1.6
Ores and metals	1.7	1.3	2.2	2.7	1.9	1.2
Fuels	38.8	48.9	48.2	35.9	30.8	32.7
Pearls, precious stones, and NMG	0.0	0.1	0.0	0.3	0.1	0.0
Chemical products	11.0	8.9	10.3	9.5	11.5	11.1
Machinery and transport equipment	4.0	5.2	5.1	12.0	11.0	8.6
Other manufactured goods	26.2	15.6	16.3	17.1	20.6	21.0
Unassigned	0.2	0.8	0.1	0.2	0.2	0.1
	100	100	100	100	100	100

Source: Author's calculation based on UNCTADStat data

Table 7.11 Composition of CEN-SAD exports with Africa, 1995–2019 (Percentage share)

Commodity	1995	2000	2005	2010	2015	2019
Food	14.7	14.2	12.2	13.9	19.0	17.9
Agricultural raw materials	9.4	4.1	2.3	1.4	1.2	1.0
Ores and metals	2.9	1.4	1.7	2.1	1.8	1.9
Fuels	32.5	49.6	52.0	45.6	35.2	38.0
Pearls, precious stones, and NMG	0.0	1.4	3.5	8.7	3.2	3.2
Chemical products	12.2	9.6	8.4	6.9	10.9	10.4
Machinery and transport equipment	5.1	4.9	3.8	8.6	11.6	9.1
Other manufactured goods	22.9	14.3	14.9	12.7	16.7	18.5
Unassigned	0.3	0.5	1.1	0.2	0.4	0.0
	100	100	100	100	100	100

Source: Author's calculation based on UNCTADStat data

Table 7.12 Composition of CEN-SAD import trade with Africa, 1995–2019 (Percentage share)

Commodity	1995	2000	2005	2010	2015	2019
Food	16.4	17.3	15.8	19.5	21.1	22.8
Agricultural raw materials	5.2	4.7	2.8	1.7	1.2	2.0
Ores and metals	1.9	1.6	3.1	2.9	1.7	2.1
Fuels	40.0	45.4	46.5	35.8	33.4	33.8
Pearls, precious stones, and NMG	0.0	0.1	0.0	0.3	0.8	0.0
Chemical products	9.9	8.9	9.9	8.8	10.3	9.9
Machinery and transport equipment	3.9	5.8	6.2	14.2	14.7	9.6
Other manufactured goods	22.4	15.5	15.5	16.6	16.7	19.7
Unassigned	0.3	0.8	0.1	0.1	0.1	0.1
	100.0	100.0	100.0	100.0	100.0	100.0

Source: Author's calculations based on UNCTAD data

Kwaw-Nimeson and Tian (2023) noted that CEN-SAD's "institutional curse" might be lifted due to a number of factors that have led to increasing flow of FDI into the region. These factors include the region's location advantages for FDI and a large array of mineral wealth that is more than any other RTA in Africa. Others have attributed CEN-SAD's problems to overlapping membership. For example, with the exception of Sudan, all the members belong to at least one or more RTAs in Africa (NEPAD, 2015). This, of course, creates a problem of which countries to trade with, where and when. The question is, To what extent can we attribute CEN-SAD's low percentage of intraregional trade to these factors? Could CEN-SAD's intraregional trade percentage been higher if it had stronger or more effective institutions and without overlapping membership? Could better institutions and non-overlapping membership make member states of CEN-SAD trade more among themselves? Based on what we have learned from CEN-SAD's trade patterns, the answers to these questions are definitely not. This is because, like other African countries, CEN-SAD's economies produce predominantly primary goods most of which they do not consume, and consume goods most of which they do not produce. So, just as predicted by classical international trade theory, they have to exchange their produce for what they are not able to produce, and given that most of this is produced outside the group and outside Africa, it is not surprising that there is less trade among CEN-SAD members and more trade with nonmembers. Strengthening the institutional capacity and removing overlapping membership are important, but they will not increase intraregional trade unless CEN-SAD members embark on diversification of their economies with greater emphasis on manufacturing industries.

7.6 Conclusion

CEN-SAD was formed in 1998 at the instigation of Libya by six countries, namely Burkina Faso, Chad, Libya, Mali, Niger, and Sudan. Within 10 years of its formation, CEN-SAD had expanded to include 29 African countries, making it Africa's largest RTA, and accounting for about 44% of its land area, 47% of its population, and 51% of its GDP in 2019. While CEN-SAD has achieved some of its objectives with particular reference to promoting intraregional trade, it has not been a stellar performance. Thus, in 1995, before it was formed, trade among the would-be members was 8% of the total export trade of the countries. In 2019, it was 7.1%. Import trade was no different. It was 5.8% in 1995 and 5.5% in 2019. CEN-SAD's trade with its members and the rest of Africa was small. For exports, it was 9.6% in 1995, and 12.5%. For imports, it was 7.5% in 1995 and 8.0% in 2019. This meant that in 1995, 90.4% of CEN-SAD's export trade was with partners outside of Africa. In 2019, it was 87.5%. With respect to imports, it was 92.5% in 1995 and 92% in 2019. The composition of CEN-SAD's trade showed that from 1995 to 2019, primary goods constituted 72.8% or more of CEN-SAD's exports, while they constituted 35% or less in imports. In contrast, 26.6% or less of CEN-SAD's exports were manufactured goods, while 63.8% or more of its imports were manufactured goods. Since its formation, CEN-SAD has been plagued with weak institutional capacity and overlapping memberships in other RTAs. These have made it difficult for the group to function effectively. However, these cannot fully explain the low intraregional trade performance. We argue that the fact that CEN-SAD members produced mostly primary products most of they do not consume and consume products they do not produce, explains the low intraregional trade performance within it. To improve intraregional trade, CEN-SAD must diversify its economy through industrialization.

References

African Capacity Building Foundation (ACBF). (2008). *Survey of the capacity needs of Africa's regional economic communities*. ACBF.

Akonor, K. (2009). *Africa's economic institutions*. Routledge.

Kwaw-Nimeson, E. & Tian, Z. (2023). *Institutional quality, foreign direct investment, and regional integration: Empirical evidence from CEN-SAD SAGE and open access*. https://us.sagepub.com/en-us/nam/open-access-at-sage

NEPAD. (2015). *Strengthening the institutional capacity of the community of Sahel-Saharan States (CEN-SAD)*. NEPAD Agency for Africa.

Oxford Analytica. (2008). *Africa: CEN-SAD reflects libyan goals to the South*. Oxford Analytica Daily Brief Service, Mar 05 2008, p. 1. ProQuest.

Chapter 8
The East African Community

8.1 Introduction

The East African Community (EAC) is one of the oldest regional trade agreements in Africa. With its origins in colonial Africa, the first East African Community fell apart after 10 years of operation from 1967 to 1977. After two decades of being defunct, the East African Community was resuscitated in 1999 and quickly began to attract attention as one of Africa's most effective regional trade agreement (RTAs). In this chapter, we examine some basic facts about the East African Community, its formation and expectation, and its performance with respect to intraregional trade. The chapter is divided into five sections and a conclusion. Section 8.2 presents some basic facts about the EAC, Sect. 8.3 discusses its formation, Sect. 8.4 deals with the goals and expectations, Sect. 8.5 explores the trade patterns, and Sect. 8.6 provides explanations for the trade performance (Fig. 8.1).

8.2 Some Basic Facts About the East African Community

The East African Community (EAC) consists of six countries, including Burundi, Congo Democratic Republic, Kenya, Rwanda, South Sudan, and Tanzania. Together, these countries cover an area of 4,783,103 km^2, which is about 15.9% of Africa's land area. The EAC in 2019 had an estimated population of 278,873,532, which was about 21% of Africa's total population. GDP, purchasing power parity of the group, was estimated at US$261,583,074,025, which is just about 10.5% of Africa's total GDP in 2019. At a glance, it appears that there are no asymmetrical relationships. However, there are a number of asymmetries. The first is the huge gap between the largest and the smallest country—Congo DR, which is the largest country in the group is about 2,345,419 km^2. Size does not always mean more natural resources,

B. Ofori-Amoah, *The African Continental Free Trade Area*,
https://doi.org/10.1007/978-3-031-59181-5_8

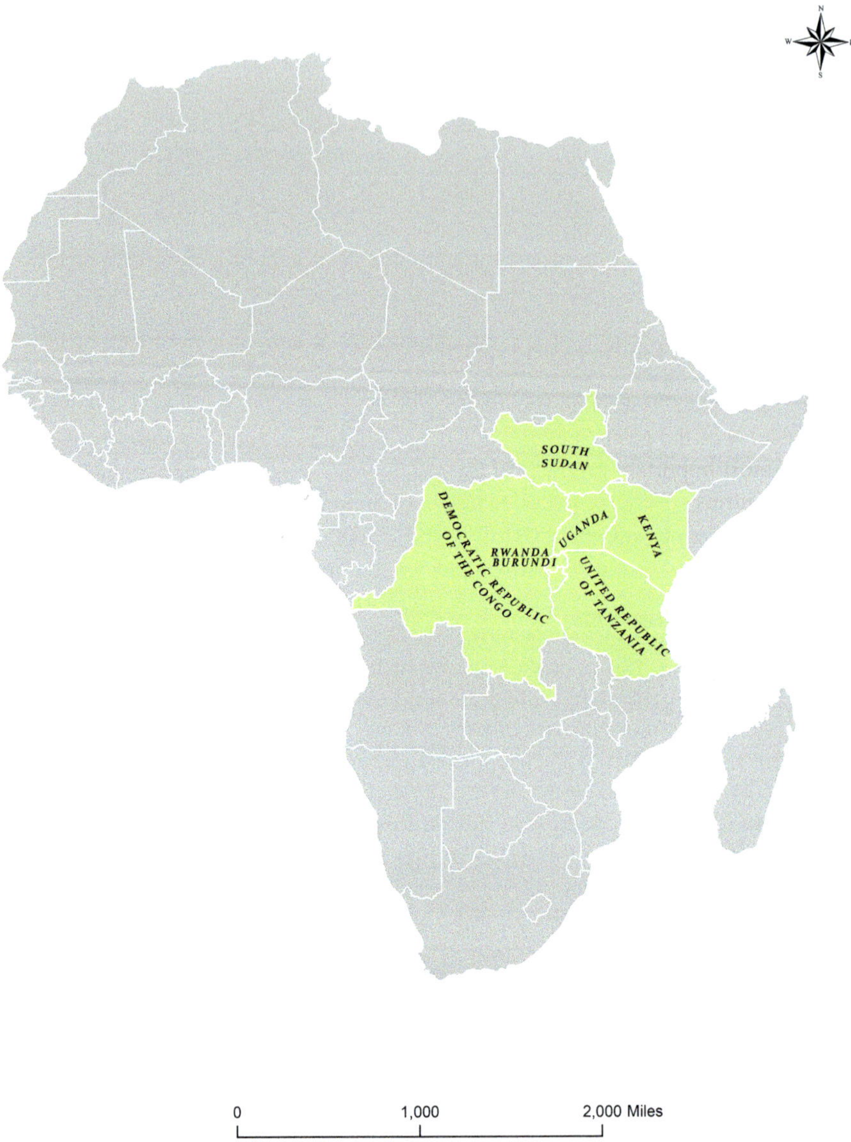

Fig. 8.1 Member states of the East African Community. (Data source: ICPAC GEOPORTA. The analysis was performed in ArcGIS Pro 3.1.0)

but in the case of Congo DR its size also comes with an enormous amount of resources—metals, precious stones, and agricultural raw materials. At the same time, there are countries, such as Burundi, that need more resources. Another asymmetry is in the generation of GDP. In 2019, Kenya alone accounted for 38% of the GDP of the community. If Tanzania's GDP, which is the second largest GDP of the

Table 8.1 Some basic facts of the East African Community, 2019

Country	Area (Km^2)	Population Est	GDP (US$)	GDP PCI, PPP (US $)
Burundi	27,830	11,874,838	2,581,268,126	783
Congo DR	2,345,410	89,906,891	51,775,830,726	1144
Kenya	582,650	50,951,450	100,379,713,697	4647
Rwanda	26,338	12,835,028	10,356,327,149	2322
South Sudan	619,745	10,447,666	–	–
Tanzania	945,090	59,872,579	61,136,873,692	2773
Uganda	236,040	42,949,080	35,353,060,634	2275
Total	4,783,103	278,837,532	261,583,074,025	

Source: Author's calculation based on UNCTADStat data

group, was added to Kenya's, the two countries—Kenya and Tanzania—would generate 61.7% of the group's total 2019 GDP (Table 8.1).

The most important products of this group include coffee, tea, gold, etc. Most of these countries specialize in coffee and tea production.

8.3 The Formation of the East African Community

Economic integration and cooperation are not new to East Africa. Gastorn and Masinde (2017) trace them back to early colonial period to the time of German East Africa (1884–1919), which consisted of Tanganyika, Burundi, and Rwanda. However, historians identify five main phases of evolution and development of the East African Community: from 1903 to 1947, 1948 to 1960, 1961 to 1967, 1967 to 1977, and since 1993. The first phase began after the construction of the Uganda Railway (1895–1901). This linked the two British territories of Kenya and Uganda and provided a basis for the establishment of several institutions that fostered cooperation among the colonies (Odhiambo et al., 2016; Gastorn & Masinde, 2017). In 1905, the British introduced a common currency (the East African Shilling) to Kenya and Uganda and established a customs union for the two colonies in 1917 (McAuliffe et al., 2012). This was followed by the establishment of the East African Currency Board in 1919. After World War I, Tanganyika became a British colony, and in 1922, it joined the customs union (Aloo, 2017). In 1933, the East African Posts and Telegraph was established. However, this was not legally secured and was only based on negotiations among the colonies.

The period from 1948 to1961 saw the merger of the Kenya and Uganda Railways and the Tanganyika Railway into the East African Railways and Harbors. Also established was the East African High Commission, which aimed at providing services in certain areas that the three colonies lacked competence. This second phase ended with Tanganyika gaining its independence from the British in 1961. It is reported that Tanganyika wanted to delay its independence to wait for Kenya and Uganda so that the three countries would form a federation immediately, but that did not happen, so on December 9, 1961, Tanganyika became independent (Odhiambo et al., 2016).

Following the independence of Tanganyika, the East African High Commission was replaced by the East African Common Services Organization (EACSO), beginning the third phase of the evolution of the East Africa Community. On October 9, 1962, Uganda became independent, and a year later, on December 10 and 12, 1963, Zanzibar and Kenya became independent, respectively. In June 1963, Kenya, Uganda, and Tanganyika announced that they would form a federation in 1964. However, efforts to settle problems with uneven distribution, which had led Uganda and Tanzania to impose restrictions on Kenyan goods, necessitated the Treaty of East African Cooperation in 1967, which established the East African Community (EAC) (Aloo, 2017). However, after 10 years of existence, the community collapsed due to several reasons, including lack of political commitment, use of different economic systems that made it difficult to conduct transactions, disproportionate share of benefits due to different levels of development, lack of private sector participation, and ideological differences under cold war politics (Odhiambo et al., 2016).

In spite of this, the three countries agreed to explore areas of future cooperation. In 1984, a Mediation Agreement to share the assets of the defunct EAC anticipated future cooperation and made it possible for future talks among the heads of state of Kenya, Tanzania, and Uganda. In 1991, at the meeting of Commonwealth heads of state in Harare, Zimbabwe, the three heads of state announced to revive cooperation and appointed a committee to work out the details. The agreement for the Establishment of the Permanent Tripartite Commission for East African Cooperation was signed by all three heads of state on November 30, 1993, and came into full force on March 4, 1996. At its second summit in Arusha in 1997, the three heads of state ordered the Permanent Commission for East African Cooperation to start working on upgrading the agreement, establishing the East African Cooperation into a treaty. On November 30, 1999, the treaty establishing the East African Community (EAC) was signed by all three heads of state. The Permanent Tripartite Commission became the Secretariat of the EAC. Burundi and Rwanda joined the EAC in 2007, South Sudan joined in 2016, and DRC officially became a member on July 11, 2022 Akonor 2008, East African Economic Community, 2022).

8.4 Goals and Expectations of EAC

Article 2 of the Treaty for East African Cooperation Act stated among other things to strengthen and regulate the industrial, commercial, and other relations for accelerated, harmonious, and balanced development and sustained expansion of economic activities the benefit of which will be equitably shared. Among others, the treaty called for (a) the elimination of internal tariff barriers and other charges of equivalent effect on trade among partner states; (b) the removal of nontariff barriers; (c) the establishment of a common external tariff (CET) for all goods imported into partner states; and (d) simplification and harmonization of trade documentation and procedures, etc. The timeline for these was set as follows: become a customs union in 2004, a common market, in 2010 and a monetary union in 2012, and eventually a political federation (Gelan & Omare, 2014, p. 531).

In 2005, the EAC became a customs union, and in 2010 a common market was established followed by a monetary union in 2012. The protocol establishing the customs union provided for removal of tariff and nontariff barriers on intra-EAC trade, establishment of a common external trade policy, a list of sensitive products that needed further protection, and institutional mechanisms needed to operate the union (Aloo, 2017). These institutions included East African Ministries and Ministers, the Common Market Council and Tribunal, the Court of Appeal of East Africa, and East African Legislative Assembly (Gelan & Omare, 2014). Free movement of goods among the partner states is governed by the provisions of the Customs Law of the Community, of the EAC Protocol on Standardization, Quality Assurance, Metrology and Testing, and the EAC Standardization, Quality Assurance, Metrology and Testing Act. Jointly managed border points to expedite movement across borders, as well as pilot border points, have registered success.

In terms of regional integration, the EAC has been commended for being the most successful of Africa's RTAs. It has been reported that compared to other regional trade agreements, EAC has been quite successful in implementing its policies, especially when it comes to trade. These include free trade, a customs union, and a common market (UNECA, 2010; AUC et al., 2016, 2019). How have these manifested themselves in EAC's trade patterns?

8.5 EAC Trade

8.5.1 *Direction of EACs Trade*

In 1995, only 17.8% of EAC's export trade occurred among its members. In 2019, it was 17.7%. The trade with the rest of Africa was consistently between 17.7% and 19.1%. Combining this with intra-EAC trade, EAC's trade with Africa appears to have increased slightly from 1995 to 2019. In 1995, it was 28.2%; in 2019, it was 33.7%. This is more than all the other regional trade agreements discussed in this book. In contrast, trade with partners outside Africa has dominated the EAC's trade, even though its volume may be decreasing. For example, in 1995, about 71.8% of EAC's trade was with partners outside of Africa. In 2019, the percentage of trade with outside Africa was down to 66.3% (Table 8.2).

The breakdown of the rest of the world is given in Fig. 8.2, which shows that Europe used to be the dominant destination of the EAC member countries until 2010. However, after 2010, Asia became the leading destination of EAC's exports. In 2019, it attracted 44.2% of the total export trade of EAC members compared to Europe's 16.5%. Northern America equally accounted for just a little more than it did in 1995. It is commendable that about one-third of EAC's exports have been directed to other African countries.

Table 8.2 Direction of export trade of the East African Community, 1995–2019 (Percentage)

	EAC	Rest of Africa	EAC and Africa	Rest of World	Total
1995	17.8	10.3	28.2	71.8	100
2000	17.9	12.0	29.9	70.1	100
2005	19.1	16.1	35.2	64.8	100
2010	18.8	18.6	37.4	62.6	100
2015	18.6	13.7	32.2	67.8	100
2019	17.7	17.7	33.7	66.3	100

Source: Author's calculation based on data from UNCTADStat

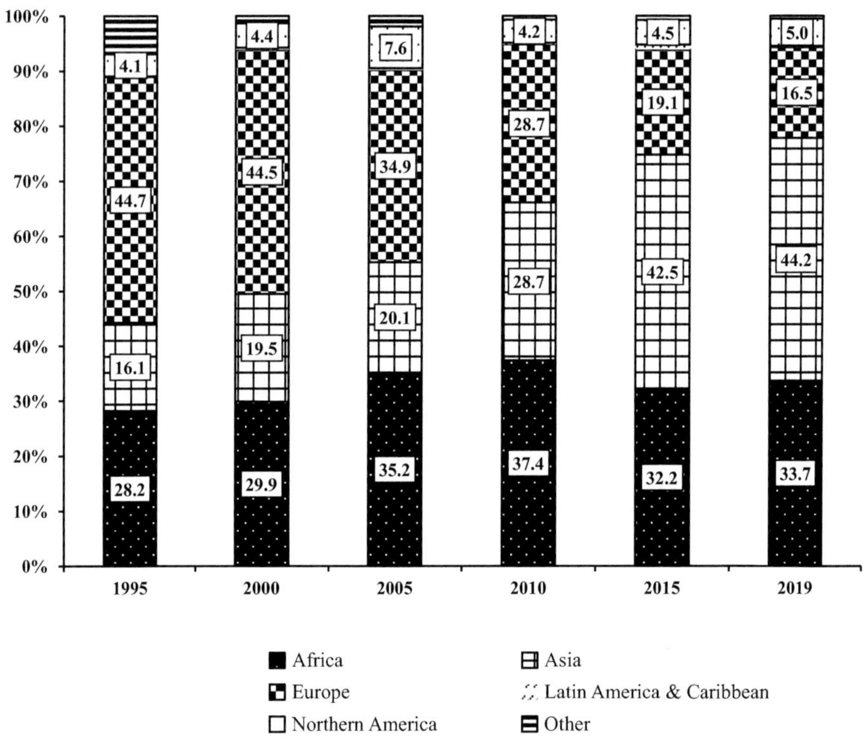

Fig. 8.2 Direction of EAC trade by major regions of the world, 1995–2019

Table 8.3 shows the top 20 exports of EAC. The table shows that with the exception of 2001, the EAC had most of its members in the top 20 export and import partners. In 2001, for example, only one country, Kenya, made the top 20 of EAC's export markets. In 2005, the number went up to five, and then six in both 2010 and 2015, and even seven in 2019 (Table 8.4).

Import trade within the EAC is much less than the export trade (Table 8.4). In 1995, it was only 10.5% of total import trade of EAC. By 2019, it was much lower—being only 8.7%. Overall, the percentage of import trade with the rest of the world from 1995 to 2019 was much higher than export trade. It was 82% compared

Table 8.3 Top 20 export markets of the EAC, 2001–2019

2001		2005		2010		2015		2019	
Country	%	Country	%	Country	%	Country	%	Country	%
UK	13.9	*Uganda	10.0	SUI	7.8	India	8.8	UAE	15.2
NLD	8.2	UK	8.3	China	6.5	*Kenya	8.6	S. Africa	6.4
France	5.9	NLD	7.0	*Uganda	6.5	*Uganda	5.1	India	6.2
*Uganda	5.7	S. Africa	5.4	UK	5.4	*Congo, DR	5.1	*Congo, DR	6.0
Norway	4.3	SUI	4.8	*Kenya	5.0	China	5.0	*Uganda	5.0
*Kenya	4.3	*Tanzania	4.5	*Congo, DR	4.7	S. Africa	4.9	*Kenya	4.6
*Tanzania	4.2	US	4.3	NLD	4.7	NLD	4.0	NLD	4.2
Germany	4.1	*Congo DR	4.3	S. Africa	4.3	UAE	3.8	US	4.0
Pakistan	4.1	*Kenya	3.4	*Tanzania	4.1	US	3.5	Pakistan	3.5
India	3.8	UAE	3.3	Sudan	4.0	UK	3.2	*S. Sudan	3.2
SUI	3.5	Pakistan	3.2	UAE	3.8	*Rwanda	3.1	*Rwanda	2.9
Egypt	3.3	Germany	3.0	*Rwanda	3.6	*S. Sudan	3.0	UK	2.9
Japan	3.1	Belgium	2.5	US	3.2	Germany	3.0	China	2.8
US	2.2	*Rwanda	2.3	India	3.1	*Tanzania	2.7	SUI	2.7
Belgium	2.2	Sudan	2.3	Germany	2.8	Pakistan	2.6	*Tanzania	2.6
UAE	1.9	India	2.1	Japan	2.2	SUI	2.0	Belgium	2.3
Hong Kong	1.5	Egypt	2.1	Pakistan	2.1	Japan	2.0	Viet Nam	2.2
S. Africa	1.5	France	2.0	Belgium	2.1	Belgium	1.9	Germany	1.6
*Congo DR	1.4	China	2.0	Egypt	2.1	Oman	1.8	*Burundi	1.5
*Rwanda	1.3	Japan	1.7	*Burundi	1.6	Egypt	1.5	Egypt	1.4
Total	80.4	Total	78.5	Total	79.8	Total	75.6	Total	81.3

Source: Author's calculation based on International Trade Centers' Trade Map data
NLD Netherlands, *SUI* Switzerland, *S. Africa* South Africa, *S. Sudan* South Sudan;
* EAC members

Table 8.4 Direction of import trade of the East African Community, 1995–2019 (Percentage)

	EAC	Rest of Africa	EAC and Africa	Rest of the world	Total
1995	10.5	1.8	12.3	87.7	100
2000	13.0	15.9	28.9	71.1	100
2005	10.1	14.7	24.8	75.2	100
2010	8.3	11.5	19.8	80.2	100
2015	8.6	8.0	16.6	83.4	100
2019	8.7	9.4	18.0	82.0	100

Source: Author's calculation based on UNCTADStat data

to 66%. Figure 8.3 shows increasing importance of Asia and declining importance of other major regions as import markets for EAC member states. Thus, even in 1995, Asia accounted for 37.7% of EAC's imports, compared to Europe's 34% and Africa's 12.3%. By 2019, Asia's share of imports had reached 62.9%, Europe's

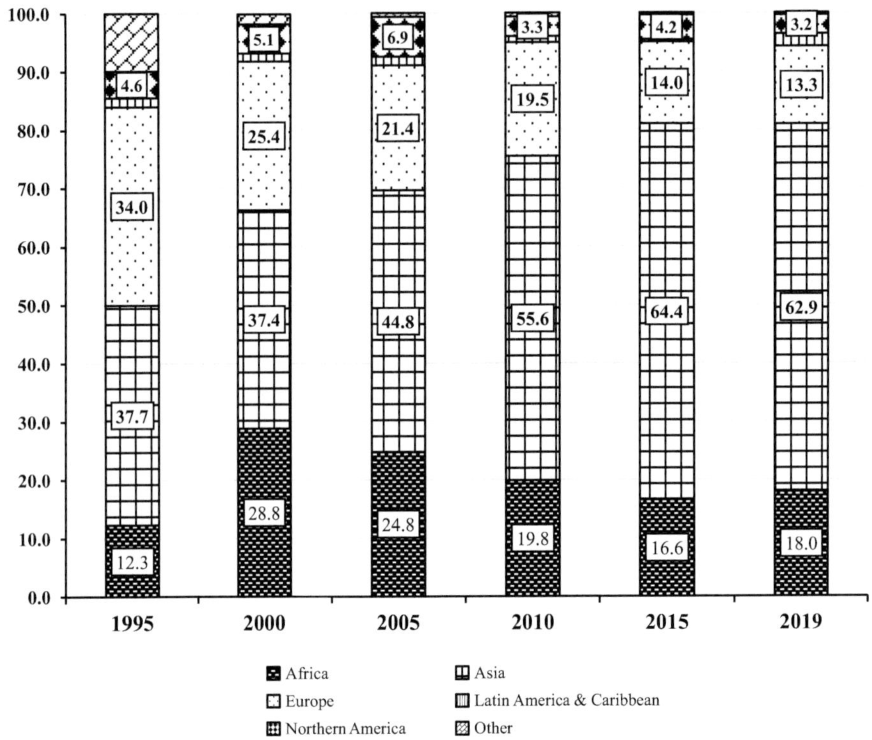

Fig. 8.3 Direction of import trade of the EAC, 1995–2019

share was 13%, with Northern America at 3.2%. Africa's share over the period bounced up and down, reaching 28.8%, its highest, in 2000 and declining afterward to 18% in 2019.

The number of EAC members that made the top 20 of the group's import markets was smaller than those on the top 20 export list. There was only one in 2001, two in 2005, 2010, and 2015, and three in 2019 (Table 8.5). With both the export and import lists, however, the contribution of EAC members to the top 20 list was small even though in 2005, Uganda was the top export destination for the group. We are confronted with two questions. The first is why has the EAC, which is a customs union, been trading more with outside partners than with its own members? The second is, Why do we have more EAC members on the group's top 20 export markets than on its top 20 import markets? We suspect that it is because of the composition of its trade.

Table 8.5 Top 20 import markets of EAC, 2001–2019

2001		2005		2010		2015		2019	
Country	%	Country	%	Country	%	Country	%	Country	%
UAE	10.4	UAE	10.3	India	11.3	S. Arabia	17.1	China	20.0
USA	8.9	S. Africa	9.7	China	11.3	China	16.4	India	11.0
UK	7.8	*Kenya	6.6	UAE	9.9	India	13.6	UAE	9.7
S. Africa	7.6	USA	6.5	S. Africa	6.9	UAE	6.2	S. Arabia	6.3
Japan	6.2	Japan	5.9	Japan	6.5	USA	4.5	Japan	4.8
*Kenya	5.8	India	5.7	UK	3.7	Japan	4.3	S. Africa	4.3
S. Arabia	4.8	China	5.6	Singapore	3.6	S. Africa	3.7	*Kenya	3.6
India	4.7	Bahrain	5.5	*Kenya	3.6	*Kenya	2.4	USA	2.9
Germany	3.9	UK	4.8	S. Arabia	3.3	Indonesia	2.1	*Tanzania	2.8
France	3.3	S. Arabia	3.7	USA	3.1	Germany	2.1	Indonesia	2.4
Belgium	3.2	Germany	3.2	Switzerland	2.8	UK	1.9	Germany	2.4
China	3.0	France	2.7	Germany	2.6	Switzerland	1.5	Egypt	1.6
Australia	2.9	Belgium	2.2	Indonesia	2.2	France	1.5	UK	1.5
Italy	2.4	NLD	2.2	NLD	2.0	Russia	1.4	Türkiye	1.4
Indonesia	2.2	Indonesia	2.0	France	1.8	Uganda	1.3	Russia	1.3
Netherlands	1.8	Italy	1.8	S. Korea	1.8	S. Korea	1.2	Netherlands	1.3
Bahrain	1.7	Sweden	1.1	Belgium	1.3	NLD	1.1	Malaysia	1.3
Singapore	1.2	Egypt	1.0	Egypt	1.3	Egypt	1.0	Uganda	1.2
S. Korea	1.1	Singapore	1.0	Italy	1.3	Italy	1.0	Thailand	1.1
Thailand	1.0	*Tanzania	0.9	*Uganda	1.2	Thailand	0.9	Italy	1.1
Total	83.9	Total	82.5	Total	81.5	Total	85.0	Total	81.7

Source: Author's calculation based on International Trade Center Trade Map data;
* EAC members

Table 8.6 Composition of export and import trade of the EAC, 1995–2019 (Percent shares)

	Primary Goods		Manufactured Goods		Unclassified Goods	
	Export	Import	Export	Import	Export	Import
1995	80.9	26.6	18.6	72.2	0.5	1.1
2000	82.7	34.1	18.6	63.5	2	2.4
2005	76.4	30.3	21.8	66.4	1.8	3.3
2010	75.3	33.9	24.2	65.2	0.5	0.9
2015	79.4	33.6	19.7	65.0	0.9	1.4
2019	83.5	35.1	16.3	64.0	0.2	0.8

Source: Author's calculation based on UNCTADStat

Table 8.7 Commodity composition of export trade of EAC

Commodity	1995	2000	2005	2010	2015	2019
Food	63.8	56.1	41.7	42.2	38.0	34.3
Agricultural raw materials	10.8	10.0	11.3	9.3	6.2	6.7
Ores and metals	1.6	3.0	4.6	9.9	6.1	4.0
Fuels	3.0	7.1	10.1	3.3	18.5	13.4
Pearls, precious stones, and NMG	1.6	6.4	8.8	10.7	10.6	25.1
Chemical products	4.1	3.8	4.7	5.4	4.1	3.7
Machinery and transport equipment	2.3	1.8	3.0	4.8	3.6	2.5
Other manufactured goods	12.2	9.7	14.2	14.0	11.9	10.1
Unassigned	0.5	2.0	1.8	0.5	0.9	0.2
Total	100	100	100	100	100	100

Source: Author's calculation based on UNCTADStat

8.5.2 *Composition of EAC's Trade*

Composition of EAC's export trade is dominated by primary commodities while its import trade consists more of manufactured merchandise (Table 8.6). For example, in 1995, primary commodities constituted 80.9% of EAC's total export trade. In 2019, it was 83.5% of total export trade. In between the 2 years, it fluctuated between 75% and 79%. Food was the largest group of exports, followed by fuel, other manufactured goods, and pearls, precious stones, and nonmonetary gold (Table 8.7). With imports, it was the reverse. Manufactured goods accounted for 72% of EAC's imports in 1995. In 2019, it was down to 64.4% but still high (Table 8.6). Machinery and transportation equipment were the largest group, followed by other manufactures, fuels, chemical products, and food (Table 8.8).

Intraregional trade of the group, as well as trade with the rest of Africa, mirror this general pattern of EAC's trade. Recall that intraregional export trade of the EAC from 1995 to 2019 has been less than 20%. Of this, Table 8.9 shows the composition of export trade within the EAC. The table shows that within the EAC, food, other manufactured goods, and chemical products were the most predominant exports of the EAC. Fuel was important but has recently declined remarkably. Over

Table 8.8 Commodity composition import trade of EAC

Commodity	1995	2000	2005	2010	2015	2019
Food	13.6	12.0	9.7	11.2	10.1	11.9
Agricultural raw materials	2.3	2.2	1.5	1.4	1.3	1.4
Ores and metals	2.1	1.5	1.3	1.4	2.9	2.5
Fuels	8.6	18.3	17.7	19.9	19.2	15.6
Pearls, precious stones and NMG	0.1	0.0	0.1	0.0	0.1	3.7
Chemical products	13.4	12.3	14.7	14.3	13.4	14.0
Machinery and transport equipment	33.2	30.8	27.6	28.3	27.3	25.7
Other manufactured goods	25.5	20.4	24.2	22.5	24.4	24.3
Unassigned	1.1	2.4	3.3	0.9	1.4	0.8
Total	100	100	100	100	100	100

Source: Author's calculation based on UNCTADStat

Table 8.9 Export trade within EAC

Year	1995	2000	2005	2010	2015	2019
Food	27.4	21.1	17.2	33.5	34.8	33.9
Agricultural raw materials	2.7	1.4	1.4	2.3	1.9	1.0
Ores and metals	3.7	3.6	2.3	2.4	2.6	2.3
Fuels	8.3	30.5	34.4	6.5	5.1	4.8
Pearls, precious stones, and NMG	0.0	0.1	0.1	6.1	0.0	15.0
Chemical products	12.8	10.1	10.9	12.0	11.8	11.2
Machinery and transport equipment	8.0	5.0	7.0	8.9	12.6	6.9
Other manufactured goods	37.0	28.2	26.6	28.0	29.7	24.7
Unassigned	0.2	0.1	0.1	0.2	1.5	0.3
Total	100	100	100	100	100	100

Table 8.10 Import trade within EAC

Year	1995	2000	2005	2010	2015	2019
Food	23.1	14.1	16.8	19.2	31.5	30.3
Agricultural raw materials	2.0	1.1	1.3	1.3	1.8	1.0
Ores and metals	4.2	3.4	2.3	4.1	3.0	2.6
Fuels	10.7	41.2	35.3	10.5	5.4	5.2
Pearls, precious stones, and NMG	0.0	0.0	0.2	0.0	0.0	18.4
Chemical products	12.7	8.5	10.8	17.1	13.2	11.4
Machinery and transport equipment	8.9	4.6	6.8	13.2	12.1	6.2
Other manufactured goods	38.4	27.0	26.5	34.3	32.1	24.8
Unassigned	0.0	0.0	0.1	0.3	1.0	0.3
	100	100	100	100	100	100

Table 8.11 EAC export trade with the rest of Africa (Percent shares)

Year	1995	2000	2005	2010	2015	2019
Food	36.3	34.4	24.2	33.5	36.0	36.6
Agricultural raw materials	2.5	1.8	1.7	2.3	2.2	2.0
Ores and metals	2.7	3.5	2.4	2.4	1.8	1.8
Fuels	9.1	20.6	23.9	6.5	8.3	8.8
Pearls, precious stones, and NMG	0.0	2.1	7.6	6.3	6.2	15.7
Chemical products	11.2	10.1	9.7	12.0	9.9	8.9
Machinery and transport equipment	6.4	3.8	6.6	8.9	9.4	5.9
Other manufactured goods	31.6	23.6	23.7	27.9	25.2	20.2
Unassigned	0.3	0.2	0.1	0.2	0.9	0.2
Total	100	100	100	100	100	100

Table 8.12 ECA import trade with the rest of Africa (Percentage share)

	1995	2000	2005	2010	2015	2019
Food	23.7	14.3	11.8	19.2	21.8	23.9
Agricultural raw materials	1.9	0.9	1.2	1.3	1.5	0.9
Ores and metals	5.3	2.9	3.1	4.1	13.3	9.5
Fuels	10.1	20.4	16.1	10.5	4.6	4.3
Pearls, precious stones, and NMG	0.0	0.0	0.1	0.0	0.0	13.9
Chemical products	12.2	11.8	11.6	17.1	15.7	12.8
Machinery and transport equipment	9.8	29.5	19.4	13.2	14.7	8.5
Other manufactured goods	36.9	20.0	36.7	34.3	27.9	26.0
Unassigned	0.2	0.1	0.1	0.3	0.6	0.2
	100	100	100	100	100	100

all, it appears that the list of export trade in manufactured goods constituted a higher percentage than primary products. With regards to imports, the largest were food imports, followed by other manufactured goods, chemical products, and machinery and equipment (Table 8.10).

EAC's trade with Africa is also small. Table 8.11 shows that the top export products have been food, other manufactured goods, and chemical products. On the import side, other manufactured goods, food, chemical products, and machinery and transport equipment made up the most important trading items. It is interesting to see that EAC's trade with the world is heavily tilted toward primary goods, yet trade within the EAC showed more engagement with manufactured goods. The implication here is that EAC members would trade with each other and with the rest of Africa if the economies of Africa were restructured to produce more manufactured goods, Africa (Table 8.12).

8.6 Explanations for the EAC's Trade Performance

Several reasons have been given for the relatively weak intraregional trade within the EAC (See, for example, Mathieson, 2016; Aloo, 2017; Gelan & Omare, 2014). Mathieson (2016) discussed 10 points, some of which we present here. First, a large number of rules governing the EAC have not been institutionalized and this has hindered the effective operation of EAC. These include the budget process, rules establishing relations among member states, and financing. Second, state bureaucracies and politics have tended to interfere with EAC policies, making it difficult to implement them. Third, a reliance on donor financing makes it difficult to implement policies that favor the EAC more than donor interests. Fourth, the hegemonic position of Kenya in the EAC and a clash of interests between Kenyan and Tanzanian elites are still problematic for the EAC. Kenya's interest is crucial for the survival of the EAC, but given that its dominance caused the collapse of the first EAC, it is a balancing act for Kenya and the EAC.

Fifth, overlapping membership also complicates the implementation of a CET. For example, Burundi is a member of the Economic Community of Central African States (ECCAS) and the Common Market for Eastern and Southern Africa (COMESA). Kenya and Uganda are also members of COMESA and the Intergovernmental Authority on Development (IGAD), while Tanzania is also a member of the Southern African Development Community (SADC). The EAC Customs Union Protocol requires member states to fulfill all their other membership obligations. This makes it difficult to implement the rules that are binding in the EAC but different from other RTAs. There have been talks of a tripartite EAC, COMESA, and SADC common external tariff (CET) that might help, but for now, overlapping memberships is problematic for enforcing EAC's CET. Sixth, lack of economic complementarities and poor infrastructure deficit and logistics take all the incentive from intraregional trade and make trading very expensive. Seventh, it appears the EAC lacks a consistent mechanism for monitoring trade among its membership. This is due to the reluctance on the part of members to establish a supranational authority and the differences in national capacity of member states in implementation and enforcement of trade rules and regulations. The result is that the EAC Secretariat does not have the mandate to monitor trade or the power to follow up with institutions charged with monitoring trade. Instead, implementation and enforcement are left with national governments.

These problems and issues have been echoed by other researchers, such as Aloo (2017) and Gelan and Omare (2014). For example, the customs union protocols were completed in 2004, and goods from Uganda and Tanzania entering Kenya did not pay any duties. However, goods from Kenya entering Uganda and Tanzania were divided into two groups. Category A goods entered duty-free but Category B goods had to pay a phased tariff of 10, 8, 6, 4, and 2% over a period of 5 years (Aloo, 2017). Now, all the protocols have been completely implemented, but goods are still subject to domestic taxes at the borders. Second, there are also exceptions to the common tariff to nonmembers when any member state wants to address adverse effects brought by implementation of the common tariff protocol. Thus, there are three bands of tariff rates that range from 0%, 10%, to 25% (Aloo, 2017).

Similarly, Gelan and Omare (2014) examined the removal of tariffs on intraregional milk trade in the EAC using a spatial equilibrium model and found that removing tariffs alone would not increase welfare within the region unless it was accompanied by trade-enhancing measures such as removal of nontariff barriers and reduction transportation cost.

All these problems are very important, but the lack of economic complementarities and competitiveness arguably are the most important factor in the EAC's low intraregional trade. EAC countries export mainly primary unprocessed products and import mainly finished consumer and capital goods. Not only that but like other African countries, they import twice as much as they export or consume twice as much as they produce in trade value terms. The result is that there is no incentive to be committed to enforcing the rules of the common market. In its assessment of Africa's regional economic integration, the United Nations Economic Commission for Africa (2010, p. 17) noted:

> The leading economic activities of the EAC member States today are agriculture, which contributes an average of 39 per cent of GDP and provides employment to 85 per cent of the population; tourism, which contributes an average of 14 per cent of GDP … and manufacturing, which contributes an average of 10.4 per cent of GDP …. Evidently, a great deal more effort must be applied to boost the region's industrial and manufacturing sector and to enhance food security.

After 10 years, not much has changed, and unless the challenge to boost the manufacturing sector is taken up, Gastorn and Masinde's (2017, p. 208) characterization of the EAC Common Market as "a label more widely applied than practiced" will continue to be the case.

8.7 Conclusion

The EAC cut its teeth in colonial Africa. However, within 10 years of postcolonial Africa (1967–1977), it collapsed due to asymmetrical relationships within its ranks. With this background, it did not take long to get back on its feet after it decided to revamp itself in 1999. Within two decades of its resuscitation, the EAC has become one of the most successful RTAs in Africa, having moved from a free trade area through a customs union to a common market. In spite of these characterizations, the EAC has not performed as well as expected in intraregional trade. In 2005, for example, intraregional trade accounted for a mere 19.1% in terms of export trade, while it was even lower—10.1%—for import trade. In 2019, the intra-EAC export trade accounted for 17.7%, and import trade 8.7%. In contrast, export trade outside Africa was 64.8% in 2005, while import trade was 75.2%. In 2019, export outside of Africa was 66.3% of total export trade and 82% of total import trade. Several reasons have been advanced for this low intraregional trade performance. These include heavy reliance on foreign capital, overlapping memberships in other RTAs, poor infrastructure, weak institutions to enforce rules governing trade, and lack of economic complementarities. We have argued that of these, the lack of economic complementarities is the most important one. This is because, without any member state that can count as an industrialized country and given the situation where the countries produce and export primary goods and consume a lot of manufactured goods, it is not surprising that there is little intraregional trade. To boost intraregional trade, EAC members must industrialize.

References

African Union Commission (AUC), African Development Bank (AfDB), & United Nations Economic Commission for Africa (UNECA). (2016). *Africa regional integration index I 2016*. Addis Ababa: UNECA.

African Union Commission (AUC), African Development Bank (AfDB), & United Nations Economic Commission for Africa (UNECA). (2019). *Africa regional integration index 2019*. Addis Ababa: UNECA.

Akonor, K. (2008). *African economic institutions*. Taylor & Francis Group.

Aloo, L. O. (2017). Free movement of goods in the EAC. In E. Ugirashebuja, J. E. Ruhangisa, T. Ottervanger, & A. Cuyvers (Eds.), *East African Community law: Institutional, substantive and comparative EU aspects* (pp. 303–325). Brill.

East African Economic Community. (2022). *History*. https://www.eac.int/customs-union. Accessed August 11, 2022.

Gastorn, K., & Masinde, W. (2017). The EAC common market. In E. Ugirashebuja, J. E. Ruhangisa, T. Ottervanger, & A. Cuyvers (Eds.), *East African Community law: Institutional, substantive and comparative EU aspects* (pp. 285–292). Brill.

Gelan, A., & Omore, A. (2014). Beyond tariffs: The role of non-tariff barriers in dairy trade in the East African Community free trade area development. *Policy Review, 32*(5), 523–543.

Mathieson, C. (2016). *The political economy of regional integration in Africa: The East African Community (EAC) report*. ECDPM.

McAuliffe, C., Saxena, S. C., & Yabara, M. (2012). *East African Community: Prospects for sustained growth*. International Monetary Fund.

Odhiambo, M., Chitiga, R., & Ebobrah, S. (2016). *The civil society guide to regional economic communities in Africa*. African Minds.

United Nations Economic Commission for Africa (UNECA). (2010). *Assessing regional integration of Africa IV: Enhancing intra-African trade*. United Nations Economic Commission of Africa.

Chapter 9
The Common Market for Eastern and Southern Africa

9.1 Introduction

The Common Market for Eastern and Southern Africa (COMESA) is the second largest regional trade agreement in Africa in terms of the number of member countries. (Fig. 9.1). After a long, slow, and arduous process, COMESA came into force in 1994. Since then it has been seen as one of the more successful RTAs in Africa. For that reason, the African Union recognized it as one of the foundation blocks of the AfCFTA. In this chapter, we examine how COMESA has performed as far as trade is concerned and the extent to which it can serve as a founding block in bringing about the African Continental Free Trade Area (AfCFTA). The chapter is in five sections. First, it presents some basic facts about COMESA. Second, it reviews the major events that led to the formation of COMESA. Third, it examines its objectives and expectations. Fourth, it focuses on the performance of COMESA with respect to trade. Fifth, it attempts to find explanations for COMESA's trade performance. Finally, it ends with a conclusion.

9.2 Some Basic Information About COMESA

As shown in Fig. 9.1, COMESA consists of 19 countries in Eastern and Southern Africa. Table 9.1 provides some basic information about these countries. From the table, these 19 countries cover a total area of 11,077,614 km^2 which is 36.8% of Africa's total land area. Its total population of 566,127,352, was about 42.7% of Africa's total population, in 2019. Its estimated total GDP purchasing power parity of US$793.3 billion in 2019, was about 31.8% of Africa's total GDP in that year. However, there are also considerable asymmetries. Five of the 19 countries, Congo DR, Egypt, Ethiopia. Libya, and Sudan, have more than a million km^2 each in land

B. Ofori-Amoah, *The African Continental Free Trade Area*,
https://doi.org/10.1007/978-3-031-59181-5_9

Fig. 9.1 Member States of the Common Market for Eastern and Southern Africa (COMESA). (Data source: ICPAC GEOPORTA. The analysis was performed in ArcGIS Pro 3.1.0)

area. Together, these five countries encompass 73.3% of the total land area of COMESA. About 54% of the total population of COMESA live in three countries—Ethiopia, Egypt, and Congo DR. About 50.8% of COMESA's GDP purchasing power parity in 2019 was due to two countries—Egypt and Kenya. If Congo DR is added the three countries' share of the total GDP rises to 62.9%.

While all but one of the countries were former colonies of Europe, their colonial experiences differed by the type of colonial administration they had. These included British, French, and Italian colonial administrations. The cultural mosaic is even more complex than the shared colonial histories. As a result, there is no one com-

Table 9.1 Some basic information about COMESA, 2019

Country	Area (Km^2)	Population	GDP (US$)	GDP Per Capita, PPP (US $)
Burundi	27,830	11,874,838	2,581,268,125	783
Comoros	2170	790,986	1,195,019,559	3188
Congo DR	2,345,410	89,906,891	51,775,830,726	1144
Djibouti	22,000	1,073,994	3,088,853,639	5482
Egypt	1,001,450	105,618,671	303,080,865,604	12,260
Eritrea	121,320	3,498,818	..	..
Eswatini	17,360	1,169,613	4,466,066,557	9018
Ethiopia	1,127,127	114,120,594	95,912,590,628	2315
Kenya	582,650	50,951,450	100,379,713,697	4647
Libya	1,759,540	6,569,088	69,252,306,372	22,764
Madagascar	587,040	27,533,134	14,191,911,512	1687
Malawi	118,480	18,867,337	11,025,370,769	1602
Mauritius	1860	1,296,279	14,045,808,843	23,835
Rwanda	26,338	12,835,028	10,356,327,149	2322
Seychelles	71,740	104,373	1,684,228,529	30,605
Sudan	1,886,068	43,232,093	32,338,079,165	4350
Uganda	236,040	42,949,080	35,353,060,634	2275
Zambia	752,610	18,380,477	23,308,667,781	3617
Zimbabwe	390,580	15,354,608	19,284,289,739	2408
Total	11,077,614	566,127,352	793,320,259,030	

Source: United Nations Population Division

mon African language among the member states, but rather a fragmented lingua franca for certain groups of countries such as Swahili and Arabic in Eastern Africa.

9.3 The Formation of COMESA

Mwale (2001) credits the formation of COMESA to the United Nations Economic Commission for Africa (UNECA) and the Organization of African Unity (OAU). The effort began in 1963 when the UNECA sent an interdisciplinary team on industrial development in eastern Africa to organize a conference for the independent nations at that time. Afterward, the Eastern Subregional Office was expanded to cover Eastern and Southern Subregional Office in 1964. The first meeting of Ministers to seriously consider cooperation and integration of countries in the subregion met is Lusaka 1965 under the auspices of the UNECA. At a follow-up meeting later that year in Addis Ababa, 11 African countries adopted and signed the Articles of Association with a charge to recommend to their Governments the establishment of an Economic Community for cooperation in the subregion (Mwale, 2001). The countries were Burundi, Ethiopia, Kenya, Madagascar, Malawi, Mauritius, Rwanda, Somalia, Sudan, Tanzania, and Zambia.

Two follow-up meetings were held in Kampala in 1968 and in Lusaka in 1969. Mwale (2001) reports that the Kampala Meeting was attended by more countries upon the invitation of the then Prime Minister of Uganda, Milton Obote. However, much of the conference focused on unity in general. The Lusaka Meeting drew more countries than before, including representatives of all the liberation movements that were going on in Africa. As a result, the meeting concluded that there could be no economic integration without peace and issued the Lusaka Manifesto, which essentially stated that African countries wanted peaceful resolution to liberation movement, but would fight to the end if that option was not granted. At that time, the United Nations set up Multinational Interdisciplinary Advisory Teams (UNDATS) to give assistance to the least-developed countries in Africa.

The 1970–1977 period was a low point in the movement toward regional cooperation. Mwale (2001) attributes this to two major developments. First, was the escalation of the wars of independence in Southern Rhodesia (Zimbabwe), Southwest Africa (Namibia), and in the Portuguese colonies of Angola and Mozambique, which pushed regional cooperation except the wars to the back burner. The second was the collapse of the East Africa Community in 1977, which raised doubts in the minds of many leaders about the future of regional cooperation. In the meantime, by 1975, it had become clear that the UNDATS were not equipped to deal with all the issues facing African countries given that they were only advisory. A Conference of African Planners in Addis Ababa in 1976 therefore recommended that the UNDATS and the UNECA Subregional offices be phased out and replaced by UNECA Multinational Programming and Operational Centers (MULPOCs). A total of five MULPOCs were established across the continent. The office for Eastern and Southern Africa was opened in Lusaka, Zambia, in 1977 (Mwale, 2001). This office was in charge of 18 countries—Angola, Botswana, Comoros, Djibouti, Ethiopia, Kenya, Lesotho, Madagascar, Malawi, Mauritius, Mozambique, Seychelles, Somalia, Swaziland, Tanzania, Uganda, Zambia, and Zimbabwe. In March 1978, renewed interest due in part to integration enthusiasts then at the helm of UNECA, particularly the new Executive Secretary Adebayo Adedeji and his staff, the first Conference of the Ministers of Trade, Finance, and Planning met in Addis Ababa to adopt the Lusaka Declaration of Intent and Commitment to a Preferential Trade Area (PTA). The conference also established an intergovernmental negotiating team (INT) and a timetable for launching the PTA. The INT met in Addis Ababa in June 1978 and established the PTA principles and protocols. In February 1979, the Lusaka MULPOC Council of Ministers met in Nairobi and decided to launch the PTA by May 1980. However, the PTA Treaty was signed and launched on December 21, 1981, in Lusaka, Zambia, by nine countries—Comoros, Djibouti, Ethiopia, Kenya, Malawi, Mauritius, Uganda, and Zambia.

Under the PTA framework, a trade liberalization process was achieved through a Common List or commodities in which member states expressed imports and export interests to be given preferential treatment in intraregional trade. The list was to be negotiated every 2 years. The first Common List was negotiated in December 1983 and came into effect on July 1, 1984, six months after the negotiation of the list per Article 6 of the PTA (Chanthunya, 2001). The PTA called for the elimination of tariffs 10 years after its implementation, which was in 1992. However, concern over loss of revenue by member states led to the adoption of a progressive reduction of tariffs of 10% every year from 1988 to 1996, 20% in 1998, and 30% in 2000. The Common List submitted by member states required matching imports and exports interest. Export interests that did not include import interests and vice versa were not included in the Common List. It was realized that it would take a long time to get all the commodities member states wanted on the Common List because of the requirement. As a result, in 1993, the Common List was abolished for giving preferential treatment to all goods produced and traded in the region, if they met the PTA's Rules of Origin (Chanthunya, 2001).

In December 1994, the agreement to change the name from PTA to the Common Market for Eastern and Southern Africa (COMESA) to reflect the true nature of the organization was signed in Kampala, Uganda. A new progressive reduction of tariff was implemented—60% in 1993, 70% in 1994, 80% in 1996, 90% in 1998, and 100% in 2000. The provisions for elimination of non-tariff barriers, which had started in 1985 with a timetable, received a boost in member states that implemented the structural adjustment programs and trade liberalization policies of the World Bank-International Monetary Fund (IMF) programs. In 1999, some of its Rules of Origin, which were deemed cumbersome, were changed. In October 2000, COMESA became a free trade area, when nine of its member states Djibouti, Egypt, Kenya, Madagascar, Malawi, Mauritius, Sudan, Zambia, and Zimbabwe removed tariffs on products originating from COMESA in line with the timetable agreed upon in 1992 by the membership (Geda & Kebret, 2007). The original members were Burundi, Djibouti, Egypt, Kenya, Madagascar, Malawi, Mauritius, Rwanda, Sudan, Zambia, and Zimbabwe. In 2006, Libya and Comoros joined the FTA (Ebaidalla & Yahia, 2014). In June 2009, it launched its customs union with the hope of becoming a monetary union by 2018 (Cheluget & Wright, 2017).

9.4 The Objectives and Expectations of COMESA

As spelt in its booklet COMESA in Brief the objectives of COMESA are as follows:

(a) To create and maintain a full free trade area guaranteeing the free movement of goods and services produced within COMESA and the removal of all tariffs and non-tariff barriers
(b) A customs union under which goods and services imported from non-COMESA countries will attract an agreed single tariff (Common External Tariff) in all COMESA Member States
(c) Free movement of capital and investment supported by the adoption of a common investment area so as to create a more favorable investment climate for the COMESA region
(d) Gradual establishment of a payment union based on the COMESA Clearing House and the eventual establishment of a common monetary union with a common currency and
(e) Gradual relaxation and eventual elimination of visa requirements leading to the free movement of persons, labor, service, right of establishment, and residence

COMESA's main institutions include the Secretariat located in Lusaka, Zambia, COMESA Business Council, COMESA PTA Bank, COMESA Insurance Agencies in Harare, Zimbabwe; the African Leather and Leather Products Institute in Addis Ababa, Ethiopia; the COMESA Court of Justice in Khartoum, Sudan, the Federation of Women in Business and COMESA Competition Commission in Lilongwe, Malawi; the Regional Association of Energy Regulators for Eastern and Southern Africa (RAERESA) and the East African Power Pool based in Addis Ababa, Ethiopia.

COMESA has been evaluated by researchers since its founding. Geda and Kebret (2007) found two sets of issues: the first was an implementation issue and the second was an approach issue. Specifically, they concluded that the performance of COMESA was constrained by variation in initial conditions, compensation issues, real political commitment, overlapping membership, lack of diversification, policy harmonization, and lack of private sector participation. The result is that COMESA had insignificant effects on bilateral trade.

Assessing COMESA as a regional economic integration, the United Nations Economic Commission for Africa (UNECA) (2010, pp. 13–14) noted the following challenges:

- Accession of all Member States to the COMESA FTA before launching the COMESA customs union
- Finalizing of the regional framework on trade in services
- Fully implementing COMESA trade and transit transportation facilitation instrument to enhance the movement of transit and cross-border traffic
- Establishing a seamless rail transportation system in the COMESA region and
- Establishing a COMESA Monetary Institute to make the necessary preparations for a COMESA Monetary Union. The COMESA Clearing House needs to accelerate the establishment of the Regional Payment and Settlement System (REPS) to become operational.

Kasekende and Abuka (1998) found that intraregional trade within COMESA since its founding has been sluggish. In 1982, it was 5.65%; in 1993, it was 5.51%. They attributed this to the fact that the relatively more industrialized economies of Kenya and Zimbabwe benefited the most. In addition, the removal of tariffs had proceeded slower than it was expected. For example, from 1994 to 1997 only two countries were able to meet the tariff-reduction targets that were set.

Other factors include lack of political will to implement what was agreed to; lack of necessary conditions—the smallness of most African markets and the similarities of most of the economies and inappropriate regional grouping; weak infrastructure; inconvertible currencies; wide disparities in industrialization levels and dependence on trade taxes; lack of common interests—countries had little trade among themselves before the formation of the RTA, while they established stronger trade ties with outsiders. It is thus unrealistic to expect that all of a sudden, these countries will change their long-established trading links. In the next section, we take a closer look at COMESA's trade pattern to ascertain the extent to which such trade patterns will support the AfCFTA.

9.5 Trade of COMESA

9.5.1 Direction of COMESA Trade

Table 9.2 shows the general pattern of COMESA's trade. The table shows that intra-regional trade has not improved much since its formation. In 1995, only 7.4% of export trade was conducted within COMESA. In 2019, intraregional export trade was still under 10%. Trade with the rest of Africa shows a similar pattern, However, the percentage share of trade with Africa increased slightly over the past decade, rising to 22.9% in 2015. In contrast, trade with the rest of the world over the same period accounted for more than 70% of total trade. Thus, like all its fellow RTAs, COMESA trades more with countries outside its group than those within it.

Figure 9.2 provides a broad breakdown of where in the rest of the world COMESA trades. The figure shows that COMESA's traditional trading partner was Europe. In 1995, about 61% of COMESA's export trade was with Europe. At that time Asia was in a distant second with only 16% of COMESA's export trade. However, over the years, the share of Europe as the top destination of COMESA's exports began declining while Asia's share rose. By 2019, Europe and Asia were at par as top destinations of COMESA's exports (Fig. 9.2). The share of other regions—Northern America—became stagnant over the years.

Table 9.3 shows the top 20 export markets of COMESA from 2001 to 2019. Table 9.3 shows that in 2001, not a single member of COMESA made the top 20 export markets of the group. One country—Uganda—made the list in 2005, while three countries made the list in 2010, 2015, and 2019.

Table 9.4 shows that COMESA's import trade within itself reached 6.2% only in 2005. Combined import trade in COMESA and Africa was only 9% in 1995. It reached 16.3% in 2005 but by 2019 it was down to 12.2%. In contrast, the import trade with the rest of the world was 91% in 1995. It went down to 83.7% in 2005, but by 2019 it was back to 87.8%.

Figure 9.3 shows that in 1995, Europe accounted for 48.7% of COMESA's imports, Asia accounted for 24.2%, and Northern America (US and Canada) 10.1%. Over the years, Europe's position as the major source of COMESA's imports declined and by 2019 it was down to 30.5%. At the same time, Asia's share as a source of COMESA's import trade increased, overtaking Europe by 2010. In 2019,

Table 9.2 Direction of export trade of COMESA. 1995–2019 in percentage shares

	COMESA	Africa	COMESA and Africa	Rest of World	Total Trade
1995	7.4	3.7	11.1	88.9	100
2000	7.6	5.4	13.1	86.9	100
2005	6.5	4.3	10.8	89.2	100
2010	6.8	4.7	11.5	88.5	100
2015	10.0	12.9	22.9	77.1	100
2019	9.6	9.6	19.3	80.7	100

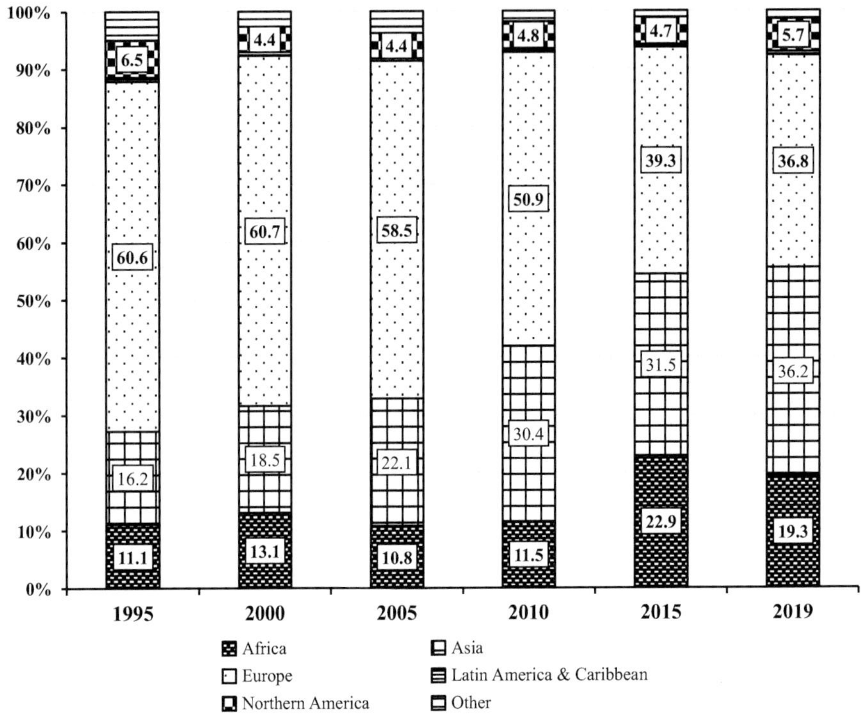

Fig. 9.2 Direction of export trade of COMESA, 1995–2019

Asia accounted for 48.5% of COMESA's import trade. Table 9.5 shows the breakdown of the top 20 import markets of COMESA from 2001 to 2019. Only one member of COMESA, Kenya, made the top 20 import markets in 2001 and 2005. For the rest of the period, 2010, 2015, and 2019, no member country made the list (Table 9.5). Overall, COMESA traded more with countries outside of Africa than inside of Africa. The obvious question is why? We argue that a greater part of this is because of the composition of COMESA's trade.

9.5.2 Composition of COMESA Trade

The composition of both export and import trade of COMESA is not very different from the trade of other RTAs in Africa. Thus, COMESA's export trade tended to be dominated by primary goods while its import trade is dominated by manufactured goods. For example, in 1995 primary goods accounted for 68% of COMESA's merchandise export. In 2019, primary goods still accounted for 69.8% of total exports (Table 9.6). In contrast, manufactured goods constituted 70% of total import in 1995. In 2019, it was down to 62.9% but still substantial.

Table 9.3 Top 20 export markets of COMESA, 2001–2019

2001		2005		2010		2015		2019	
Country	%	Country	%	Country	%	Country	%	Country	%
Italy	19.5	Italy	20.3	Italy	17.4	S. Africa	11.1	China	12.2
Germany	8.3	Germany	8.8	China	16.0	Italy	9.4	Italy	11.1
Spain	7.3	China	8.0	France	7.2	SUI	6.0	S. Africa	7.3
UK	6.5	Spain	6.3	Spain	5.1	China	6.0	UAE	7.3
France	5.9	USA	6.1	USA	3.7	UAE	5.8	Spain	4.4
S. Africa	5.1	France	5.4	SUI	3.7	*Tanzania	3.7	USA	4.4
China	4.4	UK	3.9	UAE	3.2	USA	3.6	SUI	3.0
USA	4.1	Türkiye	3.8	S. Africa	3.2	S. Arabia	3.2	France	3.0
Belgium	3.4	SUI	3.6	UK	2.7	France	3.1	UK	2.7
Türkiye	3.3	S. Africa	2.6	NLD	2.5	UK	3.0	Türkiye	2.3
SUI	2.5	NLD	2.4	Germany	2.1	NLD	2.9	Tanzania	2.1
NLD	2.2	Belgium	1.8	India	2.1	Türkiye	2.2	NLD	2.1
MOZ	1.5	Greece	1.5	S. Arabia	2.0	India	2.1	S. Arabia	1.9
India	1.3	UAE	1.4	Greece	1.9	Spain	1.9	Singapore	1.9
Tunisia	1.3	S. Arabia	1.3	Zambia	1.4	Germany	1.8	India	1.8
Greece	1.2	India	1.1	Türkiye	1.2	DRC	1.6	DRC	1.6
Singapore	1.1	Japan	1.1	Libya	1.2	Kenya	1.3	Germany	1.5
Japan	1.0	Uganda	0.9	Belgium	1.1	Singapore	1.3	Greece	1.4
Austria	0.9	Tunisia	0.9	Sudan	1.1	Belgium	1.1	Kenya	1.1
S. Arabia	0.9	Portugal	0.8	Egypt	0.8	Uganda	1.1	Malta	1.1
Total	81.7	Total	82.0	Total	79.6	Total	72.2	Total	74.1

Source: Author's calculation based on UNCTADStat data
MOZ Mozambique, *NLD* Netherlands, *SUI* Switzerland, *S. Arabia* Saudi Arabia, *S. Africa* South Africa

Table 9.4 Direction import trade of COMESA, 1995–2019

	COMESA	Africa	COMESA and Africa	Rest of the World	Total
1995	5.3	3.7	9.0	91.0	100
2000	5.7	10.0	15.7	84.3	100
2005	6.2	10.1	16.3	83.7	100
2010	5.8	8.5	14.3	85.7	100
2015	5.3	7.8	13.1	86.9	100
2019	5.1	7.1	12.2	87.8	100

Source: Author's calculation based on UNCTADStat data

With respect to export trade, the most important export trade items of COMESA have been fuel, food, ores and metals, and other manufactured goods. Some of these items have become increasingly important over the years while others have declined in the share of total export. For example, the percentage share of food in total exports has bounced 10.6% and 21.5% (Table 9.7). In the same way, fuels reached a peak as an export item in 2005 reaching 54.4% to a low point of 19.2% in 2015, while ores and metals became important export commodities from 2015.

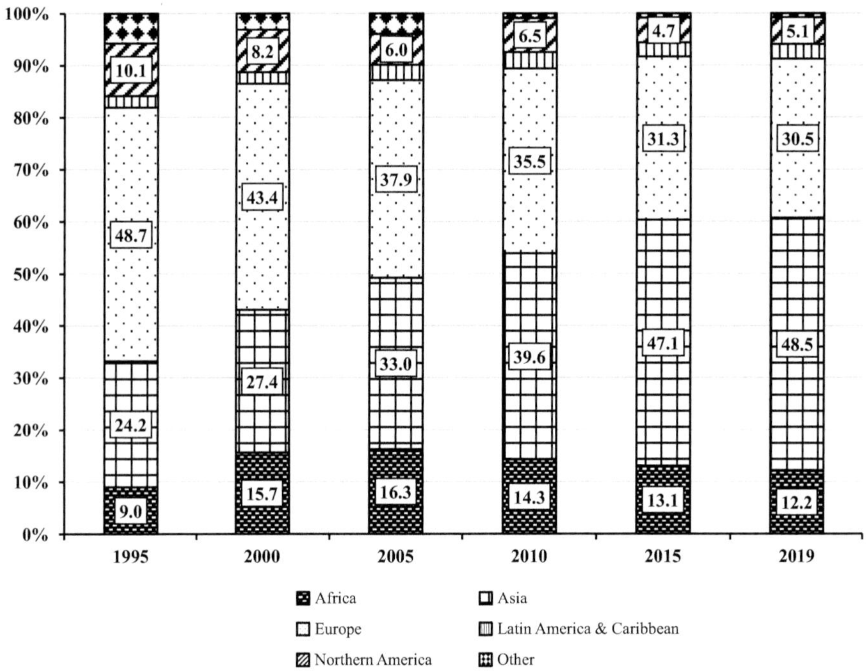

Fig. 9.3 Direction of import trade of COMESA, by major regions

Within COMESA, Table 9.8 shows the same domination of primary goods of food, fuels, ores, and metals. However, other manufactured goods and chemical products appear to be quite important in the intraregional trade of COMESA, the former ranking next to food on the list of total exports. The implication here is that if there was a stronger manufacturing base in COMESA, intraregional trade could be better. Export trade between COMESA and the rest of Africa is given in Table 9.9. The table shows that most of COMESA's export trade with the rest of Africa involves food, other manufactured goods, chemical products, and ores and metals.

The composition of COMESA's import trade over the period under consideration was heavily dominated by manufactured goods led by machinery and transportation equipment, followed by other manufactured goods, food, chemicals, and fuels (Table 9.10).

Within COMESA, the largest share of import trade was taken up by food followed by other manufactured goods, chemical products, and fuel (Table 9.11). The pattern was not different from its import trade with Africa (Table 9.12).

Table 9.5 Top 20 import markets of COMESA 2001–2019 (Percentage share)

2001		2005		2010		2015		2019	
Country	%	Country	%	Country	%	Country	%	Country	%
S. Africa	9.0	S. Africa	8.6	China	11.2	China	17.0	China	18.0
USA	8.8	China	7.2	S. Africa	7.0	India	6.2	India	5.6
Italy	6.8	Italy	5.5	USA	6.1	S. Africa	6.0	USA	5.6
Germany	6.2	USA	5.4	Germany	5.4	USA	4.9	UAE	5.4
UK	4.7	Germany	4.9	India	4.9	Germany	4.6	S. Africa	5.0
France	4.6	S. Arabia	4.6	UAE	4.1	UAE	3.9	S. Arabia	4.5
S. Arabia	4.2	UAE	4.3	Italy	4.1	Italy	3.6	Türkiye	4.1
China	4.1	France	3.7	Japan	3.5	Türkiye	3.5	Germany	3.6
Japan	3.5	UK	3.5	S. Arabia	3.4	France	3.0	Italy	3.2
UAE	3.1	India	3.5	France	3.3	S. Arabia	2.8	Russia	2.5
India	3.0	Japan	3.4	S. Korea	3.2	Japan	2.8	Kuwait	2.4
Australia	2.3	Türkiye	2.2	Türkiye	3.2	Russia	2.6	Japan	2.3
Belgium	2.1	Kuwait	1.9	UK	2.7	S. Korea	2.3	France	2.1
S. Korea	2.1	Russia	1.8	Brazil	2.0	Spain	2.1	UK	1.9
NLD	1.9	S. Korea	1.7	Kuwait	1.8	Brazil	1.9	Brazil	1.8
*Kenya	1.5	Belgium	1.7	Russia	1.8	Kuwait	1.8	Ukraine	1.8
SUI	1.3	Brazil	1.6	Ukraine	1.7	Ukraine	1.8	S. Korea	1.7
Indonesia	1.3	NLD	1.5	Malaysia	1.6	UK	1.7	Spain	1.6
Spain	1.2	Ukraine	1.5	Belgium	1.4	NLD	1.4	NLD	1.5
Türkiye	1.2	*Kenya	1.4	NLD	1.4	Belgium	1.3	Indonesia	1.4
Total	72.9	Total	69.8	Total	73.8	Total	75.0	Total	75.8

Source: Author's calculation based on UNCTADStat data; *COMESA member

Table 9.6 Composition of export and import trade of COMESA, 1995–2019 (Percentage shares)

	Primary Goods		Manufacturing Goods		Unclassified Goods	
	Export	Import	Export	Import	Export	Import
1995	68.0	28.9	31.8	70.0	0.2	1.1
2000	69.2	31.2	29.5	65.7	1.2	3.1
2005	73.5	30.6	24.3	64.2	2.2	5.3
2010	76.4	33.7	23.0	64.6	0.6	1.7
2015	64.5	32.0	23.0	67.4	0.9	0.6
2019	69.8	35.9	29.7	62.9	1.3	1.3

Source: Author's calculation based on UNCTADStat data

9.6 Explanations of COMESA's Trade

The lackluster trade performance of COMESA has been attributed to several factors and reasons, including slow implementation of removal of tariffs and non-tariff barriers (Kasekende & Abuka, 1998; Takirambudde, 1999; Carmignani, 2005; Mayda & Steinberg, 2009; Ebaidalla & Yahia, 2014; Cheluget & Wright, 2017; Ezeoha

Table 9.7 Composition of export trade of COMESA 1995–2019

Commodity	1995	2000	2005	2010	2015	2019
Food	19.5	15.3	10.6	11.5	21.5	17.0
Agricultural raw materials	4.0	3.3	2.4	1.8	2.5	2.1
Ores and metals	7.1	3.7	4.1	8.3	16.1	14.6
Fuels	36.6	45.2	54.4	49.8	19.2	28.8
Pearls, precious stones, and NMG	0.9	1.7	2.1	5.0	5.2	7.3
Chemical products	5.7	5.2	4.5	5.5	8.1	8.5
Machinery and transport equipment	3.0	3.9	4.4	5.3	9.3	7.2
Other manufactured goods	23.0	20.4	15.3	12.2	17.2	14.0
Unassigned	0.2	1.2	2.2	0.6	0.9	0.5
Total	100	100	100	100	100	100

Source: Author's calculation based on UNCTADStat

Table 9.8 Composition of export trade within COMESA

	1995	2000	2005	2010	2015	2019
Food	22.7	25.1	23.6	31.5	37.7	32.4
Agricultural raw materials	2.6	3.4	2.4	1.7	1.8	1.2
Ores and metals	2.1	3.6	5.6	9.5	10.3	9.7
Fuels	24.0	28.1	26.3	10.9	6.7	10.1
Pearls, precious stones, and NMG	0.0	0.0	0.0	0.0	0.0	2.1
Chemical products	12.2	13.8	11.9	12.8	14.8	13.3
Machinery and transport equipment	5.0	3.8	5.6	9.0	6.5	7.3
Other manufactured goods	31.3	22.2	24.5	24.3	22.0	23.9
Unassigned	0.1	0.1	0.0	0.3	0.2	0.1
	100	100	100	100	100	100

Source: Author's calculation based on UNCTADStat data

Table 9.9 Composition of export trade with Africa

YEAR	1995	2000	2005	2010	2015	2019
Food	23.2	26.5	20.2	25.7	25.7	24.2
Agricultural raw materials	3.0	6.4	4.0	2.5	2.0	1.6
Ores and metals	2.5	5.4	8.3	11.9	21.2	19.2
Fuels	18.2	19.3	18.9	8.0	4.0	7.4
Pearls, precious stones, and NMG	0.0	0.4	2.8	4.3	3.7	3.1
Chemical products	15.5	13.2	12.3	15.1	18.0	17.5
Machinery and transport equipment	6.6	7.6	7.7	9.3	6.2	6.3
Other manufactured goods	30.8	21.1	25.7	23.0	18.7	20.5
Unassigned	0.1	0.2	0.1	0.4	0.5	0.1
	100	100	100	100	100	100

Source: Author's calculation based on UNCTADStat data

Table 9.10 Composition of import trade of COMESA, 1995–2019 in percentage share

Commodity	1995	2000	2005	2010	2015	2019
Food	18.0	16.1	14.1	15.9	16.2	16.9
Agricultural raw materials	3.6	2.7	2.0	1.9	1.7	1.7
Ores and metals	1.8	2.3	2.6	3.1	2.5	3.1
Fuels	5.2	10.0	11.7	12.5	11.5	13.3
Pearls, precious stones, and NMG	0.3	0.2	0.2	0.1	0.2	0.9
Chemical products	10.4	10.6	11.1	11.0	12.7	13.4
Machinery and transport equipment	30.9	29.3	28.4	29.8	29.6	26.3
Other manufactured goods	28.7	25.8	24.7	23.8	25.1	23.2
Unassigned	1.1	3.1	5.3	1.7	0.6	1.3
	100	100	100	100	100	100

Source: Author's calculation based on UNCTADStat data

Table 9.11 Composition of COMESA's import trade within COMESA in percentage

Commodity	1995	2000	2005	2010	2015	2019
Food	24.9	24.7	26.5	32.7	35.8	34.8
Agricultural raw materials	2.7	2.8	2.5	1.6	1.5	2.7
Ores and metals	2.7	5.8	6.5	10.1	10.1	9.3
Fuels	15.8	26.3	21.2	9.8	8.2	9.0
Pearls, precious stones, and NMG	0.0	0.0	0.1	0.0	0.0	3.1
Chemical products	10.6	11.6	11.4	13.3	14.6	14.4
Machinery and transport equipment	6.1	4.5	6.8	8.3	6.5	6.1
Other manufactured goods	37.0	24.2	24.8	23.8	23.1	20.2
Unassigned	0.1	0.1	0.4	0.3	0.2	0.3
Total	100	100	100	100	100	100

Source: Author's calculation based on UNCTADStat data

Table 9.12 Composition of COMESA's import trade with Africa in percentage share

Commodity	1995	2000	2005	2010	2015	2019
Food	23.0	18.1	19.4	23.0	23.5	22.7
Agricultural raw materials	4.3	2.9	1.9	1.4	1.3	1.8
Ores and metals	2.2	5.2	4.7	5.7	5.3	5.3
Fuels	18.2	21.2	21.2	15.0	13.4	16.3
Pearls, precious stones and NMG	0.1	0.1	0.1	0.1	0.2	3.7
Chemical products	10.3	13.8	14.4	13.7	15.7	15.1
Machinery and transport equipment	10.1	14.9	14.5	15.8	17.3	13.7
Other manufactured goods	31.6	23.6	23.6	24.5	23.1	21.1
Unassigned	0.2	0.2	0.3	0.7	0.2	0.3
Total	100	100	100	100	100	100

Source: Author's calculation based on UNCTADStat data

et al., 2018; Shinyekwa et al., 2019). Kasekende and Abuka (1998) noted that only two countries had achieved the 80% tariff-reduction by October 1996. They attributed the sluggish trade performance of COMESA to several factors, including lack of political commitment, which manifests itself in the way member states deal with action agenda items and irrelevance of economic integration, lack of necessary conditions—small market size of African countries; similar country endowments that make it difficult for collusive trade policies; lack of common interest among members due to the fact that all the countries had prior trading partners outside of the group; and multiple or overlapping memberships that divide loyalty; and the conflict between COMESA and SADC that made the proposed merger to be met by a cold reception. Suggestions to improve COMESA have included breaking it up into smaller groups that will align countries with common interests together; regional approach to economic issues and problems; and political and economic reforms.

Takirambudde (1999) attributed the ineffective performance of the PTA/COMESA to several obstacles. Among them were a lack of political will, strong nationalistic tendencies of member states with no regional hegemon and identity, lack of complementarities of production structures of the economies of member states, and lack of effective judicial structures. Ebaidalla and Yahia (2014) used the gravity model to compare intraregional trade in COMESA with that of the Association of South East Asian Nations (ASEAN) and found that COMESA nations were performing well below their potential. However, they found that the difference between the potential and actual trade was trending downward. Based on the successful trading between Kenya and Uganda and Zambia and Zimbabwe Ebaidalla and Yahia (2014) concluded that distance and transport cost had negative effect on intraregional trade, and that common language, borders, and colonial links also impacted regional trade. Noting that industrialization was the main reason behind stronger intraregional trade in ASEAN, the authors recommend that export diversification be a top priority of COMESA and that countries should pay special attention to industrialization, in addition to promotion of transportation and communication networks among members.

Similarly, Cheluget and Wright (2017) noted that even though intra-COMESA trade has increased since its inception, it is still far too low compared to the trade with the developed world. Most trade items are primary products with oil and related products accounting for about 60% of the export. Other problems include poor infrastructure and corruption. Ezeoha et al. (2018) addressed the role of conflict in intraregional trade by comparing COMESA and ECOWAS. They found that ECOWAS countries bought more intraregional trade than their COMESA counterparts. This, they attributed to the fact that ECOWAS was more geographically concentrated than COMESA, and also that COMESA counted more conflicts among them than ECOWAS. In another study, Shinyekwa et al. (2019) found that COMESA has created a large market and promoted industrialization among its member states. However, they also found that COMESA still trades heavily in industrial intermediates with non-members. In particular, they observed that this trade is mostly in the importation of finished products. As a result, they recommended member states forge more integration to promote industrialization. In particular, they called on COMESA members to continue policies that promote regional integration and

COMESA infrastructure of transportation and communication; to fast track the implementation of the provisions of the regional and national industrialization policies and strategies; craft a tariff system that exempts industrial intermediates and punishes final goods and services to promote industrialization; seeking external help regarding technology transfer; and improving business environment to attract foreign direct investments.

Within the context of South-South RTAs, Mayda and Steinberg (2009) examined the trade between COMESA and Uganda. They found that Uganda's import trade with COMESA increased only slightly after the establishment of COMESA. They attributed this in part to the inelastic demand for goods in low-income countries, or to the fact that developing countries are not natural trading partners as a result of their small market sizes and similarities in natural endowments.

In their assessment of COMESA, Cheluget and Wright (2017) noted that the targets COMESA set itself to achieve, namely becoming a monetary union by 2018, doubling the per capita income, and cutting poverty in the region by half were all upended by the 2008 economic crises. By 2018, only two-thirds of the members were participating in the free trade area. They noted that COMESA is achieving some of its goals but political and economic problems were undermining progress. First, there was very little national capacity for achieving the goals it set for itself. Second, there is a lack of diversification within the region in terms of its economic base. In particular is the dearth of manufacturing in the economic sector, making it difficult to generate intraregional trade within the group. Third, fragmented regional infrastructure makes it difficult and expensive for intraregional trade. Fourth, inability to involve the private sector and for that matter leaving out the activities in the informal sector, has also been a major problem.

Beyond these, Cheluget and Wright (2017) noted that while much time had been spent on South-South trade, the bulk of COMESA's trade was still with third parties who were outside of the continent of Africa. Part of this problem, they asserted was due to the inability of COMESA countries to diversify their exports, especially through manufacturing. The result was that most of the exports from the group were primary commodities, consisting mostly of oil and related products, with very minimal contributions from agriculture and agro-processed goods. Other factors identified include corruption and inability to implement decisions of the group, inactive private sector in trading activities, limited success in building civil society in the region, and slow harmonization of services within the group.

One advantage COMESA has over some of the other RTAs in Africa is the fact that it does not have any clear hegemon such as ECOWAS and SADC. However, this has also become a weakness when it comes to its dealings with external and more powerful trading partners such as the European Union (EU). Thus, COMESA's relationship with the EU, which was its traditional trading partner has been deteriorating. The negotiation of a new EPA with the EU under the Cotonou Agreement has not been successful, while EU aid support for the region has not met what was promised. Similarly, the relationship with the United States through the African Growth and Opportunity Act (AGOA) has weakened. In contrast, China has stepped into the vacuum in a big way with capital investments and more trading opportunities.

9.7 Conclusion

With 19 countries, COMESA is one of the largest RTAs in Africa, accounting for 37% of its land area, 43% of its population, and 32% of its total GDP in 2019. It started as a preferential trade area (PTA) in 1981. In 1994, the agreement to eventually make COMESA a common market was signed. COMESA became a free trade area in 2000 and in 2009, it launched its customs union with the hope of becoming a monetary union in 2018. However, since its establishment, intraregional trade in COMESA has been sluggish. In 1995, only 7.4% of the group's exports occurred within it. This reached 10% in 2015 but went down to 9.6% in 2019. Its export trade with Africa was 11% of its total export trade in 1995. This reached 22.9% in 2015 but went down to 19.3% in 2019. In contrast, COMESA conducted 88.9% of export trade outside of Africa in 1995. In 2019, it was down to 80.7% but still a substantial portion of the total export trade. On the import side, intraregional trade was even smaller. It reached 6.2% only in 2005. For the rest of the period, intraregional import trade was more than 6% of the total import trade of COMESA. Import trade with Africa, including COMESA members was similarly not impressive.

Combined import trade in COMESA and Africa was only 9% in 1995. It reached 16.3% in 2005 but by 2019 it was down to 12.2%. In contrast, the import trade with the rest of the world was 91% in 1995. It went down to 83.7% in 2005, but by 2019 it was back to 87.8%. Clearly, COMESA trades more with outside entities than with itself and with other African countries. Explanations for this situation are many and they include distance and transportation cost, lack of export diversification, and lack of national capacities to deal with trade matters. We affirm the point made about the need for industrialization in the above discussion. We emphasize the composition of trade in COMESA as the primary reason for the sluggish performance of intraregional trade in COMESA. The predominance of primary products in the economies of COMESA provides less incentives for intraregional trade, and unless there is a major shift in the economies toward production of manufactured goods, it will be difficult for COMESA to improve its intraregional trade.

References

Carmignani, F. (2005). The road to regional integration in Africa: Macroeconomic convergence and performance in COMESA. *Journal of African Economies, 15*(2), 212–250.

Chanthunya, C. L. (2001). The COMESA free trade area: Concept, challenges and opportunities. In V. Murinde (Ed.), *The free trade area of the common market for Eastern and Southern Africa* (pp. 13–29). Ashgate.

Cheluget, K., & Wright, S. (2017). COMESA and the tripartite free trade area: Towards an African economic community? *South African Journal of International Affairs, 24*(4), 481–499. https://doi.org/10.1080/10220461.2017.1413590

Ebaidalla, E. M., & Yahia, A. M. (2014). Performance of intra-COMESA trade integration: A comparative study with ASEAN's trade integration. *African Development Review, 26*(S1), 77–95.

Ezeoha, A. E., Okoyeuzu, C., Udu, A., & Edej, J. (2018). Armed conflicts and intraregional trade flows: The cases of ECOWAS and COMESA. *African Development Review, 30*(4), 346–361.

Geda, A., & Kebret, H. (2007). Regional economic integration in Africa: A review of problems and prospects with a case study of COMESA. *Journal of African Economies, 17*(3), 357–394.

Kasekende, L. A., & Abuka, C. A. (1998). Regional trade arrangements: The COMESA experience. In Z. Iqbal & M. S. Khan (Eds.), *Trade reform and regional integration in Africa* (pp. 462–488). International Monetary Fund.

Mwale, S. G. (2001). An historical background to the formation of COMESA. In V. Murinde (Ed.), *The free trade area of the common market for Eastern and Southern Africa* (pp. 31–40). Ashgate.

Mayda, A. M., & Steinberg, C. (2009). Do South-South trade agreements increase trade? Commodity-level evidence from COMESA. *Canadian Journal of Economics/Revue Canadienne d'Economique, 42*(4), 1361–1389.

Shinyekwa, I. M. B., Lakuma, C. P., & Munu, M. L. (2019). The effects of regional economic communities on industrialization: The case of COMESA. *African Development Review, 31*(4), 506–516.

Takirambudde, P. (1999). The rival strategies of SADC & PTA/COMESA in Southern Africa. In D. C. Bach (Ed.), *Regionalization in Africa: Integration & disintegration* (pp. 151–158). James Currey.

United Nations Economic Commission for Africa (UNECA). (2010). *Assessing Africa's regional integration in Africa IV: Enhancing intra-African trade*. United Nations of Economic Commission of Africa.

Chapter 10
Other Regional Trade Agreements

10.1 Introduction

In the previous chapters, we have examined the performances of Africa's major RTAs regarding trading among them. Overall, we have seen that intraregional trade among Africa's RTAs has been low. The argument we have made is that the low performances exhibited by Africa's RTAs can be explained in large part by the low manufacturing capacity of Africa's economies and for that matter the need for African countries to trade with outsiders. In this chapter, we extend this argument to the trade patterns that exist among other RTAs. Specifically, we examine the European Union (EU), the Association of South East Asia (ASEAN), and *Mercado Común del Sur*; (MERCUSOR), (the Southern Common Market). As before, we will limit ourselves to the direction and the composition of regional trade. The chapter is in four sections. The first section is about the EU, the second section is about ASEAN, and the third is about MERCUSOR. Each section will open with a brief overview of the group—its formation, members, population, and GDP, which is then followed by presentation of trade data.

10.2 The European Union

10.2.1 Some Basic Information About the European Union

The European Union (EU) consists of 27 countries. With a total area of 3.993 million square kilometers, the EU takes up about 38% of the total area of Europe. In 2019, its population of 447,197,811 accounted for 59.9% of Europe's population, Its GDP of US$15.7 trillion in 2019 was 72.4% of the GDP of Europe. The EU membership shows several asymmetries. France, the largest country by land area is

B. Ofori-Amoah, *The African Continental Free Trade Area*,
https://doi.org/10.1007/978-3-031-59181-5_10

Table 10.1 Some basic facts of European Union members, 2019

Country	Area (Km^2)	Populations	GDP (US$)	GDP per capita, PPP (US $)
Austria	82,520	8,879,920	445,011,872,704	58,076
Belgium	30,280	11,488,980	535,376,258,147	54,278
Bulgaria	108,560	6,975,761	68,915,416,142	24,498
Croatia	55,964	4,065,253	62,246,206,341	30,544
Cyprus	9240	1,198,574	25,758,357,775	42,339
Czechia	77,206	10,671,870	252,498,032,247	42,847
Denmark	40,000	5,814,422	347,561,349,211	58,701
Estonia	42,750	1,326,855	31,045,591,753	37,851
Finland	303,930	5,521,606	268,508,200,125	50,322
France	547,557	67,248,926	2,728,870,246,706	49,072
Germany	349,390	83,092,962	3,888,326,788,627	55,653
Greece	128,900	10,721,582	205,144,152,831	30,356
Hungary	91,260	9,771,141	163,526,491,433	33,515
Ireland	68,890	4,934,340	399,122,063,504	87,380
Italy	295,717	59,729,081	2,011,285,742,552	44,376
Latvia	62,227	1,913,822	34,308,783,825	31,883
Lithuania	62,620	2,794,137	54,697,379,017	38,541
Luxembourg	2574	620,001	70,195,715,496	117,342
Malta	320	504,062	15,719,500,921	47,408
Netherlands	33,670	17,344,874	910,194,347,569	59,004
Poland	306,110	37,965,475	597,280,564,672	33,798
Portugal	91,606	10,286,263	239,986,922,639	36,172
Romania	230,080	19,371,648	249,881,592,298	31,867
Slovakia	48,080	5,454,147	105,284,375,641	31,967
Slovenia	20,136	2,088,385	54,178,877,606	40,671
Spain	499,570	47,134,837	1,393,046,093,137	41,695
Sweden	407,284	10,278,887	533,879,529,188	54,599
Total	3,996,441	447,197,811	15,691,850,452,107	

Source: United Nations Population Division

1711 times the size of Malta, the smallest country in the union. The largest eight countries—by land area—France, Spain, Sweden, Germany, Poland, Finland, Italy, and Romania, account for 73.5% of the total area of EU. About 74% of the 2019 population lived in seven countries—Germany, France, Italy, Spain, Poland, Romania, and the Netherlands. In terms of GDP, 69.7% was generated by five countries—Germany, France, Italy, Spain, and Netherlands (Table 10.1).

10.2.2 The Formation and Purpose of the European Union

Commentary on the European Union traces the idea of a united Europe to the very beginning of the European continent (Vătăman, 2010). Thus, Ancient Greece had two leagues of city states—the Delian led by Sparta and the Peloponnese led by

Athens. This vision was extended over most of Europe by the Roman Empire. The vacuum left by the Roman Empire was filled by Christianity and the so-called Holy Roman Empire. Christianity succeeded in providing a common foundation of faith for European nations. During the eighteenth and nineteenth centuries, however, the idea of a united Europe received more support from philosophers, poets, and other literary figures. Thus, philosophers including the Abbot of Saint-Pierre, J. J. Rosseau, Jeremy Bentham, and Immanuel Kant and poets such as Alphonse de Lamartine and Victor Hugo, talked about various organizational designs and structures for elimination of wars and institution of peace in Europe (Vătăman, 2010). However, while those were all ended by World War I, the horrors and devastation of the War in Europe that resulted in the formation of the League of Nations, made the idea of a united Europe even more imperative.

In 1922, Count Coudenhove-Kalergi, an Austrian political journalist published a manifesto titled "Europe's Problem is Summed Up in Two Words: Unification or Collapse" with a follow-up "Pan-Europe" in 1923. These two documents helped launch a Pan-Europe Movement, which called for a reconciliation of France and Germany as a prerequisite for European reconstruction (Vătăman, 2010). By 1929, the idea had caught the attention of both the French and German governments, and the foreign secretaries of both countries—Gustave Stresemann for Germany, and Aristide Briand for France—had supported the idea in their public speeches. Consequently, representatives of 27 European countries, all members of the League of Nations, asked France to draw up a memorandum to be brought before the League of Nations for consideration. Unfortunately, the untimely death of Stresemann in 1929 doomed the discussion of the Franco-German reconciliation as the Nazis who had gained power in Germany had no interest in reconciliation. In spite of this, France submitted its memoranda to the European governments and the League of Nations in May 1930. The memo received a lot of publicity from supporters and critics alike, with one of the most important supporting statements coming from Romania.

In September, 1930 when European nations were asked to share their views on the memoranda they were deadlocked (Vătăman, 2010). The French memo had proposed the adoption of the principles of the European Constitution and Federal Assembly. Germany counter-proposed a simple resolution that States were willing to discuss European issues only within the League of Nations. Britain proposed a committee to study the matter under the leadership of the Secretary-General of the League of Nations. The conference adopted the British proposal and the committee met in January 1931 through September 1932, but in the end, it rejected the French proposal of setting up standing committees on European unity under the League of Nations. With that France withdrew the memo, sealing the fate of the idea of European Union.

However, France was not done yet because the behavior of Germany in central Europe raised concerns that Germany might struck economic relations with the countries in the Danube Basin. To counter this, France advanced another plan calling for European Economic Union, but that also failed because Germany, Britain, and Italy did not support it. Still in 1934, Romania again made a last-ditch effort proposing the United States of Europe. The proposal called for a 10-point patriotic action that would bring Europeans together. Unfortunately, the message did not get through and 5 years later, Europe was once again plunged into another hideous war—World War II.

World War II, however became a catalyst for a new hope for Europe. Throughout the war, the realization for a more peaceful Europe grew, and at the end of the War, several European statesmen including Winston Churchill of Britain, Robert Schuman of France, and Konrad Adenauer of Germany championed the idea of a more cooperative Europe to their citizens. Churchill for example called for a Union of European States and Congress in 1946. Later that year at its meeting at Hartenstein, Switzerland, the European federalist group passed a resolution approving a training program for a European Union. A follow-up conference, the Founding Congress of the Union of European Federalists, met in 1947 at Montreax, Switzerland, and set down six principles for a future European federation. In 1948, the Congress of Europe met in The Hague, The Netherlands, and approved the principle that participating states would maintain their sovereignty, maintain unity through economic cooperation, and strengthen their defense capacities. In addition, the Congress adopted a political and economic resolution dubbed a Message to Europe, which indicated the urgency of European states to unite politically and economically within a structure that provides both security and enhances social progress (Vătăman, 2010). At the same time, there were parallel activities going on. First, on March 17, 1948, Belgium, France, Luxembourg, the Netherlands, and the United Kingdom formed the Western Union, a military alliance to defend each other in case of aggression from another country. Also, on April 16, 1948, the European Economic Cooperation (OECE) was signed in Paris, for economic cooperation.

The need for a parliamentary platform for Europe to discuss matters of mutual concern caused the two organizations to push for the establishment of the Council of Europe, on August 3, 1949. In December 1949, a French proposal to establish a European Union of States based on a presidential system was quickly followed by another French proposal that coal production in France and Germany should be placed under a joint company that would be open to all European countries. The proposal argued that such an effort would provide a basis for mutual economic development for all parties; and that such a project would also make war between France and Germany not only unthinkable but also impossible. After more discussion and consultations, the project was approved at the signing of the Treaty of Paris, which established the European Coal and Steel Community (ECSC). Among other things, the Treaty called for the creation of a common market for coal and steel. It also established a high authority as the Community's governing board, Special Council of Ministers, Common Assembly, and the Court of Justice. The Treaty came into force on July 23, 1952 when it was ratified by six countries: Belgium, France, Italy, Luxembourg, The Netherlands, and West Germany (Vătăman, 2010).

The years after the formation of the ECSC, saw more efforts at forming a European Defense Community but they failed in 1954, when the French National Assembly did not ratify the treaty. In June 1955, at the meeting of the Council of

Ministers of the ECSC, the Benelux countries floated a memorandum calling for an extension of the European integration to all sectors of the economy. The meeting appointed a committee under the chairmanship of Paul Henri-Spaak, the Belgian Foreign Minister. The committee reported back in April 1956, and the report was discussed by all members of the ECSC. On March 15, 1957, the Treaty of Rome established the European Economic Community (EEC).

The stated purpose of the EEC was to establish a common market and progressively appropriate the economic policies of Member States, to promote throughout the Community a harmonious development of economic activities, a continuous and balanced expansion, increased stability, an accelerated raising of the standard of living and closer relations between its Member States. To achieve these objectives, the Community should include.

- the elimination of customs duties and of quantitative restrictions in regard to the importation and exportation of goods, as well as of all other measures with equivalent effect
- the establishment of a common customs tariff and a common commercial policy toward third countries
- the abolition of the obstacles to the free movement of persons, services, and capital
- the inauguration of a common agricultural policy
- the inauguration of a common transport policy
- the establishment of a system ensuring that competition shall not be distorted in the common market
- the application of procedures which shall make it possible to coordinate the economic policies of Member States and to remedy disequilibria in their balances of payments
- the approximation of their respective municipal law to the extent necessary for the functioning of the common market
- The creation of a European Social Fund in order to improve the possibilities of employment for workers and to contribute to the raising of their standard of living.

In 1986, the Single Act of Europe (SEA) was signed to revise the Treaty of Rome. The act established the European Economic Community, (EEC), and the European Atomic Energy Community (EAEC), and revised and enhanced the powers of such institutions as the European Council and the European Parliament. It also set the deadline to create a single market for Europe in 1992, removing the last barrier to a single market, and provided for cooperation about common foreign policy and environmental matters (Vătăman, 2010).

Following the SEA, European leaders appointed a committee in 1988 to draft a report for economic and monetary union. The committee issued its report 10 months later and indicated that it would not be possible to forge an economic and monetary union as envisaged unless there was a new treaty. In 1990, the European Council appointed two intergovernmental conferences, one on economic and monetary union and the other on political union. At its 1991 conference in Maastricht, The

Netherlands, the European Council discussed and approved the Maastricht Treaty or the Treaty of the European Union (TEU). The treaty was signed on February 28, 1992, and in January 1993, the single market was launched. The Maastricht Treaty came into force on November 1, 1993, after it had been ratified by all member states. As indicated in its first article, the Maastricht Treaty (TEU) marked a new stage in the process of forging a closer union for the peoples of Europe. The treaty officially changed the name of the EEC to European Community (EC) and granted European citizenship to every citizen of member state. It also made possible a central banking system and the introduction of a common currency, the Euro. In addition, it committed members to implement common security and foreign policies. In March 1995, border-free travel began in seven countries—Belgium, France, Germany, Luxembourg, the Netherlands, Portugal and Spain. In January 1999, the Euro was introduced in 11 countries—Austria, Belgium, Finland, France, Germany, Ireland, Italy, Luxembourg, the Netherlands, Portugal and Spain. Denmark, Sweden, and the United Kingdom opted to stay out of the Euro at the time.

The Maastricht Treaty was amended in 1999 by the Treaty of Amsterdam, and again by the Treaty of Lisbon, which came into effect on December 1, 2009. The Treaty of Lisbon formally changed the name of the group from European Community (EC) to the European Union (EU). In addition, it clarified the powers of the Union, placed national laws under Union laws, and specified for the first time the process for member states to follow if they wanted to withdraw from the union (Vătăman, 2010).

Over this long period of formation, too the membership of the original ECSC expanded. The first expansion occurred in 1973, when Denmark, Ireland, and the UK joined the group. Greece joined in 1981, Portugal and Spain in 1986, and Austria, Finland, and Sweden in 1995. The largest expansion occurred in 2004 when 10 more countries joined. These included Cyprus, the Czech Republic, Estonia, Latvia, Lithuania, Hungary, Poland, Malta, Slovakia, and Slovenia. In 2007. Bulgaria and Romania joined raising the total number to 27 countries. In 2013, Croatia joined to make the EU, a 28-member country, but on February 1, 2020, the UK withdrew from the EU, making the EU a 27-member organization.

10.2.3 EU Trade

10.2.3.1 Direction of EU Trade

For the period under consideration, 1995–2019, most of EU's trade has been with itself. For example, in 1995, 54.6% of EU's export trade occurred within the EU. In 2005, the percentage reached 61.3%. By 2019, it was backdown to 57.8%. If EU trade with the rest of Europe is included, no less than 70% of EU export trade occurred within Europe from 1995 to 2019 (Table 10.2). As a result, EU export trade outside of Europe over the period under consideration has been less than 30% except for 1995 and 2015 (Table 10.2). This is in sharp contrast with any of Africa's RTAs that we have considered in this book.

Table 10.2 Direction of export trade of the European Union, 1995–2019 (Percentage)

Year	EU	Rest of Europe	EU and Rest of Europe	Rest of World	Total
1995	54.6	15.2	69.7	30.3	100
2000	60.1	14.6	74.7	25.3	100
2005	61.3	14.5	75.9	24.1	100
2010	59.0	14.1	73.1	26.9	100
2015	56.9	13.6	70.5	29.5	100
2019	57.8	57.8	71.0	29.0	100

Source: Author's calculation based on UNCTADStat data

Direction of EU's import trade has followed a similar trend. In 1995 53% of the import trade of the EU occurred within the group. By 2019, it was 55.1%. EU import trade with the rest of Europe ranged from 14.8% in 1995 to 11.2% in 2019. Adding these to the EU intraregional trade shows that the total import trade of EU with Europe has been above 60% over the period under consideration (Table 10.3).

The higher percentage of intraregional trade among the EU members compared to Africa's RTAs is reflected and confirmed by Tables 10.4 and 10.5. In Table 10.4 we find that there were only seven non-EU countries in the top 20 export markets of the EU in 2001. These were the US, Japan, China, Russia, Czech Republic, Hungary, and Poland (Table 10.4). Even so, four of these countries were from EU's region, which was Europe. So, only three were from outside Europe. However, from 2005, the number of non-EU members making the top 20 export markets dropped to 5—consisting mostly of the USA, China, Russia, Turkiye, and Japan (Table 10.4).

On the import side Table 10.5 shows a similar story. Only four non-EU members consistently made the top 20 import markets in the EU from 2001 to 2019. These were USA, Russia, China, and Japan. In 2019, a fourth non-EU member on the list was Turkiye. This is in contrast to what we found with the RTAs in Africa. In the previous chapters, we have consistently made the argument that the low level of intraregional trade among Africa's RTA could in part be attributed to their composition of trade. Following this argument, we will now examine the composition of EU trade.

10.2.3.2 Composition of EU Trade

Manufactured goods dominate EU trade within itself, with the rest of Europe, and the rest of the world. Thus, from 1995 to 2019, manufactured goods accounted for no less than 70% of the total EU trade (Table 10.6). This holds true also for import trade, except in 2010 when import trade was 66.5% (Table 10.6).

The breakdown of EU trade by commodity classes is shown in Tables 10.7 and 10.8. The leading commodity categories were machinery and transportation, other manufactures, chemical products, and food items. Metals, fuels, and pearls as well as precious stones feature very little in the commodity mix of EU export trade.

Table 10.3 Direction of import trade of the European Union, 1995–2019 (Percentage)

	EU	Rest of Europe	EU and Rest of Europe	Rest of the world	Total
1995	53.3	14.8	68.0	32.0	100
2000	55.9	14.5	70.5	29.5	100
2005	56.9	14.1	71.0	29.0	100
2010	54.1	13.6	67.6	32.4	100
2015	55.4	11.9	67.3	32.7	100
2019	55.1	11.2	66.4	33.6	100

Source: Author's calculation based on UNCTADStat data

Table 10.4 Top 20 export markets of the EU, 2001–2019 by percentage share

2001		2005		2010		2015		2019	
Country	%	Country	%	Country	%	Country	2%	Country	%
*Germany	13.3	*Germany	12.6	*Germany	12.8	*Germany	12.6	*Germany	12.7
*France	9.3	*France	9.0	*France	8.4	USA	7.8	USA	8.1
USA	9.0	USA	7.9	USA	6.4	*France	7.5	*France	7.4
*UK	8.1	*UK	7.0	*UK	5.8	*UK	6.4	*UK	5.6
*Italy	5.9	*Italy	5.8	*Italy	5.2	*NLD	4.6	*NLD	4.7
*Belgium	4.8	*Belgium	5.1	*NLD	4.9	*Italy	4.5	*Italy	4.6
*NLD	5.0	*Spain	5.1	*Belgium	4.6	*Belgium	4.0	China	4.1
*Spain	4.5	*NLD	4.8	*Spain	3.9	China	3.6	*Belgium	4.0
SUI	2.8	SUI	2.7	China	3.0	*Spain	3.5	*Spain	3.5
*Austria	2.3	*Austria	2.5	SUI	2.9	SUI	3.2	*Poland	3.1
*Sweden	1.9	*Sweden	2.0	*Poland	2.5	*Poland	2.8	SUI	2.9
Japan	1.7	*Poland	1.8	*Austria	2.4	*Austria	2.3	*Austria	2.3
*Poland	1.5	Russia	1.7	Russia	2.3	*CZE	2.0	*CZE	2.1
*Ireland	1.4	China	1.6	*Sweden	1.9	*Sweden	1.8	*Sweden	1.8
*Portugal	1.3	*CZE	1.4	*CZE	1.8	Türkiye	1.6	Russia	1.6
*Denmark	1.3	Türkiye	1.4	Türkiye	1.6	Russia	1.5	*Hungary	1.4
China	1.1	Japan	1.4	*Denmark	1.2	*Hungary	1.3	Türkiye	1.3
Russia	1.2	*Ireland	1.3	Japan	1.1	Japan	1.2	Japan	1.3
**CZE	1.2	*Denmark	1.3	*Hungary	1.1	*Denmark	1.1	*Denmark	1.1
*Hungary	1.0	*Portugal	1.2	*Portugal	1.1	*Slovakia	1.0	*Romania	1.1
Top 20	78.5	Top 20	77.6	Top 20	75.1	Top 20	74.3	Top 20	74.7

Source: Author's calculation based on data from the International Trade Center Trade Map
NLD Netherlands, *SUI* Switzerland, *CZE* Czech Republic; *EU members

The composition of import trade within the EU follows the same trend. The largest group of imports was machinery and transportation equipment, followed by other manufactures, chemical products, and food items.

The composition of EU export and import trade with the rest of Europe shows a similar trend. Primary commodities consisting of food items agricultural raw materials, metals and ores, fuels, pearl, precious stones, and nonmonetary gold constitute

Table 10.5 Top 20 import markets of the EU, 2001–2019 in Percentage

2001		2005		2010		2015		2019	
Country	%	Country	%	Country	%	Country	%	Country	%
*Germany	13.9	*Germany	14.5	*Germany	13.4	*Germany	13.6	*Germany	13.0
*France	8.0	*France	7.2	China	8.0	China	8.4	China	8.5
USA	7.9	*NLD	6.1	*France	6.2	*NLD	6.2	*NLD	6.1
*UK	6.4	USA	5.5	*NLD	6.0	USA	5.9	USA	5.9
*NLD	5.9	China	5.4	USA	5.3	*France	5.9	*France	5.5
*Italy	5.6	*Italy	5.3	*Italy	4.5	*Italy	4.6	*Italy	4.6
*Belgium	4.5	*UK	5.2	*Belgium	4.2	*Belgium	4.2	*Belgium	4.1
Japan	3.4	*Belgium	4.6	*UK	4.1	*UK	3.8	*UK	3.5
*Spain	3.3	*Spain	3.4	Russia	3.8	*Spain	3.3	*Spain	3.4
China	3.3	Russia	3.4	*Spain	3.2	*Poland	2.8	*Poland	3.1
SUI	2.2	Japan	2.8	SUI	2.2	Russia	2.7	Russia	2.7
Russia	2.2	*Ireland	2.2	*Poland	2.2	SUI	2.3	SUI	2.4
*Ireland	2.1	Norway	2.0	Japan	2.2	*CZE	2.2	*CZE	2.3
*Sweden	1.9	SUI	2.0	*CZE	1.9	*Austria	1.9	*Austria	1.9
*Austria	1.8	*Sweden	1.9	*Austria	1.9	*Sweden	1.6	Japan	1.7
Norway	1.6	*Austria	1.9	Norway	1.8	Japan	1.6	*Ireland	1.6
*Denmark	1.2	*Poland	1.5	*Ireland	1.7	*Ireland	1.6	Türkiye	1.6
*CZE	1.2	*CZE	1.4	*Sweden	1.7	*Hungary	1.4	*Sweden	1.5
*Poland	1.1	*Denmark	1.3	*Hungary	1.3	Norway	1.4	*Hungary	1.5
Top 20	77.5	Top 20	77.5	Top 20	75.3	Top 20	75.4	Top 20	74.5

Source: Author's calculation based on the International Trade Center Trade Map data
NLD Netherlands, *SUI* Switzerland, *CZE* Czech Republic. *EU members

Table 10.6 Composition of EU trade, 1995–2019 (Percentage)

Year	Primary goods		Manufactured goods		Unclassified goods	
	Exports	Imports	Exports	Imports	Exports	Imports
1995	17.9	25.2	76.0	70.7	6.1	4.2
2000	16.1	23.3	78.8	71.2	5.1	5.5
2005	17.3	17.1	79.1	78.3	3.6	4.6
2010	20.4	29.8	75.6	66.5	4.0	3.8
2015	19.6	26.5	77.1	70.0	3.3	3.5
2019	19.2	25.2	77.8	71.3	3.0	3.5

Source: Author's calculation based on UNCTADStat data

a smaller proportion of the trade. In contrast, machinery and transportation equipment, other manufactures, and chemical products account for most of the trading with Europe as well as with the rest of the world (Tables 10.9, 10.10, 10.11 and 10.12).

Table 10.7 Composition of export trade within the EU, 1995–2019 (Percentage)

Product	1995	2000	2005	2010	2015	2019
All food items	11.3	8.6	8.9	10.5	11.3	11.0
Agricultural Raw materials	2.6	1.9	1.6	1.7	1.6	1.5
Ores and metals	3.0	2.6	2.8	3.5	3.1	3.0
Fuels	2.4	3.6	5.0	5.5	4.8	4.5
Pearls, precious stones NMG	0.2	0.2	0.1	0.3	0.2	0.2
Chemical products	11.4	11.7	14.2	14.7	14.7	15.3
Machinery and transport equipment	34.6	37.9	36.5	33.7	35.3	36.4
Other manufactured goods	30.5	26.4	25.5	24.8	24.8	24.7
Unclassified products	4.1	7.1	5.5	5.3	4.1	3.3

Source: Author's calculation based on UNCTADStat data

Table 10.8 Composition of import trade within the EU, 1995–2019 (Percentage shares)

Commodities	1995	2000	2005	2010	2015	2019
Food items	11.0	8.6	9.0	10.6	11.4	11.1
Agricultural raw materials	2.8	2.0	1.7	1.8	1.7	1.5
Ores and metals	3.2	2.8	3.0	3.8	3.3	3.2
Fuels	2.6	3.8	5.6	6.4	5.5	5.0
Pearls, precious stones, and NMG	0.1	0.2	0.1	0.3	0.2	0.2
Chemical products	12.3	12.7	15.3	15.3	15.6	16.1
Machinery and transport equipment	33.4	37.4	36.1	33.6	35.0	36.4
Other manufactured goods	30.0	25.8	24.9	23.8	23.7	23.2
Unclassified products	4.6	6.7	4.4	4.5	3.7	3.3

Source: Author's calculation based on UNCTADStat data

Table 10.9 Composition of EU export trade with Europe, 1995–2019 (Percentage)

	1995	2000	2005	2010	2015	2019
Food	11.2	8.5	8.8	10.3	1.0	10.8
Agricultural raw materials	2.5	1.8	1.5	1.6	1.6	1.4
Ores and metals	2.8	2.5	2.6	3.2	2.8	2.9
Fuels	2.4	3.6	4.7	5.5	4.8	4.5
Pearls, precious stones and NMG	0.4	0.3	0.2	0.6	0.4	0.5
Chemical products	11.4	11.8	14.2	14.9	14.9	15.6
Machinery and transport equipment	34.9	38.3	37.1	34.0	35.5	36.2
Other manufactured goods	30.0	26.2	25.4	24.6	24.7	24.7
Unclassified products	4.5	7.0	5.3	5.3	4.2	3.5

Source: Author's calculation based on UNCTADStat data

Table 10.10 Composition of EU import trade with Europe, 1995–2019 (Percentage)

Commodity	1995	2000	2005	2010	2015	2029
Food	9.3	7.3	8.0	9.5	10.6	10.6
Agricultural raw materials	2.3	1.7	1.6	1.6	1.6	1.4
Ores and metals	3.5	3.3	3.3	4.1	3.6	3.5
Fuels	4.7	6.5	10.8	12.9	9.8	9.1
Pearls, precious stones, and NMG	0.9	1.4	0.4	0.6	0.6	0.4
Chemical products	13.0	13.3	14.9	14.9	15.6	16.1
Machinery and transport equipment	34.7	36.7	32.7	29.8	31.9	33.2
Other manufactured goods	26.8	23.2	23.0	21.8	22.3	21.9
Unclassified products	4.9	6.6	5.2	4.7	4.1	3.7

Source: Author's calculations based on UNCTADStat data

Table 10.11 Composition of EU export trade with World, 1995–2019 (Percentage)

Commodity	1995	2000	2005	2010	2015	2019
Food	10.3	7.9	7.9	9.1	9.9	9.7
Agricultural raw materials	2.1	1.7	1.5	1.5	1.5	1.4
Ores and metals	2.6	2.3	2.5	3.1	2.6	2.6
Fuels	2.4	3.4	4.7	5.6	4.8	4.7
Pearls, precious stones, and NMG	0.7	0.8	0.5	0.8	0.7	0.6
Chemical products	12.1	12.5	14.8	15.0	15.2	16.3
Machinery and transport equipment	37.1	40.4	39.1	36.7	38.1	37.8
Other manufactures	28.7	25.2	24.4	23.0	23.0	22.8
Unclassified	3.8	6.0	4.6	5.2	4.3	4.0

Source: Author's calculation based on UNCTADStat data

Table 10.12 Composition of EU import trade with World, 1995–2019 (Percentage)

	1995	2000	2005	2010	2015	2019
Food	10.5	7.7	7.9	8.6	9.6	9.2
Agricultural raw materials	2.9	2.1	1.5	1.6	1.5	1.3
Ores and metals	3.9	3.3	2.5	4.1	3.5	3.4
Fuels	6.9	9.3	4.7	14.7	11.1	10.7
Pearls, precious stones and NMG	1.0	1.0	0.5	0.7	0.8	0.6
Chemical products	11.4	10.8	14.8	12.8	13.5	13.9
Machinery and transport equipment	32.5	37.1	39.1	31.7	33.2	34.7
Other manufactured goods	26.7	23.3	24.4	22.0	23.2	22.8
Unclassified products	4.2	5.5	4.6	3.8	3.5	3.5

Source: Author's calculation based on UNCTADStat data

10.2.4 Explanation of EU's Trade Performance

There is no doubt that the European Union has been the most successful RTA in the world. Several reasons have been identified. For Dinan (2008), there are two reasons. First, the devastation of World War II and the onset of the Cold War with the Soviet threat afterward provided the urgency for a deeper integration of Europe, even with support from the United States. The fall of the Berlin Wall, the unification of Germany, and the liberalization of Central and Eastern Europe, were important factors in strengthening the EU. Second, is national leaders who were eager to promote their national interests but also saw the opportunity in a united Europe and therefore promoted the idea to their citizenry. These included French Foreign Minister, Robert Schuman, German Chancellor Konrad, and Italian Prime Minister Alcide de Gasperi, as well as Jean Monnet, the brain behind the Franco-German rapprochement after World War II. There were other national leaders that were seen as anti-EU such as France's Charles de Gaulle and UK's Margaret Thatcher. However, their opposition and critique led to important reforms. For example, De Gaulle's opposition eventually showed that he was willing to put the community's interest over national interest. Similarly, Thatcher's opposition led to heavy financial reforms (Dinan, 2008). Another leader of significance was German Chancellor Helmut Khol, who formed a closer bond with French President François Mitterrand, to push for the monetary union.

In their analysis of trade performance of the EU from 1965 to 1995 by network analysis, Krapohl and Fink (2013) identify three factors. First, a viable interdependent market existed among the original six founding countries of the EU, at the time of the Treaty of Rome. External trade partners were already at the periphery at the formation of the EU. Second, the economies of the original EC-6 were relatively symmetric, rather than asymmetric. There was no clear single hegemon. Though West Germany was a very important trading country it was more like a West Germany-France axis than a single hegemon. Third, the stability of the region allowed the trade network to develop and was able to absorb new members who formed a peripheral ring around the old core. In conclusion, Krapohl and Fink (2013, p. 480) write:

> The highly industrialized economies of the EC were able to exploit comparative cost advantages and economies of scale. Economic interdependence led to trade liberalization and regional institution-building, which in turn led to increasing interdependence. The establishment of regional institutions was a reaction to existing interdependence as well as a catalyst for further interdependence.

Lemarchand (2016) identified three features of the EU that have made it relatively successful as an RTA. These include "a determined political will, a core of highly competent international civil servants, and a set of stable governance institutions" (Lemarchand, 2016 p. 241). Other factors that have been identified include geographic proximity of the countries, the level of economic development of EU member states as measured by the means of their GDP per capita and exports volume per capita (Pietrzak & Łapińska, 2015).

Two facts stand out from the discussion of the EU trade. The first is that the EU has the highest intraregional trade of any of the RTAs in the world including those discussed in this book. The second is manufactured goods instead of primary goods constitute a far greater proportion of EU's trade. The question then is this: Is it a coincidence that an RTA which specializes in the production of manufactured goods will also have a high level of intraregional trade or is there a causal relationship between an RTA's ability to produce more manufactured goods and the level of its intraregional trade? I argue that it is much more of the latter than mere coincidence. In the meantime, let's take a look at another example outside of Africa.

10.3 The Association of Southeast Asian Nations (ASEAN)

10.3.1 Some Basic Facts About ASEAN

ASEAN consists of ten countries—Brunei, Cambodia, Indonesia, Lao, Malaysia, Myanmar, Philippines, Singapore, Thailand, and Vietnam. Together, these ten countries occupy a total area of 4,394,564 Km^2, just 9.9% of the total area of Asia. The ten countries also had a total population of about 660,617,952, in 2019, which was just 14.4% of Asia's population. In terms of GDP, ASEAN accounts for US$3,237,925,183,1250, which is 14.7% of the total GDP of Asia. Like all regional integrations, ASEAN appears to have some asymmetries. Indonesia is the dominant country of the group. In 2019, it accounted for 42.7% of the land area of ASEAN, 41% of its population, and 35% of its GDP. Thus, Indonesia's land area of 1.9 million Km^2, contrasts with Singapore's area of 716 km^2, while Indonesia's population of 270,625,567 contrasts with Brunei's population of 433,296. If we add one more country to Indonesia, the asymmetries increase in terms of area, population, and GDP. For example, in 2019, Indonesia and Myanmar accounted for 58% of ASEAN's total land area. Similarly, Indonesia and Philippines accounted for 57% of ASEAN's population, while Indonesia and Thailand accounted for 50% of its GDP (Table 10.13).

10.3.2 The Formation and Purpose of ASEAN

Established in 1967 by Indonesia, Malaysia, the Philippines, Singapore, and Thailand, ASEAN's initial purpose was to serve as security against the spread of communism in Southeast Asia. As a result, although economic integration was mentioned in its founding document, most of its successful achievements within its first 25 years were about security issues. These include the creation of a zone of Peace, Freedom, and Neutrality (ZOPFAN) in 1971, the signing of Treaty of Amity and Cooperation in Southeast Asia (TAC) in 1976, and dealing with Vietnam's invasion of Cambodia in 1978 (Krapohl, 2017c). In 1984, Brunei joined the group. The

Table 10.13 Basic information about ASEAN member states, 2019

Country	Area (KM^2)	Population	GDP Current US$	GDP Per Capita PPP
Brunei	5270	433,296	13,469,422,959	64,718
Cambodia	176,520	16,486,542	25,872,798,012	4423
Indonesia	1,877,519	270,625,567	1,119,099,868,265	12,310
Lao PDR	230,800	7,169,456	18,740,559,554	8219
Malaysia	328,550	31,949,789	365,276,379,481	29,620
Myanmar	652,700	54,045,422	68,697,759,361	4939
Philippines	298,170	108,116,622	376,823,278,561	9290
Singapore	716	5,703,569	375,472,731,271	102,431
Thailand	510,890	69,625,581	544,081,056,185	19,218
Viet Nam	313,429	96,462,108	330,391,329,476	10,562
Total	4,394,564	660,617,952	3,237,925,183,125	

Source: Author's calculation based on UNCTADStat data

coalescence of a number of factors in the 1990s got ASEAN member states to consider formation of a free trade area. The first was the decline of the communist threat and the end of the Cold War. The second was the fear that formation of free trade areas elsewhere in the world, especially NAFTA, and the rise of China as an economic giant would distract investment away from Southeast Asia, Thus, the AFTA was a way to make Southeast Asia more attractive to investment flow (Krapohl, 2017c). However, this did not mean that the member states were ready to grab the idea, because as Krapohl (2017c) reports, almost all of them had some concerns. Though all member states agreed on the idea of free trade, Krapohl (2017c) reports that there was no agreement among member states about the concrete form of the AFTA, the pace of trade liberalization, transitional periods, and how certain industries in member states would be protected. For example, domestic firms in Indonesia wanted protection; Malaysia was apprehensive about its fledgling automobile industry; the Philippines was fearful of its textile and steel industries, while Thailand thought that it would lose its petrochemical industry to Singapore's competitors. Apart from these, the group had to deal with political instability in the Philippines and Thailand. In 1992, member states finally agreed to form the Asian Free Trade Area (AFTA), by which they would reduce tariffs against each other, and abandon import-substitution and protectionism for export-led industrialization. Since then ASEAN has expanded to include Vietnam (1995), Laos (1997), Myanmar (1997), and Cambodia (1999).

10.3.3 ASEAN Trade

10.3.3.1 Direction of Trade

In the initial years from 1992 to 1995 trade direction was dominated by external partners—European Economic Community, USA, and Japan. Intraregional trade was about 18% compared to 65% in the EU. Malaysia and Singapore had some

Table 10.14 Direction of export trade of ASEAN, 1995–2019 (Percentage)

	ASEAN	Rest of Asia	ASEAN and Asia	Rest of the World	Total
1995	24.2	34.8	59.0	41.0	100
2000	22.9	35.8	58.7	41.2	100
2005	24.2	39.2	63.4	36.5	100
2010	24.4	43.1	67.5	32.5	100
2015	24.1	42.9	67.0	33.0	100
2019	22.8	43.3	66.1	33.9	100

Source: Author's calculation based on UNCTADStat data

significant trade relations, while trade between Cambodia, Laos, Myanmar, Vietnam, and Thailand was also significant. The direction of trade began to change in 1995, with Singapore slowly moving to the center of trade, but that was upended in 1997 by the Asian economic crisis leaving external partners as major trading partners.

From 1995, intra-regional accounted for more than 20% of ASEAN trade. In addition, ASEAN countries began to forge closer trading relations with their closest neighbors who were not members of ASEAN but were in close proximity to be trade partners. This raised ASEAN trade within its geographic region to more than 60% of total export trade (Table 10.14).

ASEAN's import trade followed a similar pattern (Table 10.15). Since 1995, at least 20% of ASEAN's import trade has occurred within its members, with a much greater percentage within its region. Thus, in 1995 the ASEAN's trade within its region was 64%; in 2019 it was 75%. For the period under consideration, ASEAN trade with the rest of the world is much lower than what we saw in the previous chapters regarding Africa's RTAs. In 2001, 2005, 2010, and 2015, 6 out of the 10 member states of ASEAN made the list of the top 20 export markets of the ASEAN group. These included Singapore, Malaysia, Thailand, Philippines, Viet Nam, and Indonesia (Table 10.16). In 2019, Cambodia made it seven out of ten. In 2001, the six-member states accounted for about 30.5% of the total export trade of the group. Since then the member states making the list of the top 20 export markets have accounted for no less than 22% of the total export trade.

With import trade the trend is similar. Five out of 10 members made the list of the top 20 import markets of the group, in 2001, 2005, and 2015. In 2019, there were six ASEAN members on the list (Table 10.17).

10.3.3.2 Composition of ASEAN Trade

Table 10.18 shows the composition of ASEAN merchandise trade. From the table, we can see that a greater proportion of the trade of ASEAN group consists of manufactured goods. Thus, for intra-ASEAN trade manufactured goods accounted for between 57% and 75% of both exports and imports during the period under consideration (Tables 10.19 and 10.20). The trend is the same as in the trade with the rest of Asia and (Table 10.20) with the rest of the world (Table 10.21). Once again, we

Table 10.15 Direction of import trade of ASEAN, 1995–2019 (Percentage)

	ASEAN	Rest of Asia	ASEAN and Asia	Rest of the world	Total
1995	19.0	44.6	63.6	36.4	100
2000	24.1	44.7	68.9	31.1	100
2005	25.5	46.5	72.1	27.9	100
2010	24.6	48.4	73.0	27.0	100
2015	23.0	51.1	74.1	25.9	100
2019	21.8	52.8	74.7	25.3	100

Source: Author's calculation based on UNCTADStat data

can see that intraregional trade among ASEAN countries over the period of consideration is higher than those we found with African countries. Is it a coincidence then that these countries with high content of manufactured goods also have higher intra-regional trade?

The disaggregation of the broad export product within ASEAN member states is given by Table 10.19. The table shows that machinery and transportation equipment lead the list of export products within the ASEAN. This is followed by other manufactured products, fuels, and chemical products.

Manufactured products dominate the import trade within the ASEAN group (Table 10.20). Machinery and transportation equipment have been the largest group of imported items followed by fuels, other manufactured goods, and food and chemical products (Table 10.22).

10.3.4 Explanation of ASEANs Trade Performance

Explanations for ASEAN's strong trade within itself and with its region are several. One is what has been called the ASEAN+3 process, which is ASEAN's attempt to forge closer ties with the stronger economies of three neighbors—China, Japan, and South Korea. In this regard, ASEAN has the advantage of having most of its important extra-regional trading partners to be in close proximity, geographically. It has also been pointed out that there appears to be no one or more dominant member states in ASEAN. Indonesia is a large country but it is not developed enough to dominate. At the same time, Singapore is the most relatively developed among the member states, but it is a small city state. The result is that no one country is dominant enough to place its own interest above the rest of the member states which could derail the intraregional trade. In addition to this, we also argue that more of the ASEAN member states have a higher content of manufactured goods production in their economies than we saw with African countries. This makes the ASEAN economies more competitive externally and complementary internally, causing them to engage in more intra-group and intraregional trade than what we saw with Africa's RTAs.

Table 10.16 Top 20 export markets of ASEAN, 2001–2019

2001		2005		2010		2015		2019	
Country	%	Country	%	Country	%	Country	%	Country	%
USA	17.9	USA	14.4	China	10.7	China	12.2	China	14.2
Japan	13.8	Japan	11.2	Japan	9.8	USA	10.9	USA	13.0
*Singapore	7.6	China	8.0	USA	9.5	Japan	8.8	Japan	7.7
*Malaysia	7.0	*Malaysia	6.6	HKG	7.2	HKG	6.6	HKG	6.5
HKG	5.6	*SGP	6.5	*Malaysia	6.3	*Malaysia	5.2	*Malaysia	4.7
China	4.3	HKG	6.4	*SGP	5.7	*SGP	4.9	*SGP	4.5
Taiwan	4.3	*IDN	4.9	*IDN	4.7	*IDN	4.1	S. Korea	4.2
NLD	3.9	S. Korea	3.8	S. Korea	4.3	S. Korea	3.9	*Thailand	3.5
S. Korea	3.8	*Thailand	3.6	Australia	3.6	*Thailand	3.6	*IDN	3.4
*Thailand	3.3	Australia	3.4	India	3.5	India	3.5	India	3.4
Germany	3.0	Taiwan	3.2	*Thailand	3.3	Australia	3.1	*VNM	2.9
UK	2.8	NLD	3.0	Taiwan	2.9	Taiwan	2.9	Taiwan	2.8
Australia	2.6	Germany	2.4	NLD	2.3	*VNM	2.6	Australia	2.5
*PHL	1.7	India	2.3	Germany	2.2	NLD	2.3	NLD	2.3
India	1.6	UK	2.2	*PHL	1.9	Germany	2.3	*PHL	2.2
France	1.3	PHL	1.6	*VNM	1.9	*PHL	1.9	Germany	2.1
Belgium	1.1	*VNM	1.4	UK	1.5	UAE	1.7	UK	1.4
*VNM	1.0	France	1.3	France	1.2	UK	1.5	UAE	1.1
UAE	0.9	UAE	1.2	UAE	1.2	France	1.0	*Cambodia	1.1
IDN	0.9	Belgium	0.7	SUI	0.8	Belgium	1.0	France	1.0
Top 20	88.2	Top 20	88.1	Top 20	84.5	Top 20	83.8	Top 20	84.4

Source: Author's calculation based on International Trade Center Trade Map data

HKG Hong Kong, *SGP* Singapore, *IDN* Indonesia, *NLD* Netherlands, *PHL* Philippines, *VNM* Viet Nam, *SUI* Switzerland

*ASEAN Member

Table 10.17 Top 20 import markets of ASEAN, 2001–2019

2001		2005		2010		2015		2019	
Country	%	Country	%	Country	%	Country	%	Country	%
Japan	17.2	Japan	13.9	China	13.3	China	20.1	China	21.9
USA	14.3	China	10.5	Japan	12.3	Japan	9.2	Japan	8.3
*Malaysia	7.7	USA	10.5	USA	8.8	USA	7.8	USA	8.0
*Singapore	6.1	*Malaysia	7.2	*Malaysia	6.6	S. Korea	6.9	S. Korea	7.0
China	5.9	*Singapore	6.4	S. Korea	6.0	*Malaysia	5.7	Taiwan	5.7
Taiwan	5.1	Taiwan	5.8	*Singapore	5.9	Taiwan	5.7	*Malaysia	5.5
S. Korea	4.6	S. Korea	4.7	Taiwan	5.0	*Singapore	5.7	*Singapore	4.5
*Thailand	3.8	*Thailand	4.2	*Thailand	4.5	*Thailand	4.4	*Thailand	4.2
Germany	3.5	*Indonesia	3.5	*Indonesia	3.9	*Indonesia	3.3	*Indonesia	3.4
S. Arabia	2.5	S. Arabia	3.3	S. Arabia	2.8	Germany	2.8	Germany	2.4
Australia	2.4	Germany	3.1	Germany	2.7	UAE	2.0	India	2.1
HKG	2.4	HKG	2.2	India	2.1	S. Arabia	2.0	Australia	2.0
UK	1.9	Australia	2.1	UAE	2.1	Australia	1.8	UAE	2.0
*PHL	1.7	*PHL	1.8	Australia	2.0	India	1.8	VNM	1.9
France	1.5	UAE	1.6	*Philippines	1.7	*Viet Nam	1.7	S. Arabia	1.8
*Indonesia	1.5	France	1.5	HKG	1.5	France	1.5	France	1.6
SUI	1.2	India	1.5	France	1.5	HKG	1.2	HKG	1.3
UAE	1.1	UK	1.4	SUI	1.4	SUI	1.1	UK	1.2
India	1.1	SUI	1.1	UK	1.2	UK	1.1	*PHL	1.1
Italy	1.0	Kuwait	1.0	Russia	1.0	Brazil	1.0	SUI	1.0
Top 20	86.6	Top 20	87.2	Top 20	86.2	Top 20	86.6	Top 20	86.7

Source: Author's calculation based on International Trade Center Trade Map data

S. Korea South Korea, *S. Arabia* Saudi Arabia, *HKG* Hong Kong, *VNM* Viet Nam, *PHL* Philippines, *SUI* Switzerland

*ASEAN Member

Table 10.18 Composition of ASEAN trade, 1995–2019 (Percentage)

	Primary goods		Manufactured goods		Unclassified goods	
Year	Export	Import	Export	Import	Export	Import
1995	26.4	18.2	69.7	77.5	4.0	4.4
2000	22.4	20.6	75.3	76.8	2.3	2.6
2005	27.0	25.9	63.7	65.4	9.3	8.7
2010	32.9	30.7	61.7	65.4	5.4	4.0
2015	29.0	28.0	67.7	68.2	3.3	3.8
2019	27.1	28.0	68.9	68.7	3.9	3.4

Source: Author's calculation based on UNCTADStat data

Table 10.19 Composition of export trade within ASEAN, 1995–2019 (Percentage)

Commodity	1995	2000	2005	2010	2015	2019
Food	7.7	5.6	5.5	8.2	9.6	9.7
Agricultural raw materials	3.0	1.3	1.5	1.7	1.2	1.0
Ores and metals	2.6	1.9	2.6	3.0	2.1	2.2
Fuels	10.8	13.8	19.9	23.0	21.0	19.7
Pearls, precious stones, and NMG	0.7	0.6	0.5	1.2	2.4	3.0
Chemical products	7.2	7.4	8.8	8.9	9.9	9.8
Machinery and transport equipment	48.4	55.5	39.5	35.5	36.1	35.5
Other manufactured goods	15.7	11.9	12.0	13.5	14.3	15.1
Unclassified	3.8	2.1	9.7	5.1	3.4	4.0
Total	100	100	100	100	100	100

Source: Author's calculation based on UNCTADStat data

Table 10.20 Composition of import trade within ASEAN, 1995–2019 (Percentage)

Commodity	1995	2000	2005	2010	2015	2019
Food	8.5	5.9	5.5	8.2	9.2	9.5
Agricultural Raw materials	4.0	1.8	1.7	1.9	1.5	1.2
Fuels	12.6	14.6	21.3	23.0	21.6	20.7
Pearls, precious stones, and NMG	0.9	0.7	0.6	1.3	2.4	3.4
Chemical products	6.5	7.7	8.4	8.5	9.4	9.5
Machinery and transport equipment	51.1	55.3	38.1	38.2	37.2	36.2
Other manufactured goods	13.2	11.9	12.8	14.4	15.5	15.3
Unclassified products	3.3	2.1	11.5	4.5	3.2	4.3
Total	100	100	100	100	100	100

Source: Author's calculation based on UNCTADStat data

Table 10.21 Composition of export trade of ASEAN with Asia, 1995–2019 (Percentage)

Commodity	1995	2000	2005	2010	2015	2019
Food	10.8	7.2	6.4	8.4	9.6	9.6
Agricultural raw materials	4.4	2.3	2.6	3.1	2.6	2.7
Ores and metals	3.2	2.3	2.8	3.6	3.2	3.1
Fuels	14.9	16.8	19.2	20.1	15.5	13.5
Pearls, precious stones and NMG	0.7	0.5	0.8	1.4	2.3	2.6
Chemical products	5.9	6.7	8.4	8.5	9.2	9.5
Machinery and transport equipment	38.9	48.1	37.7	37.5	39.2	39.7
Other manufactured goods	18.3	14.3	12.5	13.1	15.5	16.1
Unclassified products	3.0	1.7	9.6	4.2	2.9	3.1

Source: Author's calculation based on UNCTADStat data
NMG Nonmonetary gold

Table 10.22 Commodity composition of import trade of ASEAN with Asia, 1995–2019 (Percentage)

Commodity	1995	2000	2005	2010	2015	2019
Food	4.1	3.3	3.0	4.2	4.5	4.5
Agricultural raw materials	1.8	1.3	1.0	1.2	1.1	0.9
Ores and metals	2.2	2.0	2.2	3.0	2.8	2.7
Fuels	8.6	13.8	19.9	20.6	15.2	15.2
Pearls, precious stones, and NMG	1.0	0.8	1.2	1.4	1.9	2.0
Chemical products	7.6	7.6	7.8	8.6	9.4	9.6
Machinery and transport equipment	51.8	52.6	40.4	40.9	42.2	42.1
Oher manufactured goods	19.4	17.0	16.2	17.3	20.3	20.4
Unclassified products	3.5	1.7	8.4	3.0	2.6	2.6

Source: Author's calculation based on UNCTADStat data
NMG nonmonetary gold

10.4 Mercado Común del Sur (MERCOSUR) (The Southern Common Market)

10.4.1 Some Basic Facts About MERCOSUR

In South America, the MERCOSUR RTA is an economic behemoth. It consists of only four countries, but the four countries account for 65.4% of the total land area of South America, 62% of its population, and 67% of its GDP (Table 10.23). Within this small group however one can also identify huge asymmetries. Brazil, the largest country of the group accounts for 71.6% of the group's total land area, 79% of its population, and 77% of its GDP (Table 10.23). Argentina follows in a distant second with 23% of the group's land area, 16.9% of its population, and 18.7% of its GDP. Thus, Brazil and Argentina account for 95.1% of MERCOSUR's land area, 96;1% of its population, and 95.9% of its GDP. This means Paraguay and Uruguay the two remaining members only account for 4.9% of MERCOSUR's land area, 3.9% of its population, and 4.1% of its GDP (Table 10.23).

Table 10.23 MERCOSUR countries by area, population, GDP and GDP Per Capita PPP, 2019

Country name	Area (km^2)	population	GDP current ($)	GDP per capita PPP
Argentina	2,736,690	44,938,712	452,818,426,183	22,997
Brazil	8,358,140	211,049,519	1,873,288,158,977	15,358
Paraguay	397,300	7,044,639	37,925,338,329	13,148
Uruguay	175,020	3,461,731	61,231,149,881	24,005
Total	11,667,150	266,494,601	2,425,263,073,370	

Source: United Nations Population Division

10.4.2 Formation and Purpose of MERCOSUR

Birch (2000) traces the idea of regional integration in South America back to the revolutionary leaders of the region such as Simon Bolivar and San Martin. These leaders had a vision of creating a United States of South America. The idea was revived again in the 1930s when Frederico Pinedo, the Argentine Finance Minister, and Jose Carlos Macedo Soares, his counterpart in Brazil, floated the idea of a customs union for South America (Birch, 2000). This proposal did not work. However, through subsequent work of the United Nation's Economic Commission for Latin America (UNECLA)'s Trade Committee, in 1960 the Treaty of Montevideo establishing a Latin American Free Trade Area (LAFTA) or ALALC in Spanish) was signed by Argentina, Brazil, Chile, Mexico, Paraguay, Peru, and Uruguay. The Treaty became effective on July 1, 1961, after which it was joined by Bolivia, Colombia, Ecuador, and Venezuela. Member states agreed to remove tariffs among themselves over a period of 12 years. Birch (2000) reported that initially, intraregional trade increased within the group but that increase came at the expense of previous bilateral trade among some of the membership. For example, while trade with Mexico increased trade between Argentina and Chile decreased. Apart from this, other factors put breaks of the Treaty's initial momentum. For one thing, all the member states were also pursuing the import-substitution industrialization policy, which required protection of their infant industries from each other. Also, the bigger economies wanted to rush the pace of tariff removal to enable them to sell more to the other members, while the smaller economies were hesitant and felt that they could not compete effectively with their larger neighbors. In May 1969, six members of the LAFTA signed the Cartagena Agreement to establish the Andean Pact. The members were Bolivia, Colombia, Ecuador, Peru, and Venezuela. The objective was to forge a much stronger integration including regional industrial planning to strengthen their industrial capacity. The Andean Pact effectively killed the LAFTA. Nevertheless, members of LAFTA met again in 1980 in Montevideo, to sign a new agreement changing LAFTA into a Latin America Integration Association (LAIA or ALADI in Spanish). The new agreement allowed for bilateral agreements among member states in order to ease the concerns of the smaller and weaker economies in the group. It was within the context of this new arrangement that MERCOSUR emerged.

MERCOSUR owes its origins to a tripartite agreement of cooperation that was signed by Argentina, Brazil, and Paraguay in 1979. In response to the economic crisis of the 1980s, Argentina and Brazil became more serious about forming a free trade area for both intraregional and extra-regional trade. In addition, there was also interest in political stability. For Paraguay and Uruguay, which joined them, part of their interest was to become part of a bigger market given that they were both small countries with small markets.

The first informal talks between Argentina and Brazil occurred in 1984. In 1985, the two countries issued a joint declaration of their intent to form an economic integration. A bilateral agreement of integration, cooperation, and development was signed in 1988. In 1990, the two countries signed the Buenos Aires Act to establish a common market and recruit more members to join by 1994. In 1991, the Treaty of Asuncion, establishing a free trade area (MERCOSUR) was signed by Argentina, Brazil, Paraguay, and Uruguay. The Treaty of Asuncion was amended in 1994 by the Protocol of Ouro Preto to make MERCOSUR a customs union. In 2002, the Protocol of Olivos added dispute resolution provisions to the MERCOSUR treaty (Fink & Rempe, 2017). In 2012, Venezuela joined the group but was suspended in 2016 after it failed to comply with the group's democratic principles. MERCOSUR was created to implement the free movement of goods, services, and factors of production among member states, with the ultimate goal of becoming like the European Union for South America. The following are among the purposes of MERC OSUR (Birch, 2000 p. 1400–1401).

- permit the free movement of goods, services, and factors of production among the countries by eliminating customs duties and non-tariff barriers
- adopt a common external tariff and a common trade policy toward third countries and will coordinate positions in regional and international economic and commercial fora
- coordinate macroeconomic and sectoral policies between the countries in the areas of foreign trade, agriculture, industry, fiscal and monetary matters, foreign exchange and capital, services, customs, transport and communications, and any other areas that may be agreed upon.
- harmonize their legislation in "relevant areas" to advance the process of economic integration.

Table 10.24 Direction of export trade of MERCOSUR, 1995–2019 (Percentage share)

	MERCOSUR	South America	MERCOSUR & South America	Rest of the World
1995	19.1	37.2	56.3	43.7
2000	18.2	46.8	65.0	35.0
2005	11.7	46.2	57.8	42.2
2010	14.9	29.0	43.9	56.1
2015	13.6	25.1	38.7	61.3
2019	10.6	22.9	33.5	66.5

Source: Author's calculation based on UNCTADStat data

Table 10.25 Top 20 export markets in MERCOSUR, 2001–2019 (Percentage shares)

2001		2005		2010		2015		2019	
Country	%	Country	%	Country	%	Country	%	Country	%
USA	27.7	USA	24.2	China	10.8	China	16.2	China	23.8
*Brazil	7.6	ARG	4.8	Area Nes	9.7	USA	14.7	USA	11.3
*ARG	4.9	China	4.7	USA	7.0	Brazil	4.8	Brazil	4.4
Chile	3.9	LAIA NES	4.2	ARG	5.6	ARG	4.6	NLD	3.9
NLD	3.5	*Brazil	4.2	Brazil	5.3	India	4.1	ARG	3.7
Germany	2.9	Chile	4.0	NLD	3.4	NLD	3.9	India	3.4
China	2.8	NLD	3.3	LAIA NES	3.4	Germany	2.4	Chile	2.8
Italy	2.6	Germany	2.9	Germany	3.0	Chile	2.3	Spain	2.0
Mexico	2.4	Mexico	2.7	Am. NES	2.9	Japan	1.9	Germany	1.9
Spain	2.3	Italy	2.4	Chile	2.7	Spain	1.8	Japan	1.9
Japan	2.2	Asia NES	2.0	Japan	2.3	Mexico	1.6	Mexico	1.8
UK	2.0	Spain	2.0	Spain	1.9	Italy	1.6	Viet Nam	1.5
France	1.9	UK	1.8	Asia NES	1.8	VEN	1.5	Italy	1.4
Belgium	1.9	Japan	1.8	Italy	1.8	Uruguay	1.5	S. Korea	1.4
NLD Antilles	1.5	Russia	1.7	LCA	1.7	SUI	1.4	Malaysia	1.3
*Uruguay	1.5	France	1.4	VEN	1.6	UK	1.4	Colombia	1.3
Colombia	1.4	Canada	1.4	Russia	1.6	Viet Nam	1.3	Peru	1.3
VEN	1.2	Colombia	1.3	UK	1.6	Singapore	1.3	Canada	1.3
Canada	1.2	VEN	1.3	Mexico	1.5	Canada	1.3	UK	1.2
*Paraguay	1.1	Belgium	1.2	India	1.4	Russia	1.3	Belgium	1.2
Total	76.6	Total	73.1	Total	71.2	Total	70.9	Total	72.6

Source: Author's calculation based on data from the International Trade Center's Trade Map; NES = Not elsewhere specified; *MERCOSUR member

Table 10.26 Direction import trade of MERCOSUR, 2001–2019 (Percentage share)

	MERCOSUR	So. America	MERCOSUR & S. America	Rest of the world	Total
1995	17.7	34.4	52.1	47.9	100
2000	20.7	32.7	53.5	46.5	100
2005	19.6	28.9	48.5	51.5	100
2010	17.0	25.5	42.5	57.5	100
2015	16.1	26.4	42.6	57.4	100
2019	13.5	26.3	39.7	60.3	100

Source: Author's calculation based on UNCTADStat data

10.4.3 Trade of MERCOSUR

10.4.3.1 Direction of MERCOSUR Trade

Initially, MERCOSUR had some success. Total export trade grew by 40% between 1991 and 1998—most of it with the EU and USA. Intraregional trade rose from 13% in 1991 to 23% in 1998. In 1995, trade volume between Brazil and Argentina began to grow. There was also an investment boom, especially with foreign direct investments. However, not only has the percentage of intra-group and intraregional trade been relatively small, but it has also been declining.

Thus, intra-group export trade declined from 19% in 1995 to 10.6% in 2019 (Table 10.24). Trade with the rest of South America similarly declined from a high of 46.8% in 2000 to 22.9% in 2019, while trade with rest of the world increased from 43.7% in 1995 to 66.5% in 2019. The top 20 export markets of MERCOSUR from 2001 to 2019 are shown in Table 10.25. Argentina and Brazil have consistently been on the list every year shown in the table but their contributions have been small-12.5% in 2005, 9.8% in 2010 and 8.9% in 2019.

MERCOSUR's import trade over the period followed a similar pattern as its export trade (Table 10.26). The data show that intra-regional import trade reached a high of 20% in 2000, after which it started declining to 13.5% in 2019. Its regional trade dropped from 34.4% to 26.3%, while trade with the rest of world rose from 47.9% in 1995 to 60.3% in 2019. The top 20 import markets are given in Table 10.27, which shows the same modest contributions by MERCOSUR members similar to what we found in the export market (Table 10.27). These countries include Argentina, Brazil, and Paraguay. MERCOSUR's trade relations are much more similar to Africa's RTAs than to the EU and ASEAN. Could this also be due to the composition of trade as we saw with the African RTAs?

10.4.3.2 Composition of MERCOSUR Trade

The composition of MERCOSUR's trade is similar to the African RTAs that we have considered in this book. It consists more of primary commodities on the export side and more of manufactured goods on the import side (Table 10.28).

Table 10.27 Top 20 import markets of MERCOSUR by percentage share

2001		2005		2010		2015		2019	
Country	%	Countries	%	Countries	%	Countries	%	Countries	%
USA	22.9	USA	18.5	USA	15.3	China	18.2	China	19.5
*ARG	7.9	*Brazil	10.6	China	14.5	USA	16.0	USA	16.3
*Brazil	7.4	China	6.6	*Brazil	8.6	*Brazil	7.5	*Brazil	8.6
Germany	6.7	*ARG	6.3	*ARG	6.2	*ARG	5.4	*ARG	5.5
Japan	4.8	Germany	6.2	Germany	5.9	Germany	5.2	Germany	5.3
Italy	3.7	Japan	3.7	S. Korea	3.5	Mexico	2.8	Mexico	2.4
France	3.3	France	2.8	Japan	3.1	S. Korea	2.6	India	2.2
China	3.2	Italy	2.7	Mexico	2.5	Italy	2.4	S. Korea	2.2
Spain	2.5	S. Korea	2.4	Italy	2.4	Japan	2.3	Italy	2.2
S. Korea	2.5	Mexico	2.4	France	2.4	France	2.3	Japan	2.0
UK	2.1	Chile	2.2	Nigeria	2.1	Nigeria	2.1	France	1.8
Mexico	2.0	Nigeria	2.1	Chile	2.0	India	2.0	Spain	1.8
Chile	1.8	Algeria	2.1	India	1.8	Spain	1.8	Chile	1.7
*Paraguay	1.7	Spain	1.9	Spain	1.7	Chile	1.8	Russia	1.6
Nigeria	1.7	Colombia	1.9	UK	1.4	Bolivia	1.5	Viet Nam	1.3
Canada	1.7	*Paraguay	1.5	UK	1.3	UK	1.4	SUI	1.3
Colombia	1.7	UK	1.5	SUI	1.3	NLD	1.3	*Paraguay	1.2
SUI	1.4	Taiwan	1.3	Canada	1.3	Canada	1.2	UK	1.2
Algeria	1.2	SUI	1.3	Bolivia	1.1	SUI	1.2	NLD	1.2
Taiwan	1.2	Belgium	1.3	Russia	1.0	Russia	1.2	Bolivia	1.1
Total	81.3	Total	79.45	Total	79.4	Total	80.2	Total	80.3

Source: Author's calculation based on data from International Trade Center Trade Map
ARG Argentina, *SUI* Switzerland, *NLD* Netherlands, *SUI* Switzerland; *MERCOSUR member

Within itself, however, MERCOSUR trades more in manufactured goods than primary goods. The breakdown of these traded goods is provided in Table 10.29, which shows that exports of both food and fuel, the two largest components of primary commodities have declined slightly. At the same time the percentage share of manufactured goods exports, especially the machinery and transportation environment increased from 1995 to 2019. However, within the group, the share of manufactured goods in export trade from 1995 has not been consistent; it increased a bit from 1995 to 2005 but then started to decline afterwards. On the import side, manufactured goods dominate MERCOSUR's trade (Table 10.30).

The composition of MERCOSUR's trade with the rest of the world shows an interesting pattern. Thus, MERCOSUR has been exporting more primary goods, while importing more manufactured goods (Tables 10.31 and 10.32). This is similar to the African RTAs that we have considered in this book. The composition of MERCOSUR trade from 1995 to 2019 showed a higher component of manufactured goods compared to those African RTAs that we have considered previously. We have made the case that one of the reasons why intraregional trade is small among African RTAs is because of the high content of primary goods of their

Table 10.28 Composition of trade of MERCOSUR, 1995–2019 (Percentage shares)

Year	Primary Commodities		Manufactured Goods		Unclassified Goods	
	Export	Import	Export	Import	Export	Import
1995	59.4	24.6	39.2	74.5	1.5	1.0
2000	59.8	22.8	37.1	74.9	3.0	2.3
2005	60.7	23.3	36.9	74.4	2.4	2.3
2010	68.8	23.6	27.9	75.1	3.3	1.4
2015	68.0	23.1	28.3	75.8	3.7	1.0
2019	68.4	22.8	25.6	76.1	6.0	1.1

Source: Author's calculation based on UNCTADStat data

Table 10.29 Composition of export trade within MERCOSUR, 1995–2019 (Percentage shares)

Commodity	1995	2000	2005	2010	2015	2019
Food	25.8	17.3	12.9	16.4	20.1	22.4
Agricultural raw materials	3.9	1.6	1.3	1.1	1.0	0.7
Ores and metals	2.2	2.1	3.2	3.3	3.0	2.8
Fuels	13.2	19.4	12.4	11.5	10.4	8.6
Pearls, precious stones, and NMG	0.0	0.0	0.0	0.0	0.0	0.0
Chemical products	10.4	10.4	14.4	11.4	13.2	10.4
Machinery and transport equipment	24.3	26.0	34.0	37.9	34.1	29.6
Other manufactured goods	19.3	16.9	16.3	14.1	13.6	13.1
Unclassified goods	0.9	6.2	5.4	4.3	4.6	12.4
Total	100	100	100	100	100	100

Source: Author's calculation based on UNCTADStat data

Table 10.30 Composition of import trade within MERCOSUR, 1995–2019 (Percentage shares)

Commodity	1995	2000	2005	2010	2015	2019
Food	26.6	17.4	12.4	17.0	19.3	22.9
Agricultural raw materials	3.3	1.7	1.3	1.1	1.3	1.1
Ores and metals	2.6	2.3	3.6	3.1	3.1	3.4
Fuels	12.4	20.6	12.6	10.8	8.3	9.9
Pearls, precious stones, and NMG	0.0	0.0	0.0	0.0	0.0	0.0
Chemical products	10.7	10.4	14.9	11.8	13.3	12.1
Machinery and transport equipment	24.4	25.2	33.3	37.8	35.7	32.1
Other manufactured goods	19.3	16.4	16.3	14.1	14.2	13.4
Unclassified products	0.7	6.0	5.6	4.4	4.8	5.0
Total	100	100	100	100	100	100

Source: Author's calculations based on UNCTADStat data

Table 10.31 Composition of MERCOSUR's export trade with the rest of the world, 1995–2019 (Percentage shares)

Commodity	1995	2000	2005	2010	2015	2019
Food	28.6	22.3	23.7	29.0	37.9	38.2
Agricultural raw materials	4.7	3.0	2.6	2.7	3.5	4.5
Ores and metals	7.1	6.4	6.9	11.8	8.2	9.8
Fuels	18.3	27.5	27.2	24.1	16.8	14.2
Pearls, precious stones, and NMG	0.6	0.5	0.4	1.2	1.7	1.8
Chemical products	6.0	5.6	5.7	5.8	6.0	5.1
Machinery and transport equipment	13.0	16.3	16.1	12.6	12.3	11.1
Other manufactured goods	20.2	15.3	15.0	9.5	10.0	9.4
Unclassified products	1.5	3.0	2.4	3.3	3.7	6.0
Total	100	100	100	100	100	100

Source: Author's calculation based on UNCTADStat data

Table 10.32 Composition of MERRCOSUR's import trade with the world, 1995–2019 (Percentage shares)

Commodity	1995	2000	2005	2010	2015	2019
Food	10.2	7.1	5.2	6.1	6.3	6.2
Agricultural raw materials	2.7	1.8	1.4	1.2	1.0	1.0
Ores and metals	3.1	2.5	3.2	2.9	2.8	3.1
Fuel	8.6	11.4	13.5	13.3	13.0	12.5
Pearls, precious stones, and NMG	0.0	0.0	0.0	0.0	0.0	0.0
Chemical products	15.5	16.8	18.3	17.4	20.4	22.6
Machinery and transportation equipment	39.9	40.3	39.4	39.9	37.9	37.8
Other Manufactured Goods	19.1	17.8	16.8	17.8	17.6	15.7
Unclassified	1.0	2.3	2.3	1.4	1.0	1.1
	100	100	100	100	100	100

Source: Author's calculation based on UNCTADStat data

industry mix that make them less competitive externally, and complementary internally. If that is the case what explains MERCOSUR's low intra-group trade?

10.4.4 Explanations for MERCOSUR's Trade Performance

Explanations for the low intra-group trade have been extensively discussed by Meissner (2017), Fink and Rempel (2017), and Krapohl (2017a, b, d). Meissner (2017) points out that at the time of MERCOSUR's formation, the member states had stronger extra-regional trading partners than intraregional trade partners—namely the US, EU, and Japan. Even so, all member states benefited from the initial period of MERCOSUR. However, the Argentine Great Depression of 1998–2002 caused Argentina's influence to shrink and by 2010, Brazil had become the dominant trading hub of the organization. It became the destination of billions of European investments.

Fink and Rempel (2017) observed that the dominant position of Brazil in MERCOSUR had the potential for it to become a Rambo state, and that was what happened when the financial crisis of the late 1990s in Russia and Asia wreaked economic hardships on South American economies. Exports of mineral and agricultural products fell and the devaluation of Asian countries caused South American manufactures to decline. Extra-regional exports declined, international investors pulled back all over the developing countries, and economic growth in Brazil slowed down. In response to this Brazil devalued its currency without consulting or informing other MERCOSUR members. This threw the economies of its regional neighbors into a recession, while foreign investments continued to flow to Brazil. Argentina was hit particularly hard. Investment flow to Argentina dwindled as many investors pulled out of the country or relocated to Brazil. Argentina lost more than US$13 billion FDI in 1999 and 2000. Argentina's exports to Brazil declined especially in the automobile sector. Argentina was not able to devalue its currency because of domestic resistance and wanting to keep the Convertibility Plan, a plan that pegged the Argentine peso to the US dollar so as to eliminate hyperinflation and stimulate economic growth. A suggestion by a new economic minister to peg the peso to both the US dollar and the Euro was seen as a signal for devaluation by extra-regional partners, and this increased mistrust and inflation. The government was pressured by the IMF to eventually abandon the Convertibility Plan, which led to massive devaluation and default on public debt. However, this was too late and it was not until the end of 2002 that the Argentine economy started to slowly recover (Meissner, 2017).

Brazil's actions resulted in a tense relationship with Argentina and a subsequent trade war. Thus, Argentina put in place protectionist measures including a tariff on Brazilian iron imports and a quota on its textiles. Brazil retaliated by imposing licenses on Argentine foodstuffs and sanitary controls on other products. It also initiated an investigation into Argentine dairy products import and reinstituted domestic subsidies for farmers. MERCOSUR never attained the integration it had in the late 1990s (Meissner, 2017).

Other subsequent events show that MERCOSUR member states went from cooperative neighbors in the 1990s to uncooperative and sometimes antagonistic neighbors beyond trade matters. For example, there were three trade disputes that went before the International Court of Justice and the World Trade Organization after 2000. In 2005, Brazil made a bid for a permanent seat at the UN Security Council but none of its MERCOSUR neighbors supported it, with Argentina opposing it. Brazil and Uruguay both proposed candidates for the director general of the WTO, but Brazil's candidate did not make it after the first round, while Uruguay's went all the way to the final. Similarly, both Brazil and Colombia contested for a leadership position in the Inter-American bank. Argentina, Paraguay, and Uruguay supported Colombia's bid (Meissner, 2017).

The fragmentation of MERCOSUR entered a new phase when in 2004, Brazil initiated the formation of UNASUR, which consisted of MERCOSUR members and Bolivia, Chile, Colombia, Ecuador, Guyana, Peru, Suriname, and Venezuela. The treaty was finalized and signed in 2008. Unlike MERCOSUR which was for economic integration, UNASUR is for political cooperation and infrastructure integration. In yet another effort to neutralize MERCOSUR, Brazil entered a strategic trade partnership with the EU without informing the members of MERCOSUR, although the agreement involved issues that were not in conflict with MERCOSUR. Brazil's volatile interest in MERCOSUR can be traced to its extra-regional interests, and is a good test case of Krapohl's (2017a, b, d) hypothesis. Thus, whenever these interests aligned with those of MERCOSUR, Brazil was willing to play its role as a naturally regional leader. However, when those interests were not aligned with MERCOSUR, Brazil would begin working outside of MERCOSUR, going after its own interests. This in turn is the case because the economies of the member states of MERCOSUR are not competitive enough to break the interests and alliances that existed before MERCOSUR was established.

10.5 Conclusion

In this chapter, we have examined three RTAs from three different regions—Europe's EU, Asia's ASEAN, and South America's MERCOSUR. The chapter shows that all these RTAs started from the desire to remove trade and non-trade barriers among themselves as neighbors with the ultimate goal of improving the overall welfare of their citizens. In addition, there were also other political reasons for peace and stability. We have seen that such ideals are more difficult to achieve in practice than just signing an agreement., and none of them has reached the ultimate goals that they set themselves. Yet, we can see that two of the groups—the EU and ASEAN have been relatively successful as far as intra-group and intraregional trade is concerned. Specifically, both groups have a relatively higher proportion of their trade among themselves and within their respective regions. In contrast, MERCOSUR has not been that successful—its intra-group trade is low and so is its intraregional trade. Thus, the major trading partners of MERCOSUR members lie outside the group and also the region. This has been explained by the fact that both ASEAN and EU countries had some trading relations among their member states before forming the RTAs. In contrast, MERCOSUR member states did not have that relationship before the group was formed and as a result, the members national interests continued to lie outside the group after it was formed. This and other economic hardships created a situation where the divergence between national and group interests has caused members to choose the former over the latter. The question is why must this be the case? We argue that the reason why the national interests lie outside is because the economies were neither competitive nor complementary before the RTA, and continued to remain so after the merger because of the inability to diversify the economies to become competitive.

References

Birch, M. H. (2000). Mercosur: The road to economic integration in the southern cone. *International Journal of Public Administration, 23*(5–8), 1387–1413.

Dinan, D. (2008). Fifty years of European integration: A remarkable achievement. *Fordham International Law Journal, 31*(5), 1116–1142.

Fink, S., & Rempe, D. (2017). Trade network analysis: Economic structures of EC/EU, ASEAN, MERCOSUR, and SADC. In S. Krapohl (Ed.), *Regional integration in the Global South: External influence on economic cooperation in ASEAN, MERCOSUR, and SADC* (pp. 91–113). Palgrave Macmillan.

Krapohl, S. (2017a). Introduction – Integration theory and the new regionalism. In S. Krapohl (Ed.), *Regional integration in the Global South: External influence on economic cooperation in ASEAN, MERCOSUR, and SADC* (pp. 1–29). Palgrave Macmillan.

Krapohl, S. (2017b). Two logics on regional integration and the games regional actors play: A theoretical framework for the analysis of regional economic cooperation and defection. In S. Krapohl (Ed.), *Regional integration in the Global South: External influence on economic cooperation in ASEAN, MERCOSUR, and SADC* (pp. 33–62). Palgrave Macmillan.

Krapohl, S. (2017c). ASEAN: Extra-regional cooperation triggers regional integration. In S. Krapohl (Ed.), *Regional integration in the Global South: External influence on economic cooperation in ASEAN, MERCOSUR, and SADC* (pp. 115–146). Palgrave Macmillan.

Krapohl, S. (2017d). Conclusion: Comparing regional cooperation and defection in ASEAN, MERCOSUR and SADC. In S. Krapohl (Ed.), *Regional integration in the Global South: External influence on economic cooperation in ASEAN, MERCOSUR, and SADC* (pp. 211–235). Palgrave Macmillan.

Krapohl, S., & Fink, S. (2013). Different paths of regional integration: Trade networks and regional institution-building in Europe, Southeast Asia and Southern Africa. *Journal of Common Market Studies, 51*(3), 472–488.

Lemarchand, R. (2016). Region-building in Central Africa. In D. H. Levine & D. Nagar (Eds.), *Region-building in Africa: Political and economic challenges* (pp. 231–244). Palgrave Macmillan.

Meissner, K. L. (2017). MERCOSUR: The ups and downs of regional integration in South America. In S. Krapohl (Ed.), *Regional integration in the global south: External influence on economic cooperation in ASEAN, MERCOSUR, and SADC* (pp. 147–178). Palgrave Macmillan.

Pietrzak, M. B., & Łapińska, J. (2015). Determinants of European Union's trade – Evidence from a panel estimation of the gravity model. *E+M Ekonomie a Management, 18*(1), 18–26.

Vătăman, D. (2010). History of the European Union. *Lex ET Scientia International Journal: Juridical Series XVII, 2*, 107–101.

Chapter 11
Conclusion

11.1 Introduction

The purpose of this book was to examine the problems and prospects of the African Continental Free Trade Area by studying the performances of the most prominent regional trade agreements on the continent today that have been identified as the foundation blocks of the AfCFTA. The rationale for this quest was based on the thinking that if we want to know how well the AfCFTA will perform what better way to do that than to study the performance of a number of the organizations that have been selected to be its founding pillars? As a result, after discussing the theories and principles of international trade and regional trade agreements, this book set out to study how well the seven organizations that have been identified as founding blocks have performed to get some insights regarding how the AfCFTA will fare. Deliberately, this study was limited to the trading activities of these selected RTAs for two reasons—first, they were all trade organizations first before anything else, and second because of the role trade plays in development efforts. So, in this concluding chapter we ask, what have we learned about the theories and principles of international trade and regional trade agreements and the problems and prospects of the African Continental Free Trade Area? To what extent can the existing RTAs in Africa inform us about the problems and prospects of the AfCFTA? We answer these questions in three sections. In section two, we summarize what we have learned from the performance of Africa's seven RTAs within the context of the promises of international trade and regional trade agreements, and the performance of Africa's RTA. In Sect. 11.3, we discuss the reasons for the performances of Africa's RTAs and problems facing AfCFTA. In section three, we discuss the prospects of the AfCFTA.

B. Ofori-Amoah, *The African Continental Free Trade Area*,
https://doi.org/10.1007/978-3-031-59181-5_11

11.2 The Unfulfilled Promise of International Trade and Regional Trade Agreements in Africa

The promise of international trade to nations was first articulated in the mercantilism philosophy, which believed that a nation's wealth was determined by the amount of gold and silver it possessed. So, governments were encouraged to support more export, which brought gold and silver in, and limit import, which caused outflow of gold and silver. More importantly, mercantilism saw international trade as a zero-sum game, where one nation's gain was another nation's loss. This view was criticized by the Physiocrats and classical economists such as Adam Smith, David Ricardo, and John Stuart Mill. The Physiocrats believed that a nation's wealth depended on its agricultural development and that free trade was the best approach to amass wealth. Adam Smith also criticized mercantilism and argued that nations would benefit more if they specialized in producing goods in which they had an absolute advantage and exchanged their surpluses through trade. Ricardo argued that nations did not need absolute advantage to engage in trade; rather, they needed comparative advantage. For the next 100 years or so the law of comparative advantage became the main explanation for why international trade took place.

During the 1930s the Heckscher-Ohlin theory sought to replace the labor cost component in the law of comparative advantage with factor endowments of countries. The theory argued that labor-abundant countries should specialize in producing labor-intensive goods, while capital-abundant countries should specialize in producing capital-intensive products. By so doing both countries would consume more through specialization and division of labor. For the next 50 years factor endowments dominated international trade theory although empirical evidence was woefully weak. This and other criticisms of the theory led to firm-based and new trade theories.

Firm-based theories take their motivation from two ideas. The first is it is firms, not countries that trade. The second is the trading behavior of multinational corporation corporations. These theories highlight how corporate strategies influence when, where, and how firms conduct international trade. Still focusing on corporate behavior in a world of imperfect competition and economies of scale, the new trade theories argue that much of the world trade is conducted by oligopolies, which have the tendency to make abnormal profits. This gives national governments the legitimacy to shift some of the profits for "strategic "and other public welfare reasons using tariff and non-tariff measures. This new perspective has been criticized by proponents of free trade, yet the reality of international trade is that international trade has never been without obstacles.

Apart from this, the fairness of trade has long been questioned by researchers of the Marxist and political economy persuasions. Although he did not propose an explicit theory of international trade, Karl Marx's works on capital and surplus value contained several critiques of the classical and neoclassical international trade theories. While agreeing with Ricardo about the benefits of free trade, Marx saw free trade as an impending crisis of capitalism that would transition society into socialism due to the contradictions that came with unequal development. Intense competition among industrialized nations from the late nineteenth to the early twentieth centuries provided more fuel to the ideas of Marx. This spurned the first wave of Marxian theories that saw international trade as a tool of imperialism. The collapse of colonialism after World War II led to a second wave of Marxian theories that saw international trade as a form of exploitation of former colonies. The law of comparative advantage whether by factor cost or factor endowments was fraught with unequal exchange and other past and current exploitative rules that created dependency of peripheral countries on the core countries.

Despite the advantages of free trade, trade has never been free because of tariff and non-tariff barriers that national governments impose on trade for economic, social, and political reasons. At the same time, there appears to be a general agreement that the long-run benefit of these barriers is not commensurate with the cost of protectionism and the benefits of free trade. As a result, there has been a worldwide effort to reduce these trade barriers, most of which have taken the form of regional trade agreements (RTAs).

Like the theories of international trade, the theory of regional trade agreements raise high aspirations and expectations for countries. First, RTAs are supposed to increase trade volumes among member states by removing trade barriers. Second, they are also expected to form building blocks for larger multilateral trade organizations. Third, geographic proximity, similarity in culture, and political history among member states should lead to effective RTAs. Fourth, RTAs are also supposed to lead to convergence in economic well-being of member states.

The AfCFTA was established to attain these benefits and much more, yet, the single most important finding of this study is that Africa's regional trade agreements that have been selected to be founding blocks of the AfCFTA have not lived up to their expectations of promoting intraregional trade in Africa. Thus, after several decades of existence, the percentage of intraregional trade in Africa is very low. The overall intra-regional export trade for Africa in 2019 was 16.3% compared to Asia's 59.4%, Europe's 68%, and Northern America's 30%. Only Latin America, the Caribbean, and Oceania had lower intraregional trade, being 14.1% and 6.5%, respectively. On the import side, Africa's intraregional trade was only 14.3% compared to Asia's 62.2%, Europe's 64.9%, and Northern America's 18.5%. Latin America and the Caribbean even registered 15% of its total import trade as intraregional. Only Oceania had a lower intraregional import trade than Africa. With respect to the individual RTAs, only the EAC and SADC had more than 10% of their export trade occurring within them in 2019. It was 17.9% for the EAC and 20% for the SADC. With respect to import trade, only SADC had intraregional trade registering 19.9%. The rest were all under 10%. Contrast this with ASEAN's 22.8% of its export trade and 21.8% of its import trade in 2019. This is a problem if these RTAs are supposed to be the foundation blocks for the AfCFTA. The problem is even more serious if one considers the fact that the oldest of these RTAs (ECOWAS) has been in existence for 48 years and the youngest (COMESA) for 25 years. As a result, one is left with many unanswered questions. First, why have Africa's RTAs before the formation of the AfCFTA not led to an increased volume of intraregional trade? If geographic proximity, similarity in culture, and political history of member states of RTAs should lead to effective RTAs, why have Africa's RTAs not been effective? Finally, if Africa's existing RTAs before the AfCFTA have not been effective in achieving their goals, how can they be good models to guide the AfCFTA? In the following sections, we try to answer these questions.

11.3 Problems of the AfCFTA

Many researchers have commented on the reasons why Africa's RTAs have performed poorly with respect to promoting intraregional trade. First, is the gap between aspirations on paper and what actually occurs on the ground, especially when it comes to implementation of the trade agreements. This in turn is due to lack of political and institutional support from the various governments to back what they agree to with action. Thus, in many instances, national financial obligations have not been honored, institutional structures required for implementation have not been established, and major milestones in the evolution and development of the RTAs have been missed.

Second, poor infrastructure—specifically transportation and communication within the continent makes trading more expensive and difficult, especially for the 17 countries that are landlocked. In addition, bureaucratic red tape and unwillingness to implement rules governing free movement of goods and services continue to present problems.

Third, multiple and overlapping memberships make it more difficult to enforce rules and regulations governing a given trade agreement. Most African countries belong to at least two regional trade agreements. Fourth, some of the RTAs such as ECOWAS and the ECCAS experienced prolonged political and social unrest in the form of civil wars that hampered the operation of the RTA. In fact, the ECCAS was moribund during its first 15 years due to political and social unrest in the region. Similarly, ECOWAS was wrecked by civil wars in Liberia (1989–1996; 1999–2003), Sierra Leone (1991–2002), and Cote d'Ivoire (2002–2004, 2011). It is difficult for trade to thrive under these circumstances.

Fifth, the presence or absence of hegemonic members of the RTAs has affected the activities of the RTAs. On the one hand, the dominant positions of South Africa in the SADC, Nigeria in ECOWAS, and Kenya in the EAC have been a source of irritation since the interests of these countries appear to be outside of their regional groupings, or seen to be out of sync by the other members of their respective RTAs. On the other hand, the inability of DRC to exert its hegemonic position within the ECCAS has also been seen as an incapacitation of the ECCAS that has rendered it leaderless and weak. Sixth, the role of external influences—especially the developed countries of Europe, North America, Asia, and recently China—continues to hinder the efforts of African countries to trade with one another.

There is no doubt that these factors have affected Africa's RTAs in no small measure. However, these factors have not stopped African countries from trading. In spite of all these problems, African countries have continued trading, albeit at relatively low volumes. Instead, what we have consistently seen in the previous chapters is the fact that more of this trade has been with outside partners than partners within the respective RTAs and even within the African region. So, these factors may not necessarily be the causes of a low volume of intraregional trade. Rather the main reason for low volumes of intraregional trade among Africa's existing RTAs is the lack of economy complementarity and competitiveness of African countries that have removed all the incentives and rationale to pursue intraregional trade. In particular, African economies are mostly dependent on entities that are outside the continent in the sense that they produce primary commodities that they are not able to convert to value-added goods through manufacturing, while they consume manufactured products most of which they do not produce. As economies with very small and weak manufacturing sectors, African countries are forced to trade more with outside entities than with inside entities, in spite of overlapping RTA memberships. This fact is borne out by other relatively more successful RTAs such as the ASEAN and the EU. For example, contrary to most of Africa's RTAs, ASEAN's intraregional trade was higher than any of Africa's RTAs. The same can be said of EU's intraregional trade. The lack of any serious manufacturing economy in Africa exacerbates the situation where external influences tend to dominate the internal affairs of Africa's RTA. This situation is extended when the economic, political, and social interests of a few regional hegemons conflict or are not met by regional goals. Admittedly, all the other problems discussed above have limited the growth of intraregional trade in Africa, but I would like to emphasize that none of those problems is bigger than the current industry mix or economic structure of African countries. What then are the prospects of the AfCFTA?

11.4 Prospects of the African Continental Free Trade Area Agreement

As a continent, Africa is endowed with enormous resources needed for its economic development. It has vast amounts of mineral wealth, forest resources, water resources, and untapped renewable energy resources. While most of these resources are unevenly distributed, the formation of RTAs provides an excellent rationale for adopting a regional approach in harnessing these resources. The prospects are also good for Africa because of the shared history, common cultural trends, common history as colonies, and common bond as a people with certain cultural traits, and geographical proximity—all factors that have been identified in the theory of RTAs to be good for successful and effective RTAs. It also appears that there are people who are devoted to seeing that integration works even though the process has been quite slow. However, the success of the AfCFTA is going to take more than these foundational characteristics to make it work. At the minimum trade occurs when we need something that we are not able to produce but have something to exchange for it. So, trade among African countries can only occur more not by signing binding agreements but only if they can practically exchange more of what they have for more of what they need. At this very moment, that is impossible because there is not enough complementarity or intervening opportunities among the economies of African countries. Borrowing from the principles of spatial interaction, complementarity refers to demand and supply relationship between places, while intervening opportunities refer to alternative sources of supply that usurp an existing complementarity. Intervening opportunities thus reflect not only the existence but also the competitiveness of alternatives. In this case, the reason why African countries trade more with outside trade partners is because of complementarity between their economies. Thus, most of the goods African countries need are produced outside so it is obvious that that will dictate the direction of trade. However, if African countries begin to produce those same goods of the same quality, we can assume that African countries will begin to trade more with one another those goods. This would make those African sources intervening opportunities usurping the current trading patterns.

The point in all this is that to boost intraregional trade African countries must restructure their economies by placing more emphasis on manufacturing. Africa must industrialize! Without it, the "Africa We Want" memo that is being touted will never materialize. This is not the first time that industrialization has been mentioned in the context of regional trade agreements in Africa. Every one of Africa's RTAs has had a section on industrialization. The excellent series on assessing regional integration in Africa (ARIA) by the UNECA and its associates of the African Development Bank and African Union have mentioned this in all their volumes (UNECA, 2006a, b, 2010, 2012, 2016, 2017). Other research works such as Asante (1986), Bende-Nabende (2001), UNCTAD (2009, 2013), Odijie (2018), Oloruntuba and Tsowou (2019), van der Ven (2017) have focused on the need for industrialization within the context of Africa's RTAs. However, since the early post-colonial period of the 1960s and 1970s, there has not been any serious effort at industrialization in most African countries. Indeed, one has to go back to the early 1960s and 1970s to see explicit industrialization policies in Africa. African countries need to go back to that period when industrialization was front and center of national development policy. So, much has been written about that period and why those policies failed, but that does not mean that industrialization has no role in Africa's development. Indeed, a lot of the criticisms against those policies such as import substitution industrialization may not stand up to critical analysis if one holds them against the broad sweep of industrialization history. However, that is the subject of another book.

In the meantime, Africa needs to take industrialization more seriously and craft new industrialization policies that adopt both regional and cooperative approaches. This can be done by strategically selecting industries that use local resources and expertise. The broad classification of composition of Africa's trade is already known—food agricultural raw materials, fuels, transportation machinery and equipment, chemicals, and other manufactures. African countries can be strategic about the regional specialization in these broad categories across the RTAs, with each

RTA specializing in a specific area. In doing this, there will be the need for selective and strategic industries. Each RTA needs to conduct a comprehensive survey of its resources and potentials, decide on what type of industries will be suitable within their area, and plot out a strategy to implement the plans.

Previous work including Asante (1986) and Odijie (2018) has indicated that this is not going to be an easy task, as national rivalry and unhelpful competition can derail such efforts. There is also the China factor, which is seen as a major hindrance to Africa's trade. However, Africa's role in global trade has changed little from when China was a much lesser player in global market than it is now. Then it was Europe and the United States, and later Japan that dominated global trade. Now other countries in East Asia led by China, have found a way to dominate global trade by boosting their manufacturing output in a world that was dominated by Europe, the US, and Japan. Africa has no other choice but to industrialize if it wants to be taken more seriously on the global stage in future.

References

Asante, S. K. B. (1986). *The political economy of regionalism in Africa: A decade of the economic community of West African states (ECOWAS)*. Praeger.

Bende-Nabende, A. (2001). Foreign direct investment, regional integration, and economic growth. In V. Murinde (Ed.), *The free trade area of the common market for eastern and southern Africa* (pp. 63–110). Ashgate.

Odijie, M. E. (2018). The need for industrial policy coordination in the African continental free trade area. *African Affairs, 118*(470), 182–193.

Oloruntoba, S. O., & Tsowou, K. (2019). Afro-continental free trade areas and industrialization in Africa: Exploring Afro-Canadian partnership for economic development. *Canadian Foreign Policy Journal, 25*(3), 237–240.

UNCTAD. (2009). *Economic development in Africa: Strengthening regional economic integration for Africa's development*. United Nations Conference on Trade and Development.

UNCTAD. (2013). *Economic development in Africa report intra-African trade: Unlocking private sector dynamism*. United Nations Conference on Trade and Development.

United Nations Economic Commission for Africa (UNECA). (2006a). *Assessing regional economic integration in Africa (RIA): ECA policy research report*. UNECA.

United Nations Economic Commission for Africa (UNECA). (2006b). *Assessing regional economic integration in Africa II: Rationalizing regional economic communities*. UNECA.

United Nations Economic Commission for Africa (UNECA). (2010). *Assessing regional economic integration in Africa IV: Enhancing intra-African trade*. UNECA.

United Nations Economic Commission for Africa (UNECA). (2012). *Assessing regional economic integration in Africa V: Towards an African continental free trade area*. UNECA.

United Nations Economic Commission for Africa (UNECA). (2016). *Assessing regional economic integration in Africa VII: Innovation, competitiveness, and regional integration*. UNECA.

United Nations Economic Commission for Africa (UNECA). (2017). *Assessing regional economic integration in Africa VIII: Bringing the African continental free trade about*. UNECA.

van der Ven, C. M. A. (2017). Trade, development and industrial policy in Africa: The case for a pragmatic approach to optimizing policy coherence between industrial policy and the WTO policy space law. *Developmental Review, 10*(1), 29–80.

Index

B. Ofori-Amoah, *The African Continental Free Trade Area*,
https://doi.org/10.1007/978-3-031-59181-5